Land of Clear Light

ALSO BY MICHAEL JENKINSON

Wild Rivers of North America

Ghost Towns of New Mexico (WITH KARL KERNBERGER)

Tijerina: Land Grant Conflict in New Mexico

Land of Clear Light

*Wild Regions of the American Southwest
and Northwestern Mexico—How to Reach Them
and What You Will Find There*

BY

MICHAEL JENKINSON

*Photographs by Karl Kernberger
Maps by Mary Beth Stokes*

A SUNRISE BOOK
E. P. DUTTON & CO., INC. NEW YORK

Library of Congress Cataloging in Publication Data
Jenkinson, Michael.
    Land of clear light.
    "A Sunrise book."
    Includes index.
    1. Southwest, New—Description and travel—
1951–   —Guide books. 2. Baja California—
Description and travel—Guide-books. 1. Title.
F787.J46 1977   917.9′04′3   76–17542
ISBN: 0–87690–203–4

For my father and Hilda

Contents

Maps

Land of Clear Light

Introduction

When Spanish explorers pressed northward from the green and looted lands of the Aztecs, seeking still greater treasures from such fabled places as the Seven Cities of Cibola and the golden realm of Quivira, they entered a region of contrasts. Much of it was desert or high, grassy steppe—yet they never seemed far from abrupt, high-piled mountains which promised chill creeks and tall timber. Watercourses were unpredictable. Dry arroyo beds could become torrents raging bank to bank within a matter of seconds, subsiding within hours. The few big rivers they encountered were little more than a braiding of shallow channels through mudbanks much of the year; yet in spring and early summer they became great, raging floods that raked at inundated banks with uprooted trees. They came to expect the unexpected. A forested plateau might suddenly drop away into the depths of an abysmal chasm. Expecting gold, they discovered pearl beds. Seeking pagan souls to be converted, they trudged across vast regions where hardly anyone lived at all—yet on every hand there were traces of ancient, vanished peoples.

Despite its contrasts, the Spaniards discovered a unifying factor in this region—a certain clarity of sky and air, a sense of space and immensities. Some of them called it the Land of Clear Light.

Although no one has ever put precise boundaries on the Land of Clear Light, in the context of this book I define it as northwestern Mexico and the shoreline of the Gulf of California (or Sea of Cortez), Arizona, New Mexico, southcentral Utah, and southwestern Colorado—regions probed by sixteenth- and seventeenth-century Spaniards in quest of treasure and conversions to Catholicism.

Much of this region is substantially little changed from when the

1

explorers passed through it over three hundred years ago. Modern populations have tended to cluster in a few metropolitan areas such as Phoenix, Ciudad Juarez, Albuquerque, Chihuahua, and Tucson. One out of three residents of New Mexico, for example, lives in Albuquerque. The places I discuss in this book are islands of scant population—the outback—where paved roads fade off into jeep-trails or footpaths.

It is a region of strange and beautiful land forms—great stone towers and arches, vast and deep canyons, vaulted caverns, jagged mountain ranges. There is a feeling of mystery and antiquity in the Land of Clear Light—brooding, empty cities that were abruptly abandoned in the thirteenth and fourteenth centuries, hundreds of powerful rock paintings, effigy figures so gigantic that their dimensions can only be completely realized from an airplane.

It is a region with a rich historical legacy. I believe one will have a stronger feeling for the Navajo country knowing of the Long Walk; for Canyonlands, having read of Mormon attempts to settle the outback; and for the Sierra Madre after a visit with the widow of Pancho Villa. There is a fair amount of material on the activities, violent and otherwise, of mountain men, prospectors, cattlemen, outlaws, and other frontier folk, since they once occupied some of the backcountry I discuss.

I hope you will enjoy the Land of Clear Light, a unique and fascinating region, as much as I have.

ONE

Canyon Country
(Southern Utah and Northern Arizona)

The canyon country that covers much of central and southern Utah as well as northern Arizona is unique and breathtakingly beautiful. Until recently it was known only to a few cowhands, prospectors, and hardy Mormon settlers. Even today it remains one of North America's largest wilderness regions south of the Canadian border, since most of it is accessible only by jeep-trail, horseback, foot, or by boat on the Colorado and Green rivers. These two rivers and their tributaries have carved deep and exquisite canyons. A combination of geological factors has created thousands of rock structures in the canyons and upon the plateaus that flank them—pinnacles, serpentine ridges, vast monuments, natural bridges, arches, domes, mesas, and other assorted visual feasts. Most of the canyon country is composed of sedimentary layers, yet in places volcanic rock has bulged up to form high mountains and ranges. Boulder and Navajo mountains, the Henry, La Sal and Blue mountains, and the Bear's Ears are prominent landmarks in a region where most features are hidden beneath the horizon line, tucked into deep gorges and canyons. This wooded high country also offers delightful contrast to the slickrock lands below, which can be murderously hot during the summer months.

The regions below 6500 feet receive less than ten inches of precipitation annually, some of it in violent, localized summer thunderstorms, and part of it in sporadic winter snowfall. The summer storms often produce flash floods that fill arroyos with roiling muddy water within a few seconds, a wondrous sight to behold unless your car, camp, or person happens to be in its path.

The canyon country is a place of contrast, often monumental, even

more often quite subtle—a slowly dripping spring with ferns up an otherwise dry rock gorge; the cool pocket of shade a cottonwood throws out
against the pressing heat of summer sun. While much of the beauty of this
region comes from the vast areas of bare and sculptured rock—a vision of
the very bones of the earth itself—there are myriad diverse patches of
vegetation. The erosional forces that have swept away great sections of
what might have been a botanically unified plateau have left isolated
islands of divergent plant forms. A buzzard, cruising the thermals of a
canyon rim, might have desert flora and fauna far below off one wing tip,
and high aspen meadows lifting above the other wing.

It is a land whose forms are as unpredictable as a vivid dream.

As befits such a magnificent wilderness region, I have divided it into
three sections for the purposes of this book: the Escalante, Canyonlands,
and Navajo Country. The division is principally geographical, as historical
currents flow and ebb across all of it. "Canyonlands" addresses itself to the
northcentral section—the tapering wedge between the Colorado and Green
rivers and those sections of Canyonlands National Park to the west and
east of the Colorado and Green rivers. "The Escalante" is about the country
west and south of Land's End Plateau—San Rafael Swell, Capitol Reef
National Monument, the Henry Mountains, the Escalante River. . . .
"Navajo Country" concerns itself with the region of southeastern Utah and
northern Arizona where there are numerous cliff dwellings and other ruins.
Much of this spectacular country is today in the land of the Navajo Nation.

1. The Escalante

Most of the early exploration of the American West was stimulated by
three factors: a search for an easy water passage to the Pacific Ocean,
which would lead to the trade treasures of the Orient; a search for treasure
in the mountainous West itself—either minerals or beaver pelts; and a
reaching for distant "heathens" to be drawn into the lap of God, as defined
by Christianity. Concentrating upon the latter goal, Franciscans Atanasio
Dominguez and Silvestre Escalante left Santa Fe in August, 1776, with a
small expedition to discover a feasible route between New Mexico and the
mission at Monterey, California. They also projected finding sites for
settlements and missions. After traveling north from Santa Fe to the banks
of the Colorado River in what is now the western part of that state, they

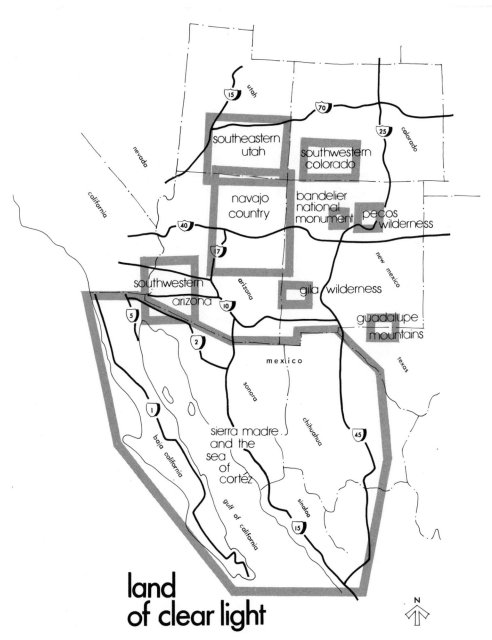

nevada

utah

california

nevada

colorado

southeastern
utah

southwestern
colorado

navajo
country

bandelier
national
monument

pecos
wilderness

new mexico

southwestern
arizona

arizona

gila wilderness

guadalupe
mountains

texas

mexico

sonora

chihuahua

baja california

sierra madre
and the
sea
of
cortez

gulf of california

sinaloa

land
of clear light

areas within heavy lines are shown in
detail in maps that follow

headed west through lands that were blank upon Spanish maps—the Uinta Basin and then the Great Basin at Utah Lake. Winter snows swirled around them before they reached the latitude they had expected to follow west to Monterey, and so they reluctantly decided to return to Santa Fe by means of a circle to the south.

Where the mountains finally dropped away, they trudged eastward over the Kaibab Plateau, using the Vermilion Cliffs as a landmark on the left, and skirting the heads of tributary canyons of the Colorado on the right. They had no Indian guides and earlier directions they had been given were vague. They came up against the deep, muddy roll of the Colorado at what is now Lee's Ferry. There were cliffs on the other side of the river; the mouth of Marble Canyon yawned to the south, Glen Canyon to the north. Attempts to ford the chill water were futile, as was an attempted crossing upon a makeshift raft. Still filled with faith, they named their campsite San Benito. Discouraged by the barriers of rock and water, they added an additional ironic word to the name—*Salsipuedes*—which means "get out if you can." The party climbed slickrock cliffs to the north, buffeted by high winds, snow, and hail. At times their diet was reduced to cactus pads flavored with berry juice. A route down to the river, let alone a practical crossing, was elusive, to say the least. After working his way out onto a rim and seeing the river five hundred feet almost directly below him, Escalante wrote in his diary: "Doubtless God disposed that we should not obtain a guide, perhaps as a benign punishment for our sins."

Forty miles above Camp San Benito Salsipuedes, a notch was found that led down to the river. It was so steep that steps were chopped into the sandstone so that the livestock would not slide off to crippling injuries or death, and somehow the party reached a sandbar lying next to the river. The ford was wide and shallow. The friars rode their horses across it without incident, and ever since this place has been known as the Crossing of the Fathers. From here the party returned to Santa Fe by way of Navajo Creek and the Hopi and Zuni villages. No route to the Pacific had been blazed, no mission sites laid out, and the treasure chest of the canyon country appeared to be thoroughly empty. Yet an important and dramatic swing of exploration had been accomplished, and more of the canyon country was becoming known.

Seventy-two years after Escalante had forded the Colorado, a Mormon party led by Jacob Hamblin reached the Crossing of the Fathers. Their Piute guides clasped hands and waded into the river, forming a line almost one hundred feet long that allowed the Mormons to pick the shallowest route. Like the Spanish friars who preceded him, Hamblin's instructions were to begin missionary work among the Indians and to keep an eye peeled for potential settlement sites.

The journey went well; the party reached the Hopi Mesas to the south

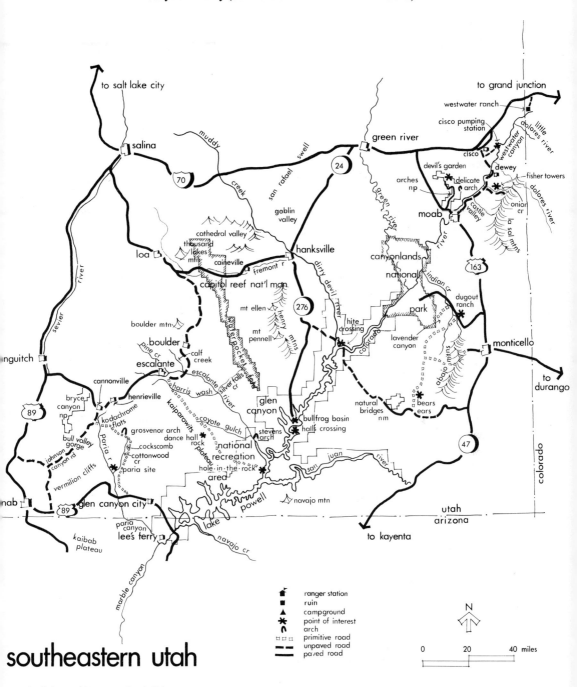

to salt lake city

to grand junction

westwater ranch

cisco pumping station

green river

little dolores river

westwater canyon

cisco

dewey

fisher towers

devil's garden

delicate arch

arches np

onion cr

dolores river

moab

castle valley

salina

muddy creek

san rafael swell

24

70

goblin valley

la sal mtns

cathedral valley

hanksville

canyonlands

163

thousand lakes mtn

caineville

national

loa

fremont r

capitol reef nat'l mon

dirty devil river

park

dugout ranch

276

indian cr

boulder mtn

mt ellen

hite crossing

lavender canyon

mt pennell

henry mtns

colorado

boulder

calf creek

pine cr

escalante

waterpocket fold

escalante river

silver falls cr

glen canyon

monticello

bryce canyon np

cannonville

henrieville

natural bridges nm

bears ears

to durango

89

harris wash

abajo mtns

kaiparowits

coyote gulch

kodachrome flats

grosvenor arch

dance hall rock

national recreation ared

bullfrog basin

halls crossing

47

stevens arch

cockscomb

cottonwood cr

paria site

hole-in-the-rock

san juan river

paria r

johnson canyon rd

vermilion cliffs

colorado

glen canyon city

navajo mtn

kaibab plateau

lee's ferry

paria canyon

lake powell

utah
arizona

to kayenta

navajo cr

marble canyon

sevier river

nguitch

nab

grovenor arch

bull valley gorge

rock plateau

89

southeastern utah

ranger station
ruin
campground
point of interest
arch
primitive road
unpaved road
paved road

N

0   20   40 miles

more detailed maps of the areas enclosed within
shaded borders will be found on later pages

and returned without incident. On a subsequent mission to the Hopis, a member of Hamblin's group was killed by Navajos who were heading into the canyon country in retreat from American military expeditions out of Fort Wingate, New Mexico. This was the first of a number of casualties in skirmishes between Mormons and Navajos, who were sometimes joined by dissident Piutes, over the next five years.

The Indian wars proved to be only temporary setbacks in Brigham Young's plans to colonize the rocky wilderness. Peter Shurtz, a man who liked lots of elbow room, put up a rock house on the Paria River that was better than one hundred miles from St. George, the nearest Mormon community of any consequence. It was here, in the magnificent isolation of a valley half a mile wide and some six hundred feet deep, that local Indians ran off Shurtz's ox and ate it. The settler later reprimanded the Indians and observed that they would now all go hungry, as he had no way to plow and plant. In the spring Indians came to the homestead to pull the plow in relays of four.

The Paria, a perennial stream that originates near Bryce Canyon National Park, has cut its way down through the White Cliffs, the Vermilion Cliffs, and through the long backbone of rock called the Cockscomb. In the eighty-five miles from its source to where it spills into the Colorado, the river meanders through some superb canyons that are, in places, only a few feet wide yet hundreds of feet high. This is wild country, likely to remain that way. The terrain and quicksand discourage jeeps and even horse-travel in many places. A great place to hike.

The farm of Peter Shurtz was about three miles below where the Paria River slashes through the Cockscomb. The village of Paria was established above the Cockscomb in 1870. Other settlements began to take shape near the headwaters of the Paria River—Cannonville, Henrieville, and Clifton. Like all Mormon settlements, whether Salt Lake City itself or small farming hamlets, they were modeled after the "Plat of the City of Zion." The plans called for the villages to be laid in a square, with broad streets, a central public area, and lots that were large enough for a vegetable garden, fruit trees, chickens, and perhaps a cow or two.

At about the same time John D. Lee and one of his wives, Emma, arrived at the mouth of the Paria River. "Oh, what a lonely dell," she exclaimed. For a number of years this was to be the name of the ranch that Lee built there. Lee appreciated the loneliness. Federal authorities were seeking him for his role in the tragic Mountain Meadows Massacre of 1857. Tensions between Mormons and "gentiles" (non-Mormons) had been growing for some time. When word reached Brigham Young that members of a wagon train had poisoned a number of springs and were planning to attack outlying Mormon settlements, he instructed Lee, a church elder, to "waste away our enemies." Accompanied by some Piute

Indians, Lee obediently set about to do just that. The rumors had been false, yet the entire party of 130 people were killed within five minutes. Only infants were spared. Although Lee was eventually captured and returned to the site of the massacre for execution, he lived for a good many peaceful years at Lonely Dell. This was the most accessible crossing of the Colorado between Moab and the lower end of the Grand Canyon. Father Escalante had been deflected here by the deep, swift river, but Lee soon began taking passengers across the river—first upon a crude raft, later on the *Nellie Powell,* a boat discarded by Major John Wesley Powell, and finally on the *Colorado,* a proper ferryboat. As traffic increased, the name Lonely Dell was heard less frequently than Lee's Ferry.

The town of Paria has been abandoned since 1912, a victim of repeated floods. A five-mile dirt spur road off U.S. 89 leads to Paria. A number of ghost town buffs, seeing "Paria (abandoned)" on their maps, head up that way and happily snap pictures of false fronts that line the single street. The wind rattles loose boards on all the right kinds of buildings—hotel, saloon, livery stable, jail. In its lonely setting of colorful desolation it is hard to imagine that anyone ever lived here, as indeed, no one ever has. All the buildings are as empty as discarded cereal boxes and are open at the rear. To find the ruins of the real Paria, one drives on for about a mile beyond this old set for a Western movie. Park your car and wade the river—the ruins of the old Mormon farming settlement are scattered along a rocky bench on the eastern bank of the river.

One of the most interesting back roads in canyon country winds its way between Cannonville and U.S. 89 near Glen Canyon City. Cannonville, an austere village of frame houses in a narrow cultivated valley, is a delightful throwback to the times when a farming village was precisely that, rather than a bustling trade center for agri-industrialists and their hired hands. The Mormon credo of self-sufficiency is very much alive in such places. Two and a half miles south of town the paved road becomes dirt and there is a fork. The right-hand fork, which eventually joins the Johnson Canyon road, reaches Bull Valley Gorge some eight miles from the junction. After crossing the bridge, a hike of about a mile up-canyon will bring you to a valley from which the sheer-sided gorge is accessible. Downstream, the high walls of Navajo sandstone rise rapidly on either side. The gorge narrows and pinches in, until in places it is like descending into the chamber of a cave where only diffused light filters down from overhead. As with most narrow chasms of the Escalante country, one should scan the horizons for approaching storms before entering, as flash floods are a constant danger.

The left fork fords the Paria River and soon reaches a place of magnificent cliffs and fins that are lavishly splashed with color. There are numerous high pinnacles which in form are rather like gigantic inverted icicles. Cowhands, more interested in flat places with something a cow might chew upon than symphonies in stone, have long called the area Thorny Pasture. In 1949 the *National Geographic* discovered the area for the outside world and changed the name of Thorny Pasture to Kodachrome Flats. Thus it is now on the maps, although local wranglers, less interested in a good film than a sturdy pickup and cold beer, still call it Thorny Pasture. Some ten miles beyond Kodachrome Flats is the weirdly eroded double arch of what old-timers called Butler Valley Arch, rechristened Grosvenor Arch by the *National Geographic*. By whatever name one chooses, it is a beautiful piece of natural sculpture—a buff-colored arch rearing 152 feet into the sky, where winds blast around curious knobs and smooth columns.

Rather abruptly, the road leaves Butler Valley and drops into Cottonwood Canyon. Here, in a vast region of scraped and naked rock, is a fifteen-mile stretch of creek whose banks are shaded by cottonwoods. There are several small springs—excellent campsites. The setting, however, is marred by a huge powerline that runs the length of the canyon. The creek is paralleled by the Cockscomb, a long upthrust of rock into which tributary washes of Cottonwood Creek have carved deep and twisting chasms. All of it is beautiful country for prowling afoot. From where Cottonwood Creek joins the Paria, one can hike back up the main river through the Cockscomb to the abandoned village.

Between U.S. 89 and Lee's Ferry is Paria Canyon, forty-two miles of canyon bordered by slickrock formations, narrow gorges where towering walls all but clamp entirely together, and occasional springs and seeps. It will never be Winnebago country, a jeep-trail, or even passable for trail bikes. The threat of flash floods, rock jams, and stretches of quicksand will soon discourage anyone who is not seriously interested in walking through the outback. Travel light and plan to spend at least five days or more, as numerous side gulches invite exploration.

During the late 1870s Mormon settlers established farming villages on the headwaters of rivers to the north and east of the Paria—Boulder, on a tributary of the deep and sheer-sided Escalante; Torrey, Fruita, and Caineville, close to where the Fremont River has blasted its way through Capitol Reef; lonely Hanksville, on the Fremont River.

Most of these towns have changed little in the past century—a few drive-in stands and garages have opened up—yet the frame or rock houses, the large garden plots, the outlying fields still constitute almost self-sufficient communities as projected by Brigham Young. Now, as when they were founded, the small sections of cultivated bottomland are surrounded by vast regions of scraped and sculptured stone.

This country behind the rock was of little interest to the original Mormon settlers, whose days were filled with working what soil could be plowed, what areas might provide pasturage. For them, God's great temples were in another world; one can hardly fault them for not noticing the exquisite natural cathedrals that lay on every side.

Cattlemen and outlaws, who were often one and the same in the Utah backcountry, gradually came to know much of the Escalante region. Prospectors fanned out into areas too rugged for cattle, where there was little or no feed. And finally, long after the first paper cup and cigarette butt hit the surface of Walden Pond, people began filtering into the outback simply to walk around in all this magnificent, useless, magical topography.

The San Rafael Reef is a ridge of jagged rock that stretches for almost a hundred miles across some of the loneliest country in America. A hiker could spend years exploring all the intricate canyons that are carved into it. It was in the reef that uranium prospector Vernon Pick made his big strike while wobbly from arsenic in creekwater. It was here that the McCarty brothers, enthusiastic and skillful bank robbers, holed up in the 1870s. The McCartys, attempting to go straight upon the proceeds of their swag, invested in cattle. Indians stole every one. So they went after the tills of yet another bank, the Farmers and Merchants of Delta, Colorado, where they were gunned down. A few years later the Swasey brothers moved into the reef, ranching. Like the McCartys, they were hostile to audit by outsiders, figuring the phenomenal increase of their stock—cattle and horses—was strictly a family affair. Other maverick businessmen of the era, such as Butch Cassidy and the Wild Bunch, spent many of their most comfortable days with the Swaseys at the reef. The focus of the Swasey hospitality was a sandstone cave where water slowly and constantly dripped from the roof. At the mouth of the cave was a meat pole, where beef hung for the Swaseys and their friends. It was old Western hospitality. There would be steak or stew and sweet water for anyone who had ridden across the dusty distance of Sinbad Desert to the crack in the towering rocks that led to the cave. Almost everyone, that is. The few lawmen that tracked into the San Rafael were spectacularly unsuccessful in bringing suspects out to civilized places where judges wore string ties and referred to leather-bound books. Mostly they got lost or shot, or determined that this vast slab of wild and weird country was out of their jurisdiction.

South of San Rafael Reef, close to Hanksville, is Goblin Valley—a place of strangely eroded and colorful rocks. To the west is Cathedral Valley, where dust devils twist beneath red, white-capped monoliths that have names like Temples of the Sun, Moon, and Stars. The almost vertical formations lift above open reaches of desert scattered with bunch grasses, juniper, pine, silverleaf, buffaloberry, rabbitbrush, yucca, and the outrageously lovely blossoms pushed out by rather drab plants when the right season is upon them. South of Cathedral Valley is a badlands of bentonite hills: odd, colorful shapes that one might imagine upon distant planets or

The Temple of the Sun, a stark rock monolith, towers above the desert floor in Cathedral Valley.

upon this earth before the first minute cluster of green appeared upon barren rock. Most of Cathedral Valley and the bentonite badlands now comprise the northern end of Capitol Reef National Park.

One of the most curious features of canyon country is the Waterpocket Fold, a furrow that extends nearly a hundred miles from Thousand

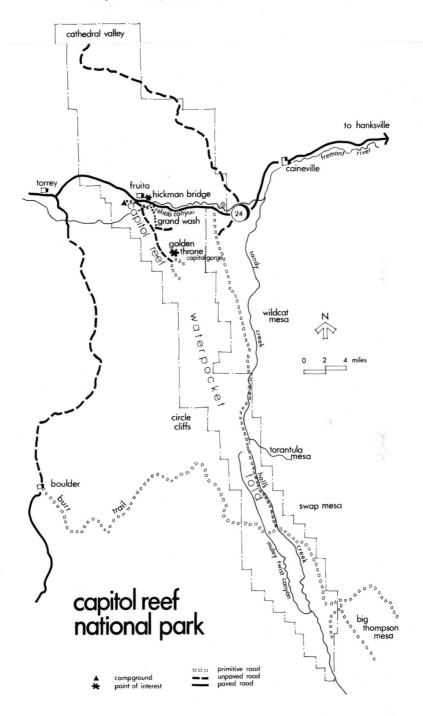

cathedral valley

to hanksville

fremont river

caineville

torrey

fruita

hickman bridge

capitol reef

cohab canyon
grand wash

24

golden
throne

capitol gorge

sandy

creek

wildcat
mesa

N

0 2 4 miles

waterpocket

circle
cliffs

tarantula
mesa

fold

halls

boulder

swap mesa

burr

trail

creek

muley twist canyon

big
thompson
mesa

capitol reef
national park

▲ campground

✳ point of interest

▫ ▫ ▫ primitive road

– – – unpaved road

—— paved road

Lakes Mountain to the Colorado River. The sedimentary layers that form the Circle Cliffs, Capitol Reef, and other escarpments have been folded sharply downward. The tilted sandstone has been eroded into countless contours and patterns. In places natural tanks have been scoured into the rock, some of them several yards across and a number of feet deep. There is cool water in all of them after rains, water in some of them even in the dry season.

Much of Waterpocket Fold lies within Capitol Reef National Park, one of the nation's newest. The visitor center for the park is close to where the Fremont River has slashed its way through the reef. Utah Highway 24 follows the river through the canyon, connecting some rather lovely, isolated farming villages, such as Loa and Torrey, to Hanksville to the east.

As it breaks out of the reef, the river tumbles over a waterfall. The broad shallow pool beneath the falls is a fine place to cool off on a hot day. Around the middle of the falls is a wonderful, smooth chute down to the pool, reached from a ledge curtained by the falls themselves. To get there one has to plunge through a forcefully dropping wall of water. If you lose your nerve—or your footing—the rush of the water will bump you down a very unsmooth chute. Most likely you will not break any bones, but bruises are guaranteed. Ask the local kids, some of whom are sure to be riding the watery chute on any given hot day, how to get to the ledge behind the falls. They will show you, and may be sympathetic with your hesitations. They figure it has been a long time since you touched the tip of your tongue to a railroad track on a freezing night, that you have forgotten about dares, how to play kick-the-can and, in general, have lost touch with reality.

The national park visitor center is close to the old Mormon settlement of Fruita. In 1886, when antipolygamy laws were passed in Utah, local settlers searched for a livable hideaway should enforcement officers arrive in an attempt to break up their pattern of family living. They selected a narrow, hidden canyon that overlooked the Fremont, which fractured into a maze of side canyons into which families or the whole community could vanish if pursued. The gorge was nicknamed Cohabitation Canyon, and the area, its name now shortened to Cohab Canyon, can be traversed by a 1¾-mile trail winding between Highway 24 and the road that leads south from the visitor center. There are a number of developed trails in this region of the reef. From Cohab Canyon one can take the Frying Pan Trail, which twists in and out of canyons, wanders across slickrock, and finally works its way over the crest of the reef itself. On the other side it joins the Cassidy Arch Trail, which leads past an arch named for bandit Butch, and emerges in Grand Wash. The entire journey runs close to six miles. The Rim Overlook Trail, four and a half miles round trip, ends where there are magnificent vistas in three directions—and one thousand feet straight down. The Golden Throne Trail is another steep haul to a high vantage

Waterpocket Fold from the Rim Trail in Capitol Reef National Park.

point; Whiskey Spring Trail affords a view of Hickman Natural Bridge and ends at a small spring set in a shady canyon. A trail leads into Capitol Gorge, which pierces the very heart of the reef. At one place the slot is only eighteen feet wide, with walls rising to over a thousand feet on either side.

Although some fine one-day rambles can be made over the park's developed trails, a notable feature of Capitol Reef National Park is its lack of roads, developed trails, or campsites; this tends to discourage the press of people eager to get a few snapshots, spend the night, and then wheel off down to the highway to the next national park on the vacation agenda. Even the one developed campsite in the park has an unhurried flavor. It is located in a peach orchard near the river, and campers are welcome in season to pick the fruit for their tables.

The southern reaches of the park are still gratifyingly wild. A dirt road, swinging south off Highway 24, heads down along the fold, past imposing mesas to the east—Wildcat, Tarantula, Swap, and Big Thompson. Although the switchbacking Burr Trail—actually a dirt road—will lead out of Waterpocket Fold and around Studhorse Peak to connect eventually with pavement at Boulder, and roads lead into the Henry Mountains and Bullfrog Basin on Lake Powell, this is mostly a region of rough jeep-trails and immensities of great country to be explored afoot.

Hall's Creek, which drains the southern end of Waterpocket Fold when there is water to be drained, is a beautiful canyon. It is named for Charles Hall, a bearded Mormon outlander who operated a ferry across the Colorado from 1881 to 1884. Hall had built the ferry with logs, planks, and pitch. When the infrequent customer would arrive, the ferry was towed upstream a way and then paddled across river on the diagonal. The toll was five dollars per wagon and seventy-five cents per horse. To even get to the ferry, one had to follow Harris Wash down to the Escalante River, ford it, trek up the steep gorge of Silver Falls Creek to a wild, broken country rimmed by the Circle Cliffs, and then find a funnel that led into a narrow canyon that was reached after a drop of a thousand feet in less than two miles. The canyon itself was so narrow, convoluted, and overhung that it was soon called Muley Twist by those who traveled to Hall's Ferry. Those who had not become lost, quicksanded, rimrocked, broken an axle, or had more unusual disasters, emerged from Muley Twist onto Hall's Creek, which they followed down to the Colorado and the ferry.

Hall's Ferry ceased operations after four years. While used, albeit scantly, the route had been one of the roughest wagon roads in America. That same route, hiked today, is one of the most lonely and lovely long walks in America. Plan at least a week to allow for side explorations.

Pioneer Mormons, who were the first non-Indians to see much of the grandeur of canyon country, were principally interested in finding pockets of land that could be cultivated or grazed and ways to get to them. Their attitude toward the spectacular rock formations was perhaps best summed up by Ebenezer Bryce, who observed of the canyon that now bears his name that it would be "a hell of a place to lose a cow." Yet Mormon colonists, urged by Brigham Young and church elders to extend the boundaries of Deseret by settlement, continued to push their way through the maze of rugged canyons.

In November of 1879 some 250 people—men, women, and children—gathered at Forty Mile Spring southeast of the village of Escalante. There were eighty-three wagons and a thousand head of stock. The expedition had been mustered to establish a settlement on Montezuma Creek, a tributary of the San Juan River. As final preparations were being made, it was discovered that a huge nearby natural amphitheater had the makings of a fine dance floor. While scouts probed the rough country ahead, the settlers square danced to the lively tunes of three fiddlers who happened to

Along the Rim Trail. The black boulders beside the trail and resting on ledges of the canyon wall are volcanic rocks carried here from miles away, in the Ice Age, by outrushing glacial melt waters.

be along. The amphitheater has since been known as Dance Hall Rock. The scouts returned with somber news—the route had not been thoroughly explored, and there seemed no feasible way to get across the ramparts of Glen Canyon.

Close to the mouth of the Escalante River the colonizers found a narrow fault. They called it "Hole-in-the-Rock." During the arduous road-

17

building that occupied them for the next six weeks, rock had to be blasted and chipped away and the loose materials used to shore up the other side of an emerging wagon road. In one particularly hazardous stretch oak poles were set into holes chopped into a cliff and tracks laid across them. Eventually all eighty-three wagons descended to the water, where a ferry had to be constructed to get them to the other side.

The pioneers spent all winter crawling across the canyon country. Sometimes blizzards swirled around them. About Gray Mesa a woman was later to write home that ". . . It's nothing in the world but rocks and holes, hills and hollows. The mountains are just one solid rock. . . ." On another mesa a forest of piñon, cedar, and juniper was so thick that trees had to be felled to let the wagons through. There was a constant need to cut "dugways" to allow the wagons to get in and out of the canyons, and up over sharp ridges. Three babies had been born before the settlers decided to halt and start the community now called Bluff, only eighteen miles from Montezuma Creek, the original goal.

The Escalante River was the last major American waterway to be named in the United States (outside of Alaska). Not surprisingly, explorer John Wesley Powell was the man who named it. The river begins upon the ten thousand-foot high Aquarius Plateau (also known as Boulder Mountain) and soon cuts deeply into sandstone, shale, and conglomerate formations. It is joined by tributaries from the Aquarius Plateau—Cherry Creek, Pine Creek, Calf Creek, and Boulder Creek. For nearly all of its entrenched, meandering course to Lake Powell, the high escarpment of the Circle Cliffs follows it to the northeast, the Straight Cliffs of the Kaiparowits Plateau to the southwest. Over the centuries, storm water sluicing down off these great rock walls and carving its way across slickrock to the Escalante has created profound and contorted side canyons. Silver Falls Creek, Harris Wash, Moody Creek, Coyote Gulch, and Stevens Canyon are all magnificent in their own right. Many of the mouths of the interesting draws that once twisted into the lower part of the Escalante are now slabbed over by the rising waters of Lake Powell.

The Escalante River gorge itself—a wonderland of towering cliffs, overhangs, natural arches, small seep springs, and other delights—is accessible by foot from several side tributaries. *By foot!* Not only do the Escalante and its numerous feeder canyons comprise a region of unique beauty, but this is wilderness. With the exception of a sixty-mile dead-end dirt road to Hole-in-the-Rock, nearly all of the Escalante Basin below the town of Escalante is roadless. The most popular route down into the canyon is by way of Hurricane Wash and Coyote Gulch. One follows the Hole-in-the-Rock road for some forty miles before turning onto a jeep-track that follows the wash for a couple of miles and then swings up onto the rim. From this point, where the trail used by cattle, game, and hikers

Deep in the gorge of the Escalante River at Coyote Gulch.

begins, the dry, sandy wash begins to narrow and deepen. In one stretch
the passage is only about eight feet wide, rimmed by sheer sandstone. As in
much of Paria Canyon, to be caught here in a flash flood would probably
be fatal. Farther down, as the walls climb higher, the wash broadens and
one comes to the first water—small seeps and stagnant pools. Some five
miles from the trail head the wash twists sharply and opens into Coyote
Gulch.

Coyote Gulch has fine stands of cottonwoods, clumps of willows, and
numerous seeps and springs that trickle into a good-sized stream. In this
solitude, this immensity of carved rock, water is often heard long before it
is seen. The seeps upon the cliff walls, usually a mere trickle of clear, cool
water, are usually marked by tapestries of vegetation—ferns, scarlet
monkeyflower, ivy, and columbine. It is about seven miles down Coyote
Gulch to the Escalante River. The gorge writhes its way deeper and deeper
into layers of ancient rock. In a number of places the walls all but shut out
the sky overhead. The outside of the meanders usually undercut the cliff.
Some of the overhangs are hundreds of feet high: vast, smooth domes that
resemble amphitheaters. Although damp, such places are virtually plantless
since sunlight only enters as a reflection from the opposite wall.

About a mile below the junction of Hurricane Wash and Coyote
Gulch is Jacob Hamblin Arch. The great window is set in a sandstone fin

A vast overhang carved out by the waters of Coyote Gulch.

Stevens Arch, also called Skyline Arch, opens 500 feet above the Escalante River.

which forces the creek to form a gooseneck around it. Eventually, the creek will cut through the wide loop, turning the arch into a natural bridge. Approaching the Escalante River, Coyote Gulch becomes wilder, with cascades fifteen to twenty feet high and angular, high boulder gardens where slabs of overhanging cliff have fallen into the canyon within the last few centuries. Men have found ways around the jumpoffs and obstructions—steps chopped into the sandstone and, in one place, a log tilted against a rock ledge, are the only feasible routes downward.

The gorge of the Escalante River itself has an intimacy lacking in such vast defiles as the Grand Canyon. Each bend of the canyon is a revelation of soaring rock and random, varied plant life that is more satisfying than the most carefully planned Japanese garden. A few miles downstream one comes to the flatwater of Lake Powell, which has already submerged such marvels as Gregory Arch and the narrow chasm of Soda Gulch. Probably the best hiking lies upriver. One passes wind-smoothed hand- and foot-holes leading up cliffs to ancient storage huts, abandoned

by the Anasazi people prior to the fifteenth century. There is Stevens
Arch, whose opening is five hundred feet above the river. The immense
window is 160 feet wide at its base. One can explore elegant side canyons
such as Stevens and Moody. Except during the high water of spring runoff,
which makes the going tricky in some sections, one can backpack the entire
waterway from Calf Creek to Lake Powell, some fifty miles of magnificence. Calf Creek campground is on State Highway 12, between Boulder
and Escalante.

To the northeast of the Escalante River, on the other side of Waterpocket Fold, are the Henry Mountains. The range was named by Powell.
The two highest summits, Mount Ellen and Mount Pennell, rise to well
over eleven thousand feet, and afford one of the finest views in all America.
From grassy meadows backdropped by stands of conifers and aspen one
can take in a vast sweep of canyon country—Waterpocket Fold, the canyon of the Dirty Devil River, the Maze, the Needles, and Lake Powell.

There are those who glowingly refer to Lake Powell as the most
beautiful reservoir in the country. They are probably right. Massive sandstone cliffs and pinnacles rise out of blue waters. Intriguing side canyons, in
which the water is still rising, twist back into slickrock. Yet those who
remember the wonders of Glen Canyon before it was buried by water
grieve as at the mutilation of all fine and unique things. They remember the
mysterious grottoes, thickets, and cottonwood groves that once were alive
with birds and small animals, and Indian ruins now lost under thickening
sediments of mud and trash. While the number of people who have
discovered the joys of backpacking and wild-river boating grows rapidly
each year, and the number of places where they may do it decreases
steadily, agencies like the Bureau of Reclamation continue to proclaim the
"recreational values" of flatwater. If all the flatwater created by the Bureau
of Reclamation and the Army Corps of Engineers in the last half-century
were laid out in strips end to end, one could all but water ski to the moon
and back.

One of the most pious myths perpetrated by federal agency and
chamber of commerce mentalities is that a project like Glen Canyon Dam
makes the outdoor treasures of our land accessible to everyone. As Edward
Abbey points out in *Slickrock* (Sierra Club, Charles Scribner's Sons, New
York, 1971), all that was formerly needed to float Glen Canyon was an
inexpensive rubber raft, or even an inner tube, and a sleeping bag. It
contained no dangerous rapids and was floated by Cub Scouts as well as
octogenarians. Today on Lake Powell one either needs to buy a boat and
incur all the expenses that go with it; rent a boat at better than seventy
dollars a day; or be jammed into an excursion boat with lots of other folks
at *thirty-five* dollars a day.

What has been fobbed off as recreation for everyone emerges as recreation for the rich.

The Escalante, perhaps the finest wild desert canyon left on our continent, faces the same dangers of "progress" that Glen Canyon lost out to. There is discussion of a dam, and, more immediately, the Utah Highway Department would like to build a scenic road from Bullfrog Basin across the Escalante country to Glen Canyon City. The road would slash across the proposed Escalante Wilderness Area and, like all pavement, would undoubtedly produce offshoots of still more pavement. Ultimately, the highway department would like to push the road all the way up across the Maze country, over the Green River, through Moab, and up through Cisco to the Colorado line.

Some shortsighted local business people warm their hands over the idea—roads equate to motels, cafés, curio shops, and money. Yet, in the long run, do they mean profits? Each decade more wilderness becomes manicured; there are more clumps of neon signs and tossed cans. Each decade more people of all ages are coming to treasure the qualities of wilderness. Like gemstones, the economic values of wilderness are subject to supply and demand. Wilderness is becoming more valuable by the year.

In a decade or so, which community will be ahead—the one that solicits the tourist who spends a night in a motel, buys a few rocks, and then "sees" the country at sixty miles an hour and is gone; or the backpacker who spends a night in the same motel, perhaps, but then outfits for two weeks in the wilderness?

Those of us who have come to know the wilderness need no debate, but must be alert to proposed projects which threaten its existence. The land of which we speak mostly belongs to the Bureau of Land Management. In other words, it belongs to us—all of us. And if highways are to be built and dams thrown across wild streams, it is our money which will pay for it. Detailed information upon the proposed trans-Escalante highway controversy can be obtained from the Escalante Wilderness Committee, P.O. Box 8032, Salt Lake City, Utah 84108; and from the Information Office, State Highway Department, State Office Building, Salt Lake City, Utah 84114.

Guide Notes for the ESCALANTE

LOCATION—Southcentral Utah. The region which includes Capitol Reef National Park, the Henry Mountains, and the drainages of the Fremont, Dirty Devil, Escalante and Paria rivers.

ACCESS—There are several routes which skirt or lead into the area. A seventy-mile stretch of Interstate 70 heads directly through the San Rafael Reef west of Green River. State Highway 24 links Hanksville and Salina, crossing Capitol Reef through the cut carved by the Fremont River. State Highway 12 meanders out of Bryce Canyon to Cannonville, Escalante, and Boulder. U.S. 89 marks the southern edge of Escalante country, running from Page, Arizona, to Kanab, Utah. These are the paved roads. Rougher roads, varying from gravel to jeep-trails, ramble through the Henry Mountains, Waterpocket Fold, and elsewhere. The glorious thing about Escalante country is that throughout a sizable chunk of the whole region there are no roads of any description. One parks one's vehicle and heads off into backcountry.

GETTING AROUND—As is the case of canyon country, some of the Escalante region is accessible to four-wheel-drive vehicles. Much of the best and most rugged country, including Escalante Canyon itself, is most readily negotiated afoot. There is boating on Lake Powell.

CAMPING—There are several developed campsites in Escalante country—close to the visitors' center of Capitol Reef National Park, Calf Creek Recreation Area, Kodachrome Basin State Park, up on Boulder Mountain, and in the Henry Mountains. Most of the region, however, is wilderness or semiwilderness, and a campsite is where you find it. From mid- to late summer flash floods often send muddy water roiling down waterways—a good time to be camped above high-water mark. Although there are springs and seeps in Escalante Canyon and some of the other gorges, this is dry country overall and so stock up water accordingly. It pays to check locally on water possibilities, as streams and springs may be seasonal.

SUPPLIES—One can stock up on supplies at several villages in the Escalante region, including Escalante, Boulder, Torrey, and Hanksville.

SPECIAL FEATURES—Like other areas of canyon country, the Escalante region has deep canyons and magnificent formations. Some of the most interesting natural features include Cathedral Valley, Goblin Valley, San Rafael Swell, Capitol Reef, Waterpocket Fold, Escalante Canyon, and Paria Canyon. The high swell of the Henry Mountains offers alpine contrast to the desert country which stretches around it.

INFORMATION SOURCES—Superintendent, Capitol Reef National Park, Torrey, Utah 84775. Escalante Chamber of Commerce, Escalante, Utah 84726. Escalante Wilderness Committee, P. O. Box 8032, Salt Lake City, Utah 84108.

2. Canyonlands

One of the most enjoyable ways of exploring Canyonlands is by boat—raft, kayak, or canoe. Two of America's great rivers, the Green and the Colorado, twist their way through deep canyons to merge at a point that is almost in the geographical center of Canyonlands National Park. The combined flows then crash down through the formidable rapids of Cataract Canyon, "Graveyard of the Colorado." The only other large river in the region, the San Juan, marks the northern edge of the Navajo Reservation and flows into Lake Powell.

Spring and autumn are the most pleasant times of the year for hiking and exploring jeep-trails; summer is my choice for river running. In early summer the rivers are high, gorged with runoff from Rocky Mountain snowfields. The bigger rapids are awesome and challenging. At this time of year one feels the scorching power of the sun, its harsh domination over desert plants and animals. Yet to escape it one need only drop over the side of the boat into chill snow water. The contrast is sensual.

Westwater Canyon of the Colorado, on the Colorado-Utah border, is an exciting portal to the canyon country. It is a canyon that should be attempted only by the experienced whitewater person or as a passenger on one of several commercial trips conducted by professional boatmen. A number of outfitters use huge neoprene "baloney boats" with outboard engines which propel them through the canyon in a single day. A trip with an outfitter who uses smaller rafts that are oar-powered is an infinitely more interesting experience. The rapids are more exciting, the quiet stretches more mellow. Wildlife is not spooked into cover before you get near it.

The traditional put-in for Westwater Canyon is at Westwater Ranch, a few miles west of Grand Junction. Below the ranch the river enters the canyon, cutting deeply through layers of sandstone, shale and limestone—beds of ancient seas pushed slowly skyward over hundreds of centuries. The mouth of the Little Dolores River, several miles downriver on the left-hand side, makes a good campsite. A wide belt of tamarisk lines the sandy shore, with numerous pockets where a couple of sleeping bags can be nestled.

Around the turn of the century there was a minor gold rush into this remote part of the country. Back from the tamarisk are the remains of a small cabin, half-dug into the rocky hillside, and close to it a section of wooden flume that was used for sluicing.

In early summer the Little Dolores is a lively stream, plunging over a waterfall about a half-mile back from the river. Later in the summer the falls are but a mossy trickle and the stream has gone, leaving a series of small pools. Minnows swim in a few of them; one wonders if the pools will dry up completely before a flash flood occurs. Will it wash tiny skeletons or live fish into the muddy Colorado? I have found myself wanting to linger, to observe the drying pools with a certain morbid curiosity. The fingerlings, darting away in ordered frenzy at my approach, probably have no sense of their danger, any more than most humans upon an abused and equally endangered planet Earth. God and scientific technology may not be enough when the pool dries up.

In midsummer there is a waist-high pool beneath the waterfall, which is only a trickle by then. The pool, far from being homogeneous in temperature, is composed of sections of chill and tepid water that curiously seem to have not the slightest boundary of blending. It is a peaceful place to spend an afternoon alternately basking in the sun or floating upon the water. The small pool creatures, after some initial panic, soon begin to ignore your presence, much as a man might get used to a dirigible if it hovered over his garden long enough. Smaller minnows, I have discovered, tend to veer away in a school as one approaches. Larger ones hide in rock crannies or small clumps of algae. Dozens of polliwogs wriggle about or lie motionless on the bottom. Tiny frog legs sprout absurdly from some of them; others have become frogs except they still retain polliwog tails, and a few look completely froglike yet so small at least three of them could nestle comfortably within a teaspoon. It is like watching a stop-action sequence in a film. Water striders rush about the surface of the water maniacally, resembling minute hydroplanes, while usually one sees a large frog or two crouching, almost camouflaged, beneath shady overhangs of stone.

Beyond the Little Dolores River the Colorado begins to tumble through some heavy-duty rapids. Funnel Falls is the first of two really large rapids in Westwater Canyon. Huge boulders reach out into the current from either shore, retarding the flow and forcing it into a whitewater chaos at midstream. In high water it is rather like riding through the breach of a dam that has just broken. Nevertheless, Funnel Falls is not as treacherous as Skull Rapids, a short distance downriver. One has to bear right to avoid a huge hole, then quickly cross to the left-hand side of the river. The main current piles up against a bulge of the canyon wall. If a boat bounces off this without capsizing it may be drawn into a giant whirlpool in a sheer-walled pocket of sandstone. Boats have circled for hours in this trap before breaking free.

On the old trail from the Doll House down to Spanish Bottom on the Colorado River in Cataract Canyon, deep in Canyonlands National Park.

Men have drowned here.

There are several other lively rapids, such as Sock-It-To-'Em and Cisco, before quiet water is reached and the canyon walls fall away. In the lower canyon one passes through a belt of Vishnu Schist, as old as any exposed rock in the world. It is not hard to imagine that the strangely eroded, polished black stone walls might have once been battlements of a city carved from a single dark gemstone by a people who lived and perished before there was any other life and when volcanoes rained fire. Before the Westwater Canyon takeout at Cisco Pumping Station, a quiet person will begin to hear and see Colorado salmon, a species of whitefish, leaping clear out of the water in eddies close to the shore—a tasty fish when browned in bacon grease.

At the Cisco Pumping Station takeout one is reminded that the twenty-six-mile run of Westwater Canyon is only for expert boaters or passengers of expert boatmen. On an overlook above the river is a marble gravestone surrounded by red and yellow plastic flowers. The inscription reads:

Charlie Ray Sherrill:
born January 11, 1943:
Lost in Westwater Canyon:
November 15, 1972

From the Cisco Pumping Station all the way down to its confluence with the Green, the Colorado is a gentle river which passes through some of the most beautiful country in the world. The village of Cisco is a huddle of buildings on a wide prairie. Bypassed by Interstate 70, most of the businesses have closed up and homes are abandoned, surrounded by rusting cars and old farm implements. A single café remains open. South of Cisco the prairie is pocked by hundreds of shallow basins which were bulldozed out in a futile effort to catch the scant rainfall for agricultural purposes. Evaporation and seepage doomed the project.

At Dewey, another hamlet, State Highway 128, here a dirt road, crosses the Colorado on a narrow suspension bridge. There are wonders in every direction. To the west is Arches National Park, 137 square miles of wildly sculptured sandstone and beautiful desert country. Eastward, Fisher, Professor, and Castle valleys contain strange and monumental formations. Dominating the skyline are the 12,000-foot high La Sal Mountains. Rearing up at the head of Fisher Valley are Fisher Towers, which an astrophysicist named Huntley Ingalls once described as "a pink, red, and orange skyscraper city in nightmare Gothic." Ingalls' description is well suited to the strangely eroded, almost sheer-sided pinnacles, but then he had a lot of time to think about it while climbing the tallest tower, the Titan, some nine hundred feet high. Ingalls and two companions spent three and a half days inching their way to the top; six hours in the long series of rappels back to the desert floor. Looking at the monolith today, the feat seems almost superhuman, especially considering that most of the rock is rotten and much of it covered with dried mud.

The sport of ascending, or attempting to ascend, desert spires has become somewhat more popular since the 1962 conquest of the Titan—but not much. The vertical faces require expert knowledge of direct-aid climbing, and are physically demanding. Hundreds of pitons must be placed and removed; numerous expansion bolts must be put into the rock. Most direct-aid climbing is made on the harder rocks, such as granite. The majority of desert spires are composed of softer sandstone, which flakes and crumbles easily. Even during winter months the rock can become scorching to the touch.

Nevertheless, a number of seemingly impossible spires with names like Castle Rock, the Vanishing Angel, Moses, Zeus, and the Owl continue

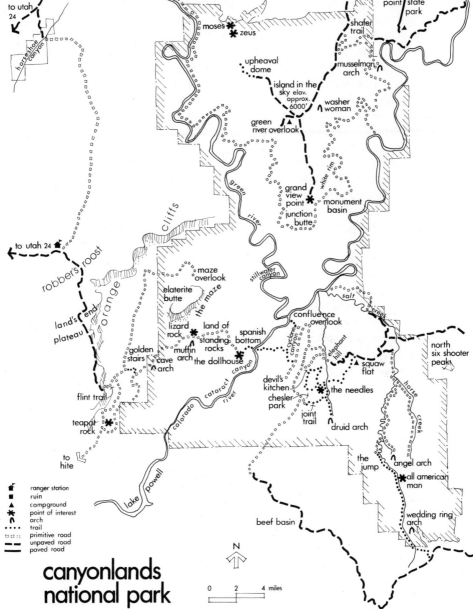

to moab

to moab

potash

horsethief
bottoms

dead horse
point state
park

to utah
24

moses zeus

shafer
trail

horseshoe canyon

upheaval
dome

musselman
arch

island in the
sky elev.
approx.
6000'

washer
woman

green
river overlook

white rim

grand
view
point

monument
basin

junction
butte

to utah 24

robber's roost

maze
overlook

stillwater canyon

salt creek

elaterite
butte

the maze

confluence
overlook

orange

cliffs

green river

land's end
plateau

lizard
rock

land of
standing
rocks

spanish
bottom

cyclone canyon

elephant
hill

squaw
flat

north
six shooter
peak

golden
stairs

muffin
arch

cave
arch

the dollhouse

devil's
kitchen

the needles

horse creek

flint trail

cataract canyon

chesler
park

joint
trail

druid arch

teapot
rock

colorado river

the
jump

angel arch

all american
man

to
hite

lake powell

wedding ring
arch

beef basin

ranger station
ruin
campground
point of interest
arch
trail
primitive road
unpaved road
paved road

canyonlands
national park

N

0   2   4 miles

to fall to skilled teams of climbers, who usually do some falling themselves in the process (although safety techniques have kept fatalities at a minimum). Moab has become a sort of base camp for this new breed of climbers.

For every spire awaiting conquest by the specialist, there are dozens of intriguing canyons and backcountry paths that can be explored by anyone with a stout pair of lungs and shoes, as well as an adequate water supply. Below Fisher Towers, for example, Onion Creek writhes its way through a maze of blood-red formations. A graded spur road leaves State Highway 128 near Fisher Towers. It is marked by an inconspicuous sign that reads "Fisher Valley." After about a mile the road begins to cross and recross the creek, whose mineral composition does indeed give it a pungent, although not overpowering, odor. The road follows the creek for the most part, leaving it to climb a higher bench for about a mile in one particularly beautiful section. Here one can hike through a narrow chasm and then be picked up at the upper end. There are myriad side canyons and grottoes, all of which are spectacular. One of them contains an old mine with a steam winch. Above the deeply cut gorge section of Moenkopi and Cutler deposits, the stream passes through a valley of pastel-hued gypsum deposits. Here the water picks up its garlicky odor, inoffensive to most people, as well as the dark arsenic seeps, highly offensive to anyone's stomach.

Above the gypsum area the stream, now clear and odorless, splits into its several sources. Almost all of them are small springs set in rock-wall glades, where willow grass grows thickly and old cottonwoods shade the flow that waters them. Still higher up Fisher Valley opens into a verdant meadow, ranchland with cliffs on three sides. And yet above that are the forests, meadows, and high-piled humps of the La Sal Range.

There are countless canyons and creeks like Onion Creek in the canyon country of Utah, passing through contrasting vegetation zones, through rock formations of staggering beauty and diversity. Yet each, in its totality, is almost as individual as a person. Unlike Onion Creek, most of them are roadless, offering one of the last great empires of wild country in America.

During the 1830s and 1840s New Mexican traders frequented a trail which ran from Santa Fe to southern California by way of central Utah. Mule trains bearing wool were herded over a thousand miles to the coast, where the cargo was exchanged for horses and mules to be driven back to Santa Fe. Some traders fattened their profits by capturing or bartering for Indian slaves in the Sevier River Country. By 1855, when Mormon colonists built a fort where the Spanish trail forded the Colorado, few traders still used the route. The Mormons arrived in mid-June and immediately set about digging ditches, planting crops, and preaching to the Ute Indians.

The outpost was named Elk Mountain Mission. The settlers had little time or inclination to enjoy the natural wonders that lay in every direction. There was no timber, firewood was scarce, and the soil was sandy. It was hot. One of the colonists wrote to his brother: "I have suffered more than I can express at present for want of water to drink; the sun's piercing rays and the sun burning your feet under you, soon dries a man up. I have been sick after being alkalied. . . ." In September Utes killed three men outside of the fort. The struggle, the danger, and the remoteness were all too much, and Elk Mountain Mission was abandoned.

By 1877 cattlemen moving into the canyon country of Utah discovered the fort of Elk Mountain Mission to be occupied by two trapper-prospectors, a French-Canadian known as Frenchie and a mulatto whose moniker was Nigger Bill. A lovely canyon north of Moab still bears the latter's name, and is highly regarded by local youths for camping, picnicking, and skinny-dipping in the clear waters of the stream. Most of the ranchers soon discovered that the best rangeland lay in the high country of the La Sal Mountains to the east and built their headquarters in that area. By this time Mormon settlers had returned to the fort and named their reestablished community Moab, which means "Far Country," the Biblical land beyond the River Jordan and the Dead Sea.

For a good many years Moab would be known as a quiet desert village, a wide place in the road on U.S. Highway 163, where summer travelers would pause to sip a soft drink beside heat-softened blacktop and wonder who would choose to live in such a God-forsaken place.

That all changed in the early 1950s, when a uranium prospector named Charles Steen came charging across his Moab yard to his house trailer, bellowing his wife's name. In his excitement he upset the clothesline, but his wife had little cause to resent the resoiled wash. Steen, a geologist whose family had lived in a tent for a time, without money enough even to buy milk for his baby, had rushed to tell his wife he had struck it rich. His Mi Vida Mine would make him a wealthy man.

A while back, a bank had refused him a $250 loan to grubstake his prospecting. After the Mi Vida came in, Steen bought the bank.

Vernon Pick, another prospector, had spent months prowling the bare rock outback. Like Steen, he made his big strike at the end of his financial tether, wading up a stream that he drank from, which almost killed him—arsenic in the water. Pick, delirious from the poison and gaunt from lack of food, staggered out of the backcountry to record a claim that would make him a multimillionaire.

Other uranium prospectors were finding rich ores in the area, and by the mid-1950s Moab was said to be the richest town in America, per capita. There was little change in life-style. An old prospector who had just sold a claim for $100,000 was asked by a reporter from a Salt Lake City newspaper what he intended to do with the bonanza. "I'm fixin' to buy my missus a rocking chair," he responded. Mostly, the wives of the new millionaires continued to live in the frame houses they had always lived in, and bought what they needed at Miller's General Store, as they always had. Only now they never had to worry about the register running over their checking account balances or the money in their pockets. The men added an extra bedroom now and again, or had a bathroom installed with flush toilets, but mostly their cash outlay was for jeeps, mining equipment, and airplanes. Some of the newly wealthy bought mansions in Salt Lake City or Denver, but most sold out soon, to return to the desert village that was home to them.

The uranium boom faded by the late 1950s, but the town lingered and, in a curious desert sense, began to flourish. There were still the cross-country travelers who paused for soft drinks, beer, a cheeseburger, a motel room—yet gradually people were beginning to come to Moab as a destination in itself.

Uranium prospectors and others before them had talked of strange and beautiful places: of narrow chasms where sunlight never touched bottom; gigantic windows of stone; thousands of square miles of carved, multihued rock.

Arches National Park, northwest of Moab, contains, among other things, eighty-eight natural arches. Some 150 million years ago a layer of sandstone was deposited when the region was probably a coastal desert. Later this bed, known as the Entrada formation, was raised to an elevation of some five thousand feet, cracking and weathering in the process. The Entrada and formations above and below it were gradually eroded into thin reefs. The alternate freezing and thawing of rainwater pried chunks of rock loose to create shallow caves that eventually, in many cases, broke through to caves on the other side of the reef, creating arches. As the freeze and thaw process enlarged the openings, wind-driven sand smoothed the apertures.

Landscape Arch, near the north end of the park, is almost as long as a football field, yet it is only six feet thick at its thinnest point. Delicate Arch rises from the rim of a smooth rock bowl, a majestic sixty-five foot salmon-colored arch that rests upon slender legs. The cowboys and sheepherders who first frequented the area, rarely given to romantic nomenclature, called it the Old Maid's Bloomers. In like fashion, they referred to the magnificent formations now officially named Double Arch as the Jug Handles. Many of the most beautiful formations are in the sections named Fiery Furnace and Devil's Garden. Other formations include the Stone Elephants, Eye of the Whale, Cave of Caves, and Dark Angel. Here, as throughout the canyon country, one grasps for names and statistics in what is perhaps an attempt to avoid the unavoidable; in a place of such over-

Indian rock art in Canyonlands National Park.

powering beauty, descriptions tend to trip over well-worn adjectives. Better to look at photographs—or better yet, go there and see.

Park headquarters is five miles northwest of Moab on Route 163. No roads penetrated the Arches area until 1937, eight years after it was set aside as a national park. Today an eighteen-mile surfaced road winds up through the middle of the park, and spur roads lead to vista points. Nevertheless, many of the finest areas of the park are still solely the domain of hikers and overnight backpackers.

Southwest of Moab is Canyonlands National Park, which encompasses majestic canyons, narrow and twisting gorges, thousands of rock formations of every conceivable size, shape, and hue, Indian ruins and rock art, some of the most challenging river rapids in America, and a great deal more. Although this is a land of rocks, where vegetation is sparse, the variety of species is profuse. In the 1880s a botanist discovered so many species of the genus *Astragalus* that he ran out of names; upon discovering yet another new species he called it *desperatus*. In late spring the canyon country is carpeted with wildflowers—evening primrose, yellow hollygrape,

and pastures of globe mallow. The white and lavender clusters of locoweed, lovely to behold, are not appreciated by stockmen. If pasturage is
poor, cattle and horses will eat locoweed. When even a small amount is
consumed their vision is distorted by the hallucinogenic properties of the
plant, especially when the animals are overheated. They tend to shy vio-
lently, buck or race madly about, and to crash headlong into fences or
trees. Should the animals eat large quantities of the plant, they become
addicted to it and will eat nothing else, standing about in a dreamy stupor
until they die of malnutrition.

There is a variety of wildlife. Bighorn sheep roam the high cliffs of
some of the steeper canyons, such as Cataract, while pronghorn antelope
graze in the open country. In the 1880s a nine-hundred-pound grizzly took
to killing cattle in the Robber's Roost country. In the five years between his
first known kill and the time the prospectors finally shot him, he was
credited with doing in 138 cattle. Presumably, the figure would be higher
when one considers he probably knocked off a number of rustled stock, but
such events were not likely to be reported to the Cattlemen's Association.
Today, although black bear live only in the Abajo Mountains that fringe

Overlooking the confluence of the Green and Colorado rivers above Cataract
Canyon.

the southeastern corner of the park, mule deer, cougars, bobcats, and coyotes are distributed throughout the region. Beavers and ducks live along the Colorado and Green rivers. Because of the wide range of habitats, bird life is extremely rich and varied.

The canyons of the Green and Colorado rivers effectively separate Canyonlands National Park into three sections, each with its own access. The wedge between the two rivers, where a road runs out to Grand View Point, is reached by roads running southwest out of Moab. Access to the western region, containing the Maze and Land of Standing Rocks, is from State Highway 24 between Green River and Hanksville. Access to the eastern side, the Needles region, is from Monticello.

Captain John Macomb entered the canyon country in 1859 with orders to ascertain the confluence of the Green and Colorado rivers and to find the most direct route between New Mexico and the southern settlements of Utah. John Newberry, the geologist with the party, was awed by the country:

> . . . while in the intervening space the surface was diversified by columns, spires, castles, and battlemented towers of colossal but often beautiful proportions, closely resembling elaborate structures of art, but in effect far surpassing the most imposing monuments of human skill. In the southwest, was a longer line of spires of . . . white stones standing on red bases, thousands in number, but so slender as to recall the most delicate carving in ivory . . . yet many, perhaps most, were over five hundred feet in height. . . . The appearance was so strange and beautiful as to call out exclamations of delight from all our party.

Captain Macomb was in a more pragmatic frame of mind when he wrote his report: "I cannot conceive of a more worthless and impracticable region than the one we now find ourselves in. . . ."

Ten years later, one-armed Major John Wesley Powell headed an expedition that started at the town of Green River, Wyoming, and followed the course of the Green to its confluence with the Colorado, then called the Grand. In Stillwater Canyon above the junction the current was smooth, "as if in no haste to leave this beautiful canyon," as Powell was later to write. The expedition's wooden boats then entered the dangerous rapids of Cataract Canyon, some of which were run, many of which were lined, before the quieter waters of Glen Canyon were reached. Powell, one of the world's great explorers, successfully voyaged one thousand miles of an unknown, rapid-torn river where anything was possible—a sheer-walled gorge where the current would spew them over a waterfall, death from starvation (at the conclusion of the journey provisions had been reduced to coffee and flour), or ambush by hostile Indians (three members of the party, who elected to leave the river and work their way to Mormon settlements, were indeed skewered with arrows). Yet Powell had come to the river as a naturalist rather than as an adventurer. All along the river he laboriously made geographical determinations, collected plants, and took note of geological formations and archeological remains.

Today one of the most enjoyable ways to explore Canyonlands continues to be by river. Rubber rafts are the most common conveyance, although wooden cataract boats and kayaks also make the run. One can put in at the town of Green River for a trip to the confluence down the Green, or at Potash, a few miles south of Moab, for a trip down the Colorado. Both rivers leisurely loop their way down to the confluence, the entrance to Cataract Canyon. Cataract, nicknamed the "graveyard of the Colorado," should be attempted only by experts or with a guided float party. Some four miles into the canyon one comes upon Spanish Bottom, a brushy flat with scattered shade trees. It is a good camping spot, although in my opinion a better one, a strip of white sand with trees at either end, lies around the next bend at the foot of some rapids. An old Spanish trail bisects the river here, heading up into the Needles country on the other side of the river. From Spanish Bottom the trail switchbacks steeply up into the Doll House, huge eroded pinnacles banded in deep red and ivory. One evening some companions and I hiked up to the Doll House and unrolled our sleeping bags in a draw where the formations loomed up on three sides. In the moonlight they seemed like gigantic chessmen. No historical records indicate use of this trail by Spaniards or New Mexicans, and it is doubtful they would have had much traffic on such an out-of-the-way and rugged route. More likely, the trail was developed by outlaws operating out of Robber's Roost, for whom its very remoteness would have had advantages.

A river map prepared by veteran whitewaterman Leslie Jones delineates forty-two rapids in Cataract Canyon, although some of these have been inundated by Lake Powell since publication of the map. The predominant sound of the canyon is the roar of a nearby rapid or the muffled growl of a more distant one. Big Drop, referred to as a "tilted waterfall," is considered the most challenging, but a number of others will give one a wild, wet, and exhilarating ride. The cliffs, in places two thousand feet high, are vividly colored. Their composition subtly or abruptly changes as the river cuts through different formations. Powell's party killed two mountain sheep on this stretch of the river. Today, boating parties frequently see the sheep, usually perched high upon the redrock crags. Lake Powell, especially on holiday weekends, can be a real let-down after the solitude and clean campsites of Cataract Canyon. On a recent voyage, when our party arrived at Lake Powell on the Fourth of July, the sound of rapids was replaced by the buzz set up by a swarm of motorboats. A vacant campsite was hard to find. We finally came upon an unoccupied stretch of beach that a power-boat party had just left. The camp, which should have been lovely, was marred by discarded cans, a broken fishing rod, and a string of rotting catfish that no one had even bothered to clean.

The western portion of Canyonlands is the most remote and difficult to get to. It contains some of the most beautiful country to be found anywhere. West of Green River, turn south on State Highway 24 and head toward Hanksville. Several miles from Hanksville, a small Mormon farming settlement, a dirt road heads across Land's End Plateau, a lonely region that was a favored hideout of Butch Cassidy, the Sundance Kid, and other members of the Wild Bunch. Robber's Roost Draw, in a redrock ravine with a spring and grass, was headquarters for the Wild Bunch and other desperados from time to time.

In this rough country all that was needed to get into the cattle business was a good horse, a long rope, and a branding iron. Utah stock could be rustled and driven across the Colorado River at one of several crossings, to be sold in Colorado or New Mexico; fresh cattle could be picked up on the way back to reverse the process. When the railroad was completed to the north, not only was the market for pilfered stock improved, but the blasting open of baggage car strongboxes came into vogue. Sheriffs and Pinkerton agents had little desire to track their quarries into the difficult country of Land's End Plateau. Water was scarce and any one of the countless curious rock formations might conceal ambushers. The inhabitants of Robber's Roost were prone to shoot any stranger on sight, though this is not to say they had no differences among themselves. Throughout the winter of 1882 bands of rival rustlers were stealing each other's stolen cattle, which led to bad feelings in general, and several dead rustlers specifically.

Robert LeRoy Parker, better remembered as Butch Cassidy, was born in 1866 to a respected Mormon family in Circleville, Utah. His boyhood idol was a cowhand named Mike Cassidy, who taught him how to quick-draw and rustle cattle. When Cassidy finally left the region—some say for Mexico to avoid a term in the slammer—young Parker adopted his name and embarked upon a life of crime. Although in recent years books and films have taken off from the Wild Bunch legend on even wilder flights of imagination, little is actually known about their activities or those of other badhats in Robber's Roost country—which is reasonable, one might say, considering they went there to avoid publicity.

The dirt road across Land's End Plateau passes a ranger station, then swings south along the rim of the Orange Cliffs. The graded road ends at the head of the Flint Trail, where a precipitous jeep-track zigzags down the Orange Cliffs. From the base of the Flint Trail the south fork makes a huge hairpin around Teapot Rock and is very rugged for several miles. One jounces into a region of extraordinary formations—Red Cove, the Golden

Stairs, Cave Arch, Lizard Rock, Muffin Arch, the Land of Standing Rocks.
. . . The jeep-trail ends close to the Doll House, where a footpath takes
off for Spanish Bottom and the Needles. From the base of Flint Trail a jeep-
track runs north and then west to an overlook of the Maze. Hiking in the
Maze, a place of delightfully demented topography, is both rewarding and
challenging. Before starting out, inquiries should be made at the ranger
station.

In parts of the Maze, and especially in Horseshoe Canyon to the north
of it, one finds powerful rock art dating from prehistoric times. Some are
tall, brooding figures—perhaps sentinels guarding ancient, long-forgotten
territories. Other figures seem to hold sickles, while yet others crouch over
pairs of sticks. Archeologists see these as representations of reapers and
seed-beaters. In Horseshoe Canyon a six-foot figure of a man has one arm
raised aloft while his other hand touches the root of a tree as if giving it
life.

The wedge of Canyonlands lying between the Green and Colorado
rivers is justifiably renowned for spectacular vistas, among other things.
Paved road access to the area is from U.S. Highway 163, eleven miles
north of Moab. Before the national park is reached a paved side-road leads
out to the narrow neck of Dead Horse Point State Park. Here the plateau
narrows to a knife-edge only a few yards wide before broadening into a
pasture of some forty acres. There are sheer drops on virtually every side.
From the point one can look down over the rock terraces that fall away to
the muddy flow of the Colorado River two thousand feet below. Beyond,
deeply eroded and colorful side canyons open into the main gorge of the
Colorado, and buttes, pillars, and pinnacles are scattered throughout the
landscape. Many are jagged and eroded, while others are as smooth as if
turned upon a lathe.

In the late 1880s cowhands stretched a wire fence with a wide gate
across the thin neck of the point. They would drive wild mustangs out onto
this natural corral and then cut the most likely horses out of the herd,
either to be saddle-broken on the spot or held for later sale. At day's end
the wranglers would drive their newly acquired horses back to their line
camp, leaving the gate open to release the culls and stallions too quick or
feisty to be captured. One evening the gate was left closed. It may have
been carelessness or done spitefully by a cowhand who had been kicked,
stomped, or bitten by one of the horses. In any case, the animals were
trapped and died of thirst within sight of the river far below.

There is an attractive campground at Dead Horse Point, with sites set
back against rock clusters with cedar trees. The visitors' center houses an
excellent museum.

The principal Canyonlands road out of Moab continues south beyond
the Dead Horse Point turnoff, continuing along the high plateau that lies

between the two great rivers. Just before reaching a narrow neck that marks the edge of Island-in-the-Sky, the Shafer Trail twists its way down eight hundred vertical feet—strictly a jeep-trail for those who do not mind having a wheel or two dangling out in space from time to time. Rancher Sog Shafer built the trail back in the twenties to work cattle between the plateau and the river. At that time it was one cow wide, but uranium miners have broadened it since then—though not much. I once rode a jeep down the Shafer Trail. The steering wheel was in the capable hands of Lin

The Maze in Canyonlands. Note the sharp drop-off in the canyon bottom.

Ottinger, who alternates his time between guiding people into the outback of canyon country and just prowling it on his own. Lin stopped the jeep at one particular tight bend on the Shafer Trail and we gazed off the brink. "They call this poison corner," he commented. "One drop will kill you."

Although Ottinger likes to ham it up with the Baltimore lawyers and Sioux Falls businessmen who take his tours, he is a resourceful man in a pinch. At one time, with his spare tire demolished by rough rock, a tire went flat from three nail-holes. He wedged rubber bands into the punctures with a screwdriver, and then reinflated the tire with a hand pump. A bit farther on the tire once more deflated. There was yet one more nail-hole. Now out of rubber bands, he soaked a screw in motor oil and screwed it into the breach, and the safari continued merrily on its way.

Among the most interesting things that Ottinger came across in the backcountry were several small slabs of rock, black with desert varnish, that were covered with deeply imbedded and well-preserved animal tracks. When paleontologists from the University of California and the University of Utah investigated the site, they identified several long-extinct species, the most exciting of which were pterosaurs. The pterosaur, a flying reptile that lived over 150 million years ago, has left tracks in only one other site known to man. The antiquity of the rock strata, much older than that of the other site, would indicate that Ottinger had found traces of the first flying vertebrates to evolve upon earth.

The Shafer Trail drops down onto the white rim, a layer of hard sandstone that is sandwiched between softer formations of dark red silt-stones. In a number of places along the edge of the rim, the siltstone has eroded out from under the harder white rim, leaving arches such as Musselman and the Washer Woman, or "mushrooms," where the white cap overhangs pinnacles of the softer material. At Walking Rocks the mush-rooms are so clustered that one can hop from one to another for some distance. The gaps between them are short but the drops become deeper and deeper the farther out one proceeds.

The White Rim jeep-trail follows the rim completely around Island-in-the-Sky, a distance of more than one hundred miles. The best way to get onto the trail is to take a dirt road that follows the river out of Moab to Potash, a large mine. When conventional shaft mining was abandoned after tunnels repeatedly became flooded, a salt solution was pumped into the mines and the potash is now recovered from the solution. A few miles beyond Potash the road becomes suitable only for four-wheel drive vehi-cles. A couple of miles farther on is Shafer Trail, connecting White Rim with Island-in-the-Sky. Farther yet, the White Rim Trail continues on, twisting and turning, skirting the abrupt heads of several magnificent canyons. One of them, Monument Basin, contains numerous slender spires and narrow reefs. Below Junction Butte, at the south apex of the trail, one looks east to the cliffs of Indian Creek and the Needles. To the south a series of benches, canyons, and talus slopes fall away to the confluence of the two rivers. Westward, the Orange Cliffs form a backdrop to the Maze and Land of Standing Rocks. On the Green River side the trail eventually drops down to the banks of the river. From Horsethief Bottoms the trail abruptly switchbacks up cliffs to the top of the plateau and eventually joins the Island-in-the-Sky road.

While the road out to Dead Horse Point is paved, the route to Island-in-the-Sky is dirt, but negotiable by ordinary passenger cars. Roads run out to the aptly named Grand View Point and to Green River Overlook, where there is a campground. Another dirt road continues out to Upheaval Dome. In a region filled with geological curiosities, Upheaval Dome is perhaps the strangest structure of them all. Concentric circles of rock surround a multihued crater, where a mineral-stained mound has pushed up. Close to the center of the crater, a tall, vertical spire rises gracefully from the mound. All of this is in vast scale—the crater itself is some three miles across. The landscape could be Martian or lunar.

In the Land of Standing Rocks, Canyonlands National Park.

Early geologists in the region speculated that Upheaval Dome might be a vast meteor crater. Yet the unshattered curves of towering red cliffs indicate slow warping under tremendous pressure rather than a meteor. Gradually scientists became aware of the salt beds that lie beneath the dome, and how they had pushed upward to bulge the overlying rock strata until it burst open from the pressure. Erosion had broken through the rock rim on the northwest side to form Upheaval Canyon. One can hike up the canyon from the Green River if boating, or from the White Rim jeep-trail.

Salt is responsible for much of the surreal landscape of Canyonlands. A few hundred feet under alluvial deposits, a salt bed as much as two and a half miles thick is found in an area as large as Maryland. The bed is lighter than rock and like paste when pressured from below with the intense forces of the inner earth. It rises into faults and other weak places in the overlying rock, heaving belts of sedimentary rock upward where surface water eroded them into patterns unlike anything else found upon the earth. At least this is what most scientists will tell you, although when you're camping out in Canyonlands and your fire drops to coals and you get to studying the giant gargoyles rising on every side, more magical explanations are sometimes in order.

Explorers had long since traced the sources of the Nile and planted flags in the eternal snows of both the North and South poles before anyone (who left much of a record) filtered into the strange and baffling topography of the Needles country. By and large, the men who first came to know this region were cowhands, whose job was to work the stock into what meager pasturage was to be found. Their appreciation of the Needles was somewhat blunted in that the formations made it difficult to move cattle or find them, water was in scant supply and often unreliable, and there was simply more rock than feed.

Kent Frost, who had grown up in the Monticello area and on a ranch in the La Sal Mountains, had long been intrigued by stories he had heard from wranglers about the Needles. Yet when he backpacked into the area in the spring of 1940 it was still as magnificently mysterious as the Mountains of the Moon in Africa. Few, if any, people had ever been into the myriad places too dry, narrow, or rocky for cattle. In his book, *My Canyonlands,* he writes:

> The next day I hiked across Beef Basin and over the ridge into Fable Valley, arriving there as it started getting dark. I was lucky to find a large cave—and doubly lucky because in my hand was a rabbit that I had shot with my .38 pistol. I made a trip down to the creek for water and put the rabbit on to boil. Coyotes were howling up and down the canyon. A hoot owl chimed in. Several Indian cliff dwellings could be seen near the creek in the dusk. It was an eerie place. I did not leave my fire all night. . . .

Kent Frost is now in the guide business jeeping parties into the core of the Needles country, a place all but unknown three decades ago. Fifteen miles north of Monticello a paved road heads west from U.S. Highway 163. After traveling some thirty miles through redrock canyon country one reaches Squaw Flat, where there is a campground and a ranger station. The pavement ends not far from Squaw Flat at the base of Elephant Hill, a mile-long stone staircase that puts the durability of a four-wheel drive vehicle and the skills of its driver to the test. Beyond are the Needles themselves. The thousands of towers, many of which are gigantic, rise up in a fantasy of shapes and hues—ivory, red, orange, and chocolate. A number of impressive arches lie up side canyons. One might well be viewing a deserted, prehistoric metropolis or a city of the future. Although jeep-trails lead to such landmarks as Cyclone Canyon, the Devil's Lane, and Confluence Overlook, vehicles are now prohibited from Chesler Park and most other sections of the Needles to conserve the delicate ecology.

There are miles of hiking trails to be explored. One of the most fascinating is the Joint Trail. The jeep-trail out of the Devil's Lane has a short spur that ends in Chesler Canyon. The footpath starts up a typical Canyonlands wash—a dry, sandy bottom, except in flash floods, contained by high sandstone walls. The gorge narrows as the trail works its way up rocky terraces where there are sand dunes held in place by grasses and wildflowers, junipers, piñon pine, and desert shrubs scattered about. From each higher vantage point the panorama of the Needles becomes broader. After climbing a series of stone steps, the trail enters a cool cavern formed by overhanging rocks the size of apartment buildings. At the end of this curious cave is a natural window opening onto a canyon view of rock gargoyles and narrow, water-carved passages. Beyond are sheer-walled cracks, or joints, that give the trail its name. Eons ago subterranean pressures made a number of long splits in the rock, and over the centuries erosion has removed much of the debris. Smooth rock walls loom vertically above the fissures. In places on the main trail the crack is less than three feet wide and the sky seems but a blue ribbon far overhead. Side joints are everywhere, most of them pinching out to a vise no human could wriggle through, although a thin person might exit from the rock mass from a few of them if he did not get stuck or lost. Rather suddenly, another flight of steps leads up into sunlight and an overlook of the grassy meadow known as Chesler Park.

From here one can continue to hike on to Druid Arch, back to Squaw Flat and the Devil's Kitchen, or over any one of the many intriguing paths that lead out of the park.

The ramble to Chesler Park up the Joint Trail need take no more than an hour. The total round-trip distance to Druid Arch is six miles. From Squaw Flat it is a thirteen-mile round trip to the Arch, by way of a

Chesler Park, in "The Needles" district, Canyonlands National Park.

beautiful trail that works its way up Elephant Canyon. One should always carry water when hiking Canyonlands, but it should be noted that there are some waterholes in Elephant Canyon. Druid Arch itself is awesome—a vast rock window that is 360 feet high. One might well see it as the remnants of some temple to ancient, forgotten gods.

Topographical maps, nice to have even when prowling somewhat predictable terrain, are pure joy and may be survival tools in the psychotic

iking toward Chesler Park through
e confining gorge of the Joint Trail.

landscapes of Canyonlands. These can be supplemented by trail maps—
both jeep and foot—which are available from the ranger at Squaw Flat. It
is possible to drive a four-wheel-drive vehicle for several miles up three
spectacular canyons—Salt Creek, Horse, and Lavender. All three watercourses have arches. Horse Creek, as well as containing a number of
Anasazi ruins and rock art, is the approach to delicate Castle Arch as well
as massive Fortress Arch. Angel Arch is up a side draw from the twisting
course of Salt Creek. At the Jump, a sharp drop in the canyon, jeeps must
be left and one proceeds on horse or afoot. The trail passes close to the All-
American Man, a four-foot-high rock painting of a balloon-bodied figure
done in red, white, and blue pigments. There are numerous other examples
of rock art in the canyon. After passing Wedding Ring Arch the trail
reaches the dirt road to Beef Basin near the head of Salt Creek. Lavender
Canyon contains a number of arches and is reached by jeep-trail out of
Dugout Ranch on Indian Creek. The end of the jeep-trail is some sixteen
miles from the ranch. Although one should bring an ample supply of water,
as the stream is alkaloid, the end of the jeep-trail is a splendid base camp
for exploring the upper end of the canyon. Cliffs at the head are some
thousand feet high. One can hike to several nearby arches—Train, Cleft,
Caterpillar, and Pedestal—or to various Indian ruins.

One could hike for years in Canyonlands—both in the national park
and surrounding regions—and find something new and special every day.
The region that Captain Macomb described as "worthless and impracticable" is probably just that, by and large, to men who wish to domesticate
the land for their economic progress. But for those who come only to look
and enjoy, it is one of the most unique and fascinating wilderness areas
upon the planet.

Guide Notes for CANYONLANDS

LOCATION—Southeastern Utah. The region covered in this section includes
Canyonlands National Park, Arches National Park, Dead Horse Point State
Park, and a section of Glen Canyon National Recreation Area. The higher
elevations include portions of Manti–La Sal National Forest.

ACCESS—A brace of major national highways cuts through southeastern Utah,
but as is so often the case in spectacular desert country, they somehow
manage to avoid nearly all of the high spots. Cross-country tourists generally
fan themselves with road maps and wonder what will be on the motel tele-

vision when they get to Salt Lake City or Grand Junction. For the outback buff, however, these highways provide access to the minor roads, jeep-trails, and hiking routes of Canyonlands. U.S. Highway 163, between Monticello and Crescent Junction, sprouts a number of paved spur and gravel roads that lead into canyon country—Needles, Needles Overlook, La Sal Mountains, Dead Horse Point, and Island-in-the-Sky. State Highway 128 links Interstate 70 and U.S. 163 by following the Colorado River past the mouths of Castle and Fisher valleys. The isolated western section of Canyonlands National Park can be approached by State Highway 24, which veers southwest from Interstate 70 toward Hanksville.

GETTING AROUND—Although a number of backcountry roads, especially in the Island-in-the-Sky region, are passable for passenger cars, the bulk of motorized travel in Canyonlands is by four-wheel-drive vehicles. In many remote areas, such as the Maze, rangers advise that at least two vehicles travel together. In case of breakdown, civilization is far away, and reliable water sources few and far between. Beautiful though it may be, this can be a harsh environment for the unprepared. Summer temperatures are often well over one hundred degrees; in the winter they may linger well below zero for days. Where the jeep-tracks are pinched out by looming rock, the magnificent hiking country of Canyonlands begins. Spring and autumn are the most pleasant times for trekking this area, but if you are properly equipped, winter has a magic of its own.

Summer, in the author's opinion, is a miserable time for extensive hiking in this region. It is simply too damned hot. On the other hand, spring and summer are probably the best times for boating the canyon country. While Colorado and Green river water might be a bit murky to serve your Aunt Matilda at a lawn party, I have imbibed a fair amount of it over the years without ill effects. The trick is to let it settle out overnight in a saucepan or other container. And in the summer one can always counteract the heat by jumping in the river.

CAMPING—Within Canyonlands National Park there are only two developed campgrounds: at Squaw Flat and Green River Overlook. Only the Squaw Flat campground has piped water. There are also developed campgrounds at Dead Horse Point State Park and Arches National Park. There are several campsites in the Manti–La Sal National Forest. The backpacker will find innumerable attractive camping places throughout the canyon country. Water and fuel are scarce. Be sure to carry enough water for your needs, which vary according to individuals and time of year. Even in mild temperatures most people need at least a couple of quarts a day on the trail—not counting that which is used to prepare dehydrated foods. Where fuel is scarce, as in the canyon country, a small backpacking stove is desirable. In Canyonlands National Park all fuel must be carried in.

SUPPLIES—A reasonable array of backcountry gear and chow is available at Monticello and Moab. A limited selection of supplies is available at Canyonlands Resort, just outside the park in the Needles section.

SPECIAL FEATURES—One of the loveliest, most varied, and largest wilderness areas to be found upon the continent. Here the geological and climatic conditions have combined to create a wonderland of slickrock. Majestic canyons have been carved by the Colorado and Green rivers and their respective tributaries. Contrast is perhaps the most special quality of this region—springs where least expected, abrupt vegetation changes, high mountains looming over canyons.

INFORMATION SOURCES—Superintendent, Canyonlands National Park, Moab, Utah 84532. Superintendent, Arches National Park, c/o Canyonlands National Park, Moab, Utah 84532. Baker Ranger Station, Manti–La Sal National Forest, Monticello, Utah 84535. Moab Chamber of Commerce, 702 S. Main Street, Moab, Utah 84532. Monticello Chamber of Commerce, Monticello, Utah 84535. Moab Rock Shop, 137 N. Main Street, Moab, Utah 84532. American River Touring Association, 1016 Jackson Street, Oakland, California 94607.

3. Navajo Country

In the house of long life, there I wander.
In the house of happiness, there I wander.
Beauty before me, with it I wander.
Beauty behind me, with it I wander.
Beauty below me, with it I wander.
Beauty above me, with it I wander.
Beauty all around me, with it I wander.
In old age traveling, with it I wander.
Dawn Boy's Song on Entering White House

According to Navajo legend, First Man and First Woman emerged from the lower worlds with earth from the four sacred mountains there. Some was mixed with white shell and became the *Sis Najani,* sacred mountain of the East. It was secured to the earth with a bolt of lightning. More of the sacred soil was mixed with turquoise to form *Tso Dzil,* the sacred mountain of the South, that was fastened to the earth by a flint knife. Other soil from the lower worlds was mingled with abalone shell, fastened to the earth with a sunbeam. This was *Doko'o'slid,* sacred Shining-on-Top Mountain of the West. And, finally, yet more soil was mixed with jet and became *Dibe Ntsa,* sacred Bighorn Sheep Mountain of the North. It was attached to the earth with a rainbow.

Between the four sacred mountains lay *Dinetah*—land of the Navajos, stretching across northeastern Arizona and spilling into corners of New Mexico, Colorado, and Utah.

It is a land of sharp contrasts. High-timbered mountains, like the Chuskas, fall away to stretches of multicolored prairie that have subtle swells like the surface of an inland sea. Yet here, quite abruptly, one comes to red sandstone cliffs topped by white domes so smooth it seems they might have been molded by gentle hands when gods yet walked the earth and the rock was still soft. And there, looming above sandy washes, tower the great spires of dark volcanic rock that loom against the sky.

The colors of Navajo blankets and rugs reflect the hues of Dinetah, which constantly change with the light of hour and season. The bold designs have their counterpart in the rock of Navajo country as well as its legends. To the Navajo, the natural world—vegetation, waters, animals—and the shape of the land—mountains, canyons, and monoliths—all have their place in the ancient sacred stories. Thus there is Cabezon Peak in New Mexico, a black volcanic plug that is said to be the head of the monster killed by the Twin War Gods, the blood spilled in that monumental encounter long since having become lava beds stretching to the south and east from Grants. There is Navajo Mountain, the head of a female giant; Beautiful Mountain, the feet of another giant; El Huérfano, up near the San Juan River, which means "orphan" in Spanish, and to the Navajos is the center of the world (a strange and poetic juxtaposition); and Agathla, a great, dark tower rising up from the floor of Monument Valley. Upon these summits are the deities who hold up the sky. Between earth and sky, the sun, moon, and stars are supported and moved by the winds.

The knowing of plants, animals, the high rocks and land that stretches between like the hide of old drums, is a personal thing, a gift. Men can make of it things of beauty for other ears, hands, eyes. They can make medicine in the form of sand paintings, erased at sundown, that may have more curative properties for the Navajos than the American Medical Association would like to admit. Legends come from the land. The design of the art—blankets, silverware, and more recently, paintings—comes from the land. As do legends and chants. Horses, sheep, blankets, and squash blossom necklaces are personal property. The land is not. Nor are the songs a man may build upon the old forms of ancestral chants.

In Dinetah a man may have no sheep, nor goats—yet if he has a song he is considered rich in that land.

Most Navajo songs relate to the creation story, for it, in turn, is reflected in the natural world of the present time and traditional ways of doing things. The story begins in the Dark World. There were five entities: Begochiddy, the Great God, who was both man and woman, an offspring of the sun; First Man, son of Night and Blue Sky Above Sunset; First Woman, whose parents were Dawn Light and Yellow Sky of Sunset; Coyote, the curious rover, the prankster; and Hashjeshjin, the Fire God. Begochiddy built mountains and planted reeds or sunflowers in the four directions of the Dark World. He created insects. When he said there should be one law, Hashjeshjin was angered, and began to burn the Dark World. Begochiddy stuck a giant reed in the central Red Mountain and all he had created climbed into it. The reed grew into the next world above, while the fires burned below them, as they do today.

They were now in the Blue World. Here Begochiddy built mountains like those of the Dark World, and replanted reeds and sunflowers. He created Twin Bees. He planted cotton, which he later caused to rise up as four clouds. Under them grew four sacred plants. This world, too, the Fire God threatened to burn, and so Begochiddy placed all the created things into another hollow reed which grew up into the Yellow World above.

Agathla, in Monument Valley, one of the summits where Navajo gods uphold the sky.

Here in the Yellow World the Great God created springs and streams. He made many people, animals, fish, and birds; he created cyclones and lightning and lived in a rainbow house. The sky was dark, but light came from the mountains. Most living things and even gods had special places where they usually stayed in this Yellow World, although Coyote trotted everywhere, keeping track of creation. There was rejoicing at the first wedding. After a time, the young wife began to neglect her duties, spending much time at the river. There she met and came to love a Water Horse, who appeared to her as a young man. When her husband learned of this there was trouble between them, as well as with her mother. Begochiddy placed all the men on one side of the river and all the women on the other. After a few years some of the women yearned for men so much that they coupled with rocks and cactus. They became heavy, as with children, but gave birth to monsters. Grieving at what had happened, they begged the Great God to let them return to their men, promising to attend to their duties. Begochiddy finally forgave them.

Where the two rivers of the Yellow World crossed each other there was a whirlpool. Salt Woman saw a baby floating in it and told Coyote, who took the baby and hid it in his blanket. After four days a huge and terrifying noise came from the edges of the world. A crow went to the East and returned to tell of a black storm; a hummingbird found a yellow storm in the West; a magpie reported a blue storm to the South, and a white storm was seen to the North by a dove. The storms were all moving toward the center of the Yellow World, and the gods placed all that had been created into a hollow reed. Flood waters from the storms rushed upon the base of the reed. The reed was not tall enough to reach the next world. Begochiddy made a cloud above it, and the Spider People wove a web around it for safety.

The ants tried to dig to the next world, but could not. Locust placed an arrow upon his forehead and sprang up through a crust of mud and water to the fourth world. He was attacked by a powerful white bird. Locust was very strong and wise, and after they tested each other with many trials of magic, the bird fled to the East, frightened. When Locust returned, Begochiddy went up into the fourth world, emerging on an island. He traveled upon a rainbow to a white cloud in the East, where he was greeted by Talking God, the god of the *Yehbechai* ("Night Chant"). In clouds to the North, South, and West, he found House God and the two Seed-bringing gods. These four gods pushed back the waters, which ran off in rivers to form the ocean. Where the waters had been there were monsters. Begochiddy blew upon the monsters and they became strange rocks.

Water from the third world was welling up into the fourth. A council was held, and it was wondered who might have done wrong. Begochiddy asked Coyote to open his blanket, and there upon it was the stolen baby. It

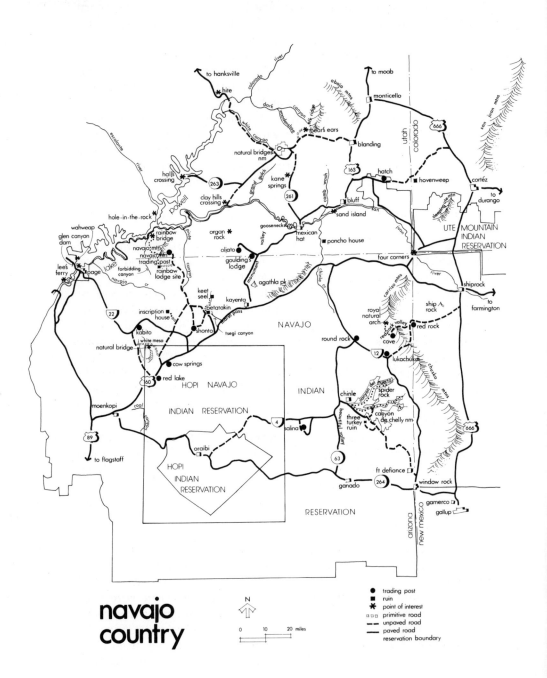

navajo country

N

0   10   20 miles

● trading post
■ ruin
✱ point of interest
□□□ primitive road
--- unpaved road
— paved road
     reservation boundary

was the child of Water Monster. The child was thrown back into the third world and the flooding ceased. There was no fire in the fourth world, and so Coyote descended to where the Fire God was sleeping beside burning rocks and stole some flame.

All the gods and chiefs gathered into a great Council, where they sang the "Beginning of the World Song." The spirit of the earth was created, and the spirit of the sky, rain, and clouds. Turquoise Man was placed as the spirit inside the Sun, which was of fire with a rainbow around it. The Moon was made of ice, with White Shell Man as its spirit. The seasons were placed in their proper directions, and spirits raised the sun, moon, and stars in the sky. Winds were sent to hold them up, and cyclones held up the earth at its edges.

Begochiddy breathed life into all creation and it began to move at its own speed, in its own rhythms.

And Begochiddy saw that the Earth and life upon it were good. . . .

There is a group of scholarly men who, when speculating upon where the Dineh, or Navajo people, have come from, are more interested in the language structure of the Navajos than in their creation stories. They are called anthropologists, and for the record, also spend little time seeking the Garden of Eden or the remains of the Ark. They classify the Navajo language as Athapaskan, a general linguistic grouping that extends up through Canada and into Alaska. By the fifteenth-century arrival of the first Spaniards on the upper Rio Grande, anthropologists tell us, the Navajos were principally occupying a mountainous area in what is now northern New Mexico.

The Dineh were ever on the move, willing to absorb strays from other tribal groupings, and extremely adept at learning from others, borrowing ideas, and giving them new dimensions. Utes joined them, as did some Pueblo people. They learned methods of agriculture, began to graze sheep, and to weave. There were exchanges of ancient beliefs and chants, and each tribal group and clan grew ceremonially stronger from the knowing.

By the mid-1700s there were Navajos in Canyon de Chelly, which is in eastern Arizona, and its principal tributary, Canyon del Muerto. Although many clans were content to live in peace, working with their flocks and crops, other Navajos continued to raid Hopi, Zuni, and Spanish villages. The Spaniards, and later the Americans who took the area from Mexico in 1846, sometimes made treaties with the "chief." With a long history of monarchs, popes, and presidents, western Europeans in the Southwest erroneously assumed that the Indians, like them, had a single figure of power atop the political structure, with whom an agreement could be made for an entire tribe.

They completely failed to realize that the strong headmen of the Navajos could only speak for their particular groups or clans. Other Navajos, especially if there were hunger among them, had no formal restraints upon raiding.

The United States Army of the 1860s, a goodly portion of which had been committed to suppressing Indian raids in the Southwest, was totally unaware of this diplomatic nuance. Given the general sentiment of the times concerning Indians, it is doubtful that even if the Army had been aware, the result would have been much different.

In the winter of 1863–64 General James H. Carleton sent out Kit Carson with an army of volunteers to subdue the Navajos. There was little actual fighting. The Indians would withdraw into the crannies of their rugged country, and the soldiers, many of whom had been raided by Navajos in the past, burned hogans, slaughtered livestock, and destroyed food stores and orchards. Although a few bands holed up in the mountains or went north and west to the Monument Valley country, most of the Dineh began to trickle into Fort Defiance to surrender, cold and half-starved. It was all over within six months.

What the Navajos call the Long Walk began. It was decided that the same 8500 Navajos who had surrendered would be relocated at the Bosque Redondo on the Pecos River, in New Mexico, over three hundred miles away. The old, the sick, and babies were carried in wagons—everyone else plodded the entire distance, each evening's camp yet farther from Dinetah, the homeland. Bosque Redondo proved to be tragic for the Navajos. Many died of diseases against which they had no resistance. In this alien land their knowledge of plants and seasons meant nothing. Crops failed. Raiding parties of Plains Indians plundered their flocks of sheep. There was almost no fuel. Some Navajos, with mankind's unbreakable need to survive, attempted to cope with the new environment, herding what sheep they had and faithfully eating the government provisions which, to them, were scarcely palatable. Others looked out over a flat, colorless land, thought of Dinetah, where each spire of rock, winding arroyo, plant, and animal had a place in the design of creation of which the singers chanted. They looked without seeing at this new place and slowly, quietly, died over a period of months.

After four years a new peace treaty was signed and the Navajos were allowed to return to their homeland to begin the difficult task of restoring croplands and building up flocks of sheep and goats. While at Bosque Redondo some of the men had been taught silversmithing. Painstaking, patient craftsmen with a rich store of traditional designs, the Navajos soon began to turn out exquisite jewelry of silver and turquoise. After the return of the Navajos to Dinetah, traders began to open posts in scattered locations. The women had resumed weaving, and blankets as well as jewelry began to pass over counters in the trading posts in exchange for food and other supplies.

Probably the most widely used route to Canyon de Chelly is State Highway 264, which comes in from the west out of the Hopi Reservation, and from the east out of Gallup, New Mexico. If you are coming from Gallup, the semideserted coal town of Gamerco, three miles out of town and just off the highway, is worth a once-over. In contrast to most of the Gallup trading posts that attract tourist trade, the post at Gamerco is usually filled with Indians—buying, selling, transacting pawn, or just hanging out to watch the activity. The nearby hole-in-the-wall café, Rosie's, dishes up good mutton stew or a bowl of red chili with an altogether satisfying bite to it. Farther down the road, at Window Rock, the tribal headquarters, the fare runs more to the likes of Colonel Sanders' Finger-Lickin' Good and Tastee Freeze. Forget it. Near Ganado, where the old Hubbell Trading Post is preserved as a National Historic Site, State Highway 63 cuts north from 264 through Beautiful Valley to Chinle at the mouth of Canyon de Chelly. Although modern motels are mushrooming in the once-isolated settlement, I prefer to hang my hat at the oldest accommodation, Thunderbird Lodge. There is also a campground under an extensive grove of cottonwoods nearby.

To preserve the backcountry values of the canyons, as well as to protect the ruins and the privacy of the Navajos living in them, no hikers are allowed in the canyons unless accompanied by Park Service personnel or an authorized Navajo guide. An exception to this is the trail down into the canyon from White House Ruin overlook. Horses can be rented at the mouth of the canyon. Conditions permitting, there are also four-wheel-drive excursions operated out of Thunderbird Lodge—old Army troop trucks are expertly jockeyed up the canyons by young Navajos.

Each season has its own special beauty here. In the spring water from melting snow meanders down the canyons, creating treacherous sections of quicksand. Smoke curls up from hogans, and there is a sense of expectancy and activity as fields are readied for planting. The red-orange walls of the canyon glow with nuances of color during the summer months and the sun heats the rocks, warming the bottomlands where sunflowers sway above growing corn. There are beautiful, violent thunderstorms during the late summer. By the time all of the cottonwoods have turned yellow in autumn, the peak of the visitor season has passed—my favorite season for back-packing here or just about anywhere else in the Southwest. In winter frigid air is locked into the bottomlands, held there by warmer air above it. Most of the Navajos move out for the season, and it is then that the canyons seem the most somber and monumental.

At the entrance to Canyon de Chelly, the sandstone walls are only a few feet high. Gradually the walls rise higher and higher, until at the eastern end they lift a thousand feet from the sandy floor. Many of the walls in Canyon de Chelly and Canyon del Muerto are sheer or overhanging, cleanly sliced, while others are great swirls of rock, rather resembling vast, petrified sand dunes—which is exactly what they are. During the Permian period, some 230 million years ago, the inland seas which had covered much of America began to dry up. Mountain ranges were pushed skyward, blocking moist prevailing winds. Much of the Southwest became a desert as barren as the Sahara and Gobi are today. Sand dunes hundreds of feet deep piled up in what is now the Canyon de Chelly region, and gradually hardened into rock. New formations were deposited on top of them. On one of them, the Chinle, dinosaurs walked, and trees grew whose mineralized remnants we now call petrified forests.

Fifty million years ago a section of the earth forty miles wide and a hundred miles long was pushed up into roughly the shape of a standing wave, with the gradual slope of the back side facing west and the sharp drop of the crest on the east. Through this barrier, the Defiance uplift, mountain streams gnawed out Canyon de Chelly and Canyon del Muerto.

A paved road parallels Canyon de Chelly to the south, with access to five overlooks. East of Spider Rock turnoff the road becomes dirt and is interesting in most seasons, muddy and miserable after a rain or when snow has melted. This road leads out to Fort Defiance, twenty-eight miles away. A five-mile spur wanders its way out to a bench high above Three Turkey Ruin, a place of solemn beauty. Inside the canyons themselves, however, the only roads are wheel-ruts cutting across sand. Navajos who live in the canyon travel back into it either on foot, horseback, horse-drawn wagons, or with pickups.

The canyons are peaceful places. The traveler passes through cottonwood groves and skirts cornfields and peach orchards of the Navajo farms. The peach trees are believed to have been planted by the Hopi before the coming of the Dineh. There is no indication the Hopi ever took up permanent dwelling in the canyon; they apparently only set up temporary camps to harvest the fruit from time to time. A common sight in the canyons is flocks of sheep and goats being herded by children, and in places one may see a woman weaving.

It was Spider Woman, according to Navajo belief, who taught the Navajos how to weave. Spider Rock, a monolith that juts up from the floor of upper Canyon de Chelly, is deservedly the most photographed sight in the national monument. The slab-sided column is more than eight hundred feet high. A popular legend has it that the Navajos tell misbehaving children that Spider Woman lives upon the summit of the pinnacle, and that the white cap of rock is a layer of victims' bones. Speaking Rock, a similar but not-quite-detached spire across the canyon, is said to inform Spider Woman when prey is approaching, whereupon the sinister woman drops down a web of her weaving to the canyon floor, scoops up the unfortunate, and reascends to her perch to devour him.

The Navajo, whose myths are tightly woven into the land he inhabits, tells of many monsters that inhabit Dinetah—mountains that are slain giants, The Rock that Claps Together, Tracking Bear, the Rock Monster that Kicks People Off. . . .

The child-eating woman of Spider Rock, however, may be something of a put-on for the eager pilgrim who arrives with cameras and notebooks. Until recently, it appears, a goodly number of the older or more isolated canyon Navajos had not heard of Spider Woman being upon that rock, although most had heard of a fine weaver who once worked beside a hogan close to it. An attempt to buttonhole a young Navajo hanging around the canyons—a guide, say—will get the truth-seeker nowhere. The Navajos, whose humor is generally subtle and considerable, are masters at deadpan

The author in the Canyon de Chelly.

and deflection. In any case, the story is a good one, and Spider Rock in its setting is always better than I remembered every time I go back.

Two miles above the junction of Canyon de Chelly and Canyon del Muerto is White House Ruin, set in the recessed niche of an immense cliff. The buildings are angular and fortresslike, with few windows, the color of the cliff itself. One structure, however, the name-giver, stands in sharp white contrast to the rest. The niche is practically inaccessible from the canyon floor, where another large ruin rises against the cliff. When this village was inhabited, some six hundred years ago, the lower ruin was four or five stories high, with ladders giving access to the upper. Inside, the large structures are hivelike, multicelled—living and storage units arranged in proximity to ceremonial *kivas,* chambers for religious activities. Navajos sometimes refer to the people who once lived in this and other cliff villages as the "Swallow People," or the Anasazi, which means "the Ancient Ones." The Anasazi lived in the region several hundred years before the Navajos.

The trail from the rim to White House Ruin switchbacks down through piñon and juniper, past flowering bushes—cliff roses, service-berry, and mock-orange—which blossom their own vivid colors against red

White House Ruin, where the homes of the ancient Anasazi cling to the cliff like deserted swallows' nests.

stone in late spring. One New Year's Day friends and I headed down the trail to White House Ruin, accompanied by two bloodhounds. There was a light dusting of fresh snow upon the piñon and juniper; the creek was frozen solid. One of the dogs charged out across the ice, huge paws splaying in all directions. She lost her footing completely. She scrambled up, slid down again, and then threw that great mournful head back and howled. There are certain places where, at the right time of season and day, the echo is almost perfect. The creek below White House Ruin is such a place. The yowls of what seemed a dozen hounds came bouncing back up canyon. Both dogs were now baying mightily. The bedlam set up by the actual animals and the reverberation of the phantom pack died away only when we had bodily carried the hound off the ice, slipping and sliding all over the creek.

There are several notable Anasazi ruins in Canyon del Muerto. Antelope House Ruin lies beneath an overhanging cliff, as do nearly all of the canyon ruins. The high, tightly constructed walls lean with the weight of centuries. There is rock art throughout the canyons, and one of the finest panels is close to this ruin: red and white antelopes whose movement is frozen forever against sandstone. This is a comparatively recent painting. Many Navajos attribute the work to a great artist of their tribe, Little Sheep, who lived in the early 1800s. It was also he, some claim, who created the beautifully executed blue and white cow which gives Standing Cow Ruin its name.

In Canyon del Muerto there is a remarkable pictograph depicting a line of mounted Spanish *conquistadores*. Most carry lances, and one of the white figures wears the brown robe of a priest. Once Spanish settlements were established, Navajos soon lost their initial fear of horses and began to run some of them off, probably solely for food at first. Within less than a generation, young boys and old men alike had become superb riders. Navajos raided Spanish villages and took away livestock and sometimes women. The Spaniards, in turn, plundered Indian encampments, and kidnapped children for the slave trade.

A punitive expedition, led by Lieutenant Antonio Narbona, rode into the canyons in the winter of 1804–05. The Indians holed up in a high ledge protected by an overhang in Canyon del Muerto. In the past they had held off attacking Utes with stones and arrows from this vantage. The Spaniards were guided to a point above the ledge by a young Navajo seeking revenge on the head men of the canyon, who would not allow him to marry a girl of his own clan. The girl and her family and relations, warned of the treachery, fled up a side canyon to the rim. From there they watched helplessly as Narbona's soldiers fired down into the shallow cave from rimrock on the opposite side of the canyon.

The first soldier to reach the ledge was attacked by a Navajo woman wielding a knife. They grappled briefly, then plunged over the edge, an event which explains the Navajo name for the place—*Ah-tah-ho-do-nilly* —which means "two fell off." Non-Indians now refer to the ledge as Massacre Cave. Narbona reported killing 115 Navajos, and later, in a grisly attempt to prove the claim, sent the Spanish governor at Santa Fe 84 pairs of ears, with an apology for some that were missing. Although Narbona reported taking some prisoners, Indians say only one old man survived the massacre.

Across the canyon from Massacre Cave is Mummy Cave Ruin, one of the most awesome of all Anasazi sites. Perched upon a rock ledge beneath an overhanging cliff, the pueblo appears as a mysterious, imposing citadel with a massive watchtower at one end. No one knows why such towers were constructed. Possibly they were for defense; probably there was also a ceremonial significance.

There is much about the Anasazi that is unknown. Yet anthropologists, patiently working with scattered clues, are bringing more and more details of their lives into focus. Over a period of better than a thousand years the Anasazi flourished throughout the plateau country of the Southwest. At first a nomadic people who hunted and gathered wild plants, they gradually evolved the complex culture which built the great cliff and canyon pueblos.

Around 200 A.D. the Anasazi began crude cultivation of canyon bottomlands. During the summer they lived in brush shelters close to the fields; the winters they passed in high, dry caves. Although not possessed of bow and arrow, they developed a sort of catapult, the *atlatl,* which greatly increased the velocity and range of their spear-throwing. They wove fine, water-tight baskets that were sealed with pitch; grain was stored in them as well as water. Hot stones were dropped into them to stew meat and vegetables. Game was not only hunted by spear, but trapped in nets of yucca fiber and human hair; some have been found that are two hundred feet long. Footgear, a necessity in a land of rock, took the form of sandals made of yucca fiber.

After a couple of centuries the crude shelters evolved into pit houses with circular rooms some five feet deep covered with a thick thatch of reeds, grasses, and dirt. Each house had a firepit and smoke hole. The Anasazi now planted beans, corn, and squash. In addition to domesticated dogs, they now also raised turkeys. Crude pottery was being made, and the bow and arrow came into widespread use, probably borrowed from other tribes with whom they came in contact.

By the seventh century the Anasazi were building pueblos of apartments, with the pit-house design lingering in the form of religious *kivas.* Pottery was becoming more refined, more beautiful—bold, colorful designs were being applied over a smooth white slip. Trading became more extensive, and a number of new products were being used, including cotton. The Anasazi now wore garments of fur and cotton, exquisite robes of feathers. Tools and religious fetishes were more numerous and well-made than those of earlier times.

By the late thirteenth century all the great canyon and cliff pueblos had been built. It was in the last stage of building that the towers were constructed—mostly windowless, mysterious, foreboding.

And then, abruptly, the Anasazi were gone from these places forever.

From tree-ring studies it is known there was a severe drought in the Southwest from 1276 to 1299. The watchtowers also suggest the possibility of the fear of attack—either by other tribes or enemies of a different sort, the kind only talked of in the safety of the *kiva*.

In any case, anthropologists speculate that the Anasazi worked their way toward the Rio Grande River or the region of the Little Colorado to establish new villages. Their descendents are the modern-day Pueblo and Hopi tribes.

Beneath the tower of Mummy Cave Ruin a young Navajo shared a different view with me one hot August afternoon.

"These Navajos believe those old people died up there," he said, giving the slightest lift of his chin toward the ruin. "Some kind of curse. They didn't do things right. Can't kill game. Corn won't grow."

He smoked a bit. Then looked up at the tower.

"These Navajos lived here a long time. They don't use those buildings." He snubbed out his cigarette.

"Those old people never left. They died up there. That's why these Navajos don't use those buildings. The dead people are still there."

Eighty miles north of Canyon de Chelly is another place where the Anasazi once lived and are gone—Hovenweep. The very sound suggests ruin and desolation. The word is, in fact, Ute for "deserted valley."

Driving north from Cortez, Colorado, on U.S. Highway 666, there is no suggestion of what one will find at Hovenweep National Monument. The country is a series of swells, too gentle to slow a tractor much; red clay croplands stretch off toward the snow-covered crest of the San Juan Mountains to the east and roll westward to the horizon. The prim farmhouses are scattered, mostly two-story white frame dwellings with porches. Some sixteen miles out of Cortez, a gravel road branches out to the west, marked by a sign to Hovenweep. After about a mile the farmhouses are behind you, but still the fields stretch on and on, seemingly fenceless, and one begins to wonder if they have been plowed and planted all the way to California.

The fields finally fall back and the country quickly becomes drier—cattle range with sparse vegetation and lots of bedrock showing through. The road becomes dirt, rough in places. Four miles beyond the Utah border lies Hovenweep National Monument Headquarters and Square Tower Ruins.

The towers, constructed of beautifully fitted stone, rise from the edge of a small, steep-sided canyon. The fact that there are no real windows— only small slots commanding views of a nearby spring, the rubble of what was once a sizable pueblo, and principal trails—would indicate these were watchtowers. Yet who the enemies were, or even if they were real, is as mysterious as the towers themselves, the secret of a people dead for more than seven centuries.

Although ancestors of the tower-builders had lived in the Four Corners region since before the birth of Christ, it was not until the beginning of the thirteenth century that they moved to the heads of draws feeding into Hovenweep Canyon. As well as the towers, they built pueblos against the canyon walls and apparently thrived . . . for less than a century. For even as the great towers rose into the sky, the sky itself yielded less and less water, and a long drought was upon the land. It may be that there was simply not enough water to grow crops for so many people, or perhaps the enemies they had watched for drove them from their villages.

Yet the towers remain, some walls rising more than twenty feet, even though most of the mortar has washed away over the centuries. The spring at the head of the draw still trickles into a rock basin much as it must have in that ancient time. Hunkering by the spring, which is sheltered by an overhanging cliff, the inner eye can see a pueblo thrusting out from the cliff where there is now only talus and pottery shards; women in yucca sandals approaching the pool with water pots; a dark, watchful face at a slot in the highest tower.

A great many people once lived in this draw, farming it, carrying water from the spring. Moving down the quiet, sun-struck canyon one notices the quantity of ruins. Here is the rubble of a small pueblo, there some boulder houses. The draw has many oddly shaped slabs of rock, fallen from the rims and carved—some by water, mostly by wind. Wherever possible, the Hovenweep people built under and against these rocks, using the natural forms for a roof and even a wall or two. In heat-shimmer the sculpted boulders and rock walls of a vanished culture assume curious shapes: one looks like a bulbous wine bottle in a wicker holder. Down-canyon, a large tower lifts from a pinnacle of rock in the canyon. Hovenweep. Deserted valley. If there be noble ghosts, I think they would be here, not confined to night, but brooding behind fashioned rock walls in full daylight.

The San Juan River marks the northern boundary of the Navajo Reservation for much of its meandering journey through southern Utah. The eighty-one-mile float trip from Bluff, Utah, to Clay Hills Crossing makes a fine voyage. Before construction of Glen Canyon Dam one could float on down into the Colorado and take out at Lee's Ferry, but the rising waters of Lake Powell have now pushed up-river beyond Clay Hills Crossing. If you are rafting this is the only practical takeout, unless one is making the shorter twenty-four-mile run from Bluff to Mexican Hat. Clay Hills Crossing is reached by taking State Highway 263 southwest out of Natural Bridges National Monument toward Hall's Crossing on Lake Powell. Eighteen miles down this paved road an eleven-mile rough dirt track (four-wheel drive advised) forks off the highway and leads to the crossing.

    If you are voyaging in canoe, foldboat, or kayak and you have plenty of time and supplies, there is an option of continuing down the San Juan

One of the Square Tower ruins, beautifully constructed relics of the vanished Anasazi people, in Hovenweep National Monument.

Mexican Hat.

arm of Lake Powell to the main lake, then proceeding north past Hole-in-the-Rock and the mouth of the Escalante River to Hall's Crossing—a distance of more than seventy-five miles. Another possibility is to head southwest past Rainbow Bridge Marina to Wahweap near Page, a distance of close to a hundred miles.

Bluff is a quiet village of hewn red rock and houses scattered beneath shade trees. When the Hole-in-the-Rock pioneers settled the town in 1880 the population was 225, and, as the Utah Federal Writers Project of 1941 comments, "it has never since reached that figure." The colonists, we are told, built houses of crooked cottonwood limbs,

> whose walls bowed in and out with wonderful irregularity. . . . [They] roofed them with quick coats of sand, which feathered out into a crop of runty sunflowers and stinkweeds, if the weed-seed had time to sprout before the wind carried the sand away. But whether it raised weeds or blew [them] away, it never turned the rain, which dripped dismally from it long after the sky was clear. These houses had doorways without doors, windows without glass, and floors which required sprinkling

at intervals to lay the native dust and tempt the soil to harden. [Utah Federal Writers Project, American Guide Series, Hastings House, N.Y., 1941]

Four miles out of Bluff, on the highway to Mexican Hat, a short graded spur leads to Sand Island, a campground on the river. There are panels of pictographs here, some of which portray Kokopelli, the flute player. This is a good put-in for the San Juan. It is also a popular picnicking place for travelers, and most boaters will probably want to head downriver a few miles before selecting a campsite.

The San Juan winds its way past rock formations of virtually every shape, size, and combination of colors. There are grassy, sandy benches beside the river, many of them with substantial cottonwood groves. On rock walls and slabs behind some of these glades are panels of rock art—designs of great beauty and power. The river moves at a fine clip yet seems gentle—until one gets into some sand waves. One minute you seem to be on a peaceful stretch of water, and the next, without the warning growl of rapids, you find yourself plunging through billowing waves. The waves are caused by the shifting of sediment on the river bottom. The only

The meandering Goosenecks of the San Juan River.

real rapids of any consequence is Government Rapids, some twenty miles upriver from Clay Hills Crossing.

Much of the voyage is through canyons, some of whose walls are 2500 feet deep. The river writhes its way through the entrenched meanders of the Goosenecks, where the flow, 1500 feet below the rim, swings out in wide loops that cover six miles. A bird flying over the necks would cover only a mile.

Before leaving Bluff throw away your plastic wallet calendar and give your watch to a small boy with a fishing rod. Drink enough cold beer to drown any recollections of schedule. Then you are ready for the river.

As John Ruskin observed, when informed of the invention of the steam engine: "There was always more in the world than a man could see, walked he ever so slowly. He will see no more by going fast, for his glory is not in going but in being." There is a special quality about the San Juan which seems to invite this sense of being. The river flows leisurely through canyons where exposed layers of rock represent millions of years of deposits from lost landscapes—broad, waveless seas and swamps where great reptiles quivered the mud as they moved, the sands left by winds forgotten before there was memory. All along the river are things left by the Anasazi —large, dark figures painted upon red rock; small pueblo ruins up side canyons; hand- and footholds chopped into vertical rock leading up to small caves and yet other ruins. Camp early. If you are on the south side of the river, the Navajo side, you may hear a bell tinkling back off in the willow and tamarisk—an old patriarch of a goat, leading a flock of sheep. You are not likely to see the herder, although probably he or she will be patiently observing you, with curiosity, all the time you are there.

During the 1890s there was a gold rush to the San Juan River and Glen Canyon. Much of the impetus came from prospectors figuring that any region that rugged was bound to conceal something of value. There had been stories—a golden statue of Jesus cached by a Spanish wagon train in the Henry Mountains, a mysterious Navajo silver mine, and, finally, the reports of men who had actually panned some color along the San Juan and Colorado rivers. During the 1890s several hundred men trekked into the area, living under overhanging cliffs, in lean-tos, and in caves. Most picked up their mail and supplies at Hite Crossing, where there was a store. The pickings were lean, however, and most of the men, as well as the few women living there, drifted on to more promising areas.

Around the turn of the century a huge dredge was constructed at considerable effort and no small expense. The cost of the whole operation has been estimated in the neighborhood of $100,000. The first cleanup netted $30.15. When the second cleanup returned $36.80 the project was abandoned. Some years later a party of river runners camped by the abandoned dredge, pulling off some boards for a fire to boil coffee. The first president of the dredging company, Julius Stone, was on the trip and reminisced. Sipping his coffee, Stone pronounced it excellent and remarked it was the only return he had ever received on his personal investment in the dredge.

"This cup of coffee cost me five thousand dollars."

The flow of the San Juan varies from year to year. It is normally a river of heavy flow, but in 1909 the water was very low. Expanses of river bottom were exposed, and here prospector James Douglas discovered a sand bar chock-full of gold dust. He took a fair amount out before the river rose, covering the bar. Douglas hung around Mexican Hat year after year, patiently waiting for a low-water season to uncover his bonanza. After twenty years of waiting, he jumped off the Mexican Hat bridge and drowned. Five years later the river went completely dry.

Grand Gulch, which opens to the San Juan up-river from Clay Hills Crossing, is a deep, meandering canyon with a number of Anasazi ruins and rock art sites. The thirty-six-mile-long canyon is rugged, straight-walled, and isolated. It has also recently been designated as a primitive area by the Bureau of Land Management. One can enter the canyon at its mouth on the San Juan or from Kane Spring near its head. Kane Spring, on Highway 261, is about ten miles from Natural Bridges National Monument. It is about a five-mile hike to Grand Gulch from Kane Spring. People planning to ramble through Grand Gulch are required to register at the Bureau of Land Management's office in Monticello, where information on water availability and the like, as well as maps, is available. As with all primitive areas, motorized vehicles of any kind are prohibited.

The first time I visited Natural Bridges National Monument, about fifteen years ago, it was accessible only by an axle-splitting dirt road. Ranger Headquarters was a small house trailer, and the ranger himself boiled up a pot of coffee as he commented that we were the first people he had seen in a few days. We sat out on some rocks, sipping the dark, thick brew out of tin cups as I asked him about trails into the bridges, while he, in turn, inquired as to what was happening out in the wide world beyond Comb Wash. Having read a newspaper that morning in Blanding, we told him, and he seemed to be very pleased to be exactly where he was, on the wilderness side of Comb Wash.

Last year I returned to Natural Bridges over blacktop. There was a large Park Service building done in the rustic modern school of architecture. There were some excellent displays, and I wandered out to talk to a ranger, trying, no doubt, to recapture the mellow memory of the conversation over ranch coffee more than a decade before. The young ranger I buttonholed was affable, talkative, and very concerned about meeting a quota in terms of visitor hours.

Zeke Johnson, the first custodian of the monument, was paid a dollar a month from the government in 1916—an income which he fleshed out by renting horses and serving as guide. When Johnson became custodian, this was one of the least-visited areas in America. People would ask him why he chose to live in such a remote place. He was apt to respond that he was "so close to the Four Corners that no sheriff could ever catch him," or with similar whimsies. Johnson could be deadly serious when vandalism came to his attention. A man from Blanding and his son cut their names into one of the bridges. The custodian suggested the man remove the blemish. He refused, and not long after the man received a letter from the National Park Service in Washington. According to Johnson, "the letter told the culprit that 'unless he immediately complied with Custodian Johnson's instructions, he would have a free ride at his own expense from Blanding to Washington, D.C., to be arraigned before the U.S. Government.' He soon hunted me up and asked what he should do. I said, 'Just do as I told you, track back out there and take off those initials.' He offered me twenty bucks if I would do it, but I told him nobody could do it but him, and it was a five-day horseback trip in those days." The culprit not only did it, but became a local advocate for preserving beautiful places.

Natural Bridges National Monument contains some fine, rugged canyon country, several Anasazi ruins, and the three graceful bridges themselves. The bridges were originally named by early explorers for their wives or other relatives—Edwin, Caroline, and Augusta. Later on the Park Service decided Indian names might be more appropriate to the character of the bridges and the country around them (Edwin and Augusta do rather sound like formal folks who wear wing collars and bustles while negotiating the wilds of Central Park in a carriage). Piutes lived in the area, but it was soon discovered they had one name for all the bridges—*Ma-Vah-Talk-Tump*—which means "Under the Horse's Belly." Park officials, feeling this less than completely lyric, turned then to Hopi nomenclature, reasoning this proper since the Anasazi are considered their cultural ancestors.

Owochomo Bridge is the smallest of the spans, 180 feet long and chiseled to a mere 9 feet in thickness at the middle. The name means "Flat Rock Mound," and refers to a nearby promontory. The bridge is pale salmon in color, with lateral streaks of vermilion and patches of green and orange lichen. Three miles down Armstrong Canyon by trail is Kachina Bridge. Pictographs on an abutment resemble Hopi masked dancers. Sipapu Bridge, several miles up White Canyon, is the largest of the bridges; it is 208 feet long, 53 feet thick, and 220 feet high. These statistics describe the beauty of this structure in its setting about as well as the beauty of a woman could be projected from her weight, measurements, color of eyes and hair.

The name, Sipapu, tells the armchair visitor more. In Hopi belief the spirits of all men were once under the crust of the earth. Animals, who were in communication with the gods, and still are, knew of this and dug a hole for man to emerge out of. Coyote dug for a while, as did many other animals, but it was Badger, the strongest digger of them all, who finally broke through to the underworld. Man came up through this opening, the Sipapu, and flourished upon the surface of the earth. If there comes a time when there is no place upon the surface of the earth for man to dwell with dignity, honor, and kindness, he must return back through the Sipapu.

The image of the Sipapu has been likened by non-Indians to the birth process. But of course. We are all born into mystery and die with our roots still growing out of the same mystery. All our myths are strikingly similar, whether we express them in Tibetan paper prayer wheels close to the roof of the world, responsive readings in clapboard churches with flaking paint in America's midlands, or in the creation songs of the Hopi, Navajo and

The richly colored, 180-foot span of Owachomo Bridge is one of the glories of Natural Bridges National Monument.

other people. The holy books, the songs, the myths, all give us fragments of
the mystery, indicating we all come from the same place.

Sipapu Bridge is well named. The arc of stone spans a canyon where a
tangle of desert shrubs lifts greenly, vividly. It is massive, wonderfully
balanced in shape and form. Here, indeed, is a place of such dignity that no
songs nor poems can define it; yet it is of itself both a song and a poem,
and worthy of the name Sipapu.

To the northeast of Natural Bridges National Monument is Elk Ridge,
a spur of the Abajo Mountains whose fringes have been excitingly eroded
by some very special canyons—Dark, Woodenshoe, and White—twisting
to the Colorado; Comb Wash and Grand Gulch meandering to the San
Juan. All of these canyons will lead a person of stout legs to places of
magical beauty. About ten miles from the monument a rough dirt road
passes between the Bear's Ears in Manti–La Sal National Forest. These
two hulks of rock (9095 and 8508 feet in altitude) command some of the
finest views in all of Utah. On a clear day one can see the San Juan
Mountains, sleeping Ute Mountain, and Mesa Verde in Colorado; the
Carrizo Mountains in Arizona; and the spires of Monument Valley on the
Arizona-Utah border. Closer at hand is White Canyon, with its natural
bridges; the deeply eroded Grand Gulch; and the San Juan River. Dominating the horizon to the southwest is the high dome of Navajo Mountain, a
massive, volcanic blister of over ten thousand feet in elevation. From the
Bear's Ears the magnificent complexity of prairie, towering monoliths, and
slickrock canyons that make up Navajo country lies below you and
stretches off into the horizon.

As a youth John Wetherill herded cattle on his parents' Alamo Ranch,
named for a grove of cottonwoods in which the ranch house was situated.
He and his brothers explored the nearby canyons of Mesa Verde, finding
pottery, baskets, skeletons, axes, mummies, and other objects left from the
time of the Anasazi. Later, Wetherill prospected the San Juan River
country and wandered up among the giant rocks of Monument Valley. He
found little to speak of in the way of minerals, but came away profoundly
impressed with this wild and little-known country. After five years of
working as a trader in the Chaco Canyon region, Wetherill and two
companions headed back toward Monument Valley with three wagons full
of personal effects, tools, and trade goods. The year was 1906. At a spring
the Navajos call Oljato—"Moonlight Water"—the wagons halted. This
was where Wetherill hoped to build his post.

He was met by Hoskinini-begay, the tall, graying son of a great chief.
With grave dignity he told Wetherill to leave. The trader responded by
proposing a rabbit hunt and feast:

"You get the rabbits, and I'll furnish flour and sugar and coffee."

The Navajos were impressed with his quiet way of speaking, the fact that he carried no guns. They agreed to feast and talk. In three days there were enough rabbits. Wetherill had a bed of coals for cooking them, and he made bread and served coffee. All day long Indians came to Oljato, eating rabbit and fresh bread, sipping coffee, listening and sometimes speaking. Wetherill pointed out that, with a post at Oljato, they would not have to travel long distances to trade—ninety miles to Round Rock, seventy miles to Red Lake, or eighty miles to Bluff. The Navajos debated softly among themselves, often voicing the thought that no white man had ever settled in this part of Dinetah, that bad might come from it.

An old man reminded them of a long-ago time, when the rains failed and the Dineh survived on piñon nuts and roots. Clothes were made of cedar bark and people built platforms in trees for protection against ravenous packs of wolves. The white man brought sheep, he told them, and from then on there were always mutton ribs to roast and wool for clothing. People forget how hard those times were long ago, he continued. A trading post here would be of help to them.

The feasting and talking began at sunrise and continued through the day. At sunset Chief Hoskinini and Hoskinini-begay told Wetherill he could build his post at Moonlight Water.

With the arrival of his wife, Louisa, as well as more supplies from Gallup, Wetherill laid a board across two coffee boxes and was ready to trade. Navajos were hired to help them cut timber and build the trading post. Gradually, Dineh began to ride or walk to Oljato, at first merely to look and listen, later to trade. Men and women dressed in velvet blouses and calico trousers or skirts. Most wore jewelry of turquoise and silver. The trust and friendship between the traders and the Dineh deepened. When supplies at the post ran out, and Louisa, alone at the time, had no food but corn she ground in her coffee mill, Hoskinini-begay arrived on his gray mule and dropped off some provisions he had ridden ninety miles to Round Rock to purchase.

Knowing of his great interest in the Anasazi, Navajos would sometimes tell Wetherill of cliff dwellings and other ruins they had chanced upon. The Navajos, believing these places *chindi,* "haunted by the dead," never entered them and would avoid going near them unless after strayed stock.

Word of the ruins was beginning to spread in scientific circles. In 1909 Dr. Byron Cummings of the University of Utah hired Wetherill to lead him into the backcountry. After exploring some ruins in Navajo Canyon, they came to a major cliff dwelling in an aperture of high-walled Nitsin Canyon. A half-obliterated date, either 1661 or 1861, provided a name for this site—Inscription House. Here was a combination of building techniques: one room had sandstone cliff for the back wall, wattle and plaster for another, a third of adobe, and finally a side of masonry.

The party headed into Tsegi, one of the most beautiful canyon systems in all the Southwest—sandstone cliffs and stands of spruce and aspen.
They worked their way up a tributary of the main canyon where there were
cottonwoods and wild roses, finally to a cave city upon a high ledge
beneath an overhanging cliff. The ruin seemed huge—it stretched along the
ledge for 350 feet. Later, archeologists would find 160 rooms, and establish this as the largest and best-preserved Anasazi site in Arizona. It is
called Keet Seel, which means "broken pottery" in the language of the
Dineh.

Word of the discoveries was sent back to Oljato. Louisa Wetherill and
her children came to look at Inscription House and Keet Seel. At a major
fork of Tsegi Canyon she lingered to talk with a Navajo woman while her
husband and Dr. Cummings investigated a nearby Anasazi burial. Louisa
Wetherill, or Asthon Sosi—"Slim Woman"—as the Navajos affectionately
called her, was a remarkable person. At Oljato she often ran the trading
post while her husband was off purchasing supplies or guiding parties into
the outback. Dineh came to regard her as one of them, asked her advice on
important matters, and told her many things of their lives in this land of
strong light. Now this Navajo woman, wife of Nide-kloi, "the Whiskered
One," told her there was a large cliff dwelling up a side fork of the canyon.
She had seen it while gathering plants for dye.

But there was other business to be attended to, and by the time
Wetherill and Cummings started up the side canyon in search of this new
ruin, Louisa had returned to Oljato. The men were guided by Nide-kloi's
son-in-law. The steep-sided stream was running high with clear water, and
care was taken to keep the horses out of patches of viscous quicksand.
Abruptly the guide reined up and gestured to the canyon wall above them.
There, in a gigantic vaulted cave, was indeed another cliff city, fashioned
walls blending with the symmetrical sandstone walls which soared above
them. The new ruin, named Betatakin, was not quite as large as Keet Seel.
Yet, in its setting, Betatakin is the finest of all the empty villages of the
Anasazi—a vision of magic beauty.

Wetherill and Cummings had still another vision—the rock rainbow.
The One-Eyed Man of the Salt Clan had first spoken of it to Louisa
Wetherill. He had guided parties for the Wetherills to the natural bridges of
White Canyon in Utah, and now spoke of a larger bridge behind Navajo
Mountain. He had seen it, he said, because he had horses in that country.
It had once been used for ceremonies. But the old men who knew the
songs, the prayers, of the Rock-Rainbow-that-Spans-the-Canyon, had died,
and no man now knew them. Few even could find their way there. The One-
Eyed Man of the Salt Clan died the following autumn.

Wetherill asked many Indians about the bridge, but only a few had
heard vague references to it and none knew how to get there. Finally an

elderly Piute, Noshja, stated that he and his son had come upon such a bridge while seeking strayed horses. Wetherill and Cummings made plans to travel to the bridge using Noshja and his son as guides. Meanwhile, W. B. Douglas of the General Land Office had also heard of the bridge while preparing to survey boundaries of a national monument which would protect the ruins of Tsegi and Nitsin Canyons—the areas that are now Navajo National Monument. Douglas was somewhat dubious as to the legitimacy of Cummings' archeological work in the area. Wetherill, ever the Quaker diplomat, felt the best way to quell the growing dispute between the two men would be for them to have a personal meeting.

In Moonlight Valley, near Organ Rock, the Douglas party caught up with the Wetherill-Cummings expedition, which had delayed as long as they could at Oljato before departing for the fabled bridge. Cummings was on a tight schedule, as he had to be back at the university in time for commencement of classes. It was decided the two groups would jointly seek the bridge. With Douglas was Mike's Boy, a Piute who had been with Noshja when he saw the bridge. They started off.

This is tough country for a man afoot, harder for horses. The party worked its way across the deep slickrock canyons that have cut their way northward from the slopes of Navajo Mountain to the San Juan River. In Piute Canyon Noshja was expected to join them, but the old Indian, impatient when the explorers did not arrive on the appointed day, was moving his sheep and goats to better grazing. He would, he promised, send his son Noshja-begay along shortly to help guide the party. At Beaver Creek there was a running stream between pines and aspen. Neill Judd, a student of Cummings' and a member of the expedition, wrote of the country beyond Beaver Creek that

> Old Noshja had pictured a complexity of rolling sandstone, twisting ravines, and craggy cliffs—a mild description as we came to know. . . .
> Bare rock stretched before us. Billows of bare red stone, carved and scoured by wind and sand, reaching mile after rocky mile and always downward from Navajo Mountain into the intricate network of canyons that surrounds it. I still marvel at Wetherill's ability or instinct to lead us over those wind-swept surfaces, around dangerously narrow ledges, past apparently insuperable barriers, without visible evidence of earlier travel to guide him. But he did, and brought us finally to the rounded crest of the "smooth rocks. . . ." ["Return to Rainbow Bridge," Neill M. Judd, *Arizona Highways*, August 1967, pp. 30–39]

Here, Judd reports, they came to the first discernible trail since leaving Beaver Creek; steps in steeply sloping rock said to have been chopped with stone axes by Hoskinini and his band when he led his people into hiding from the United States Army, which had forced most of the

Navajo bands onto the Long Walk to Bosque Redondo.

Hoskinini himself had died only two months after this journey had started for the rock rainbow. As befits a great chief, he was laid to rest in a small hogan under rocks, his moccasins on the wrong feet so that his spirit might not make tracks like a human, and they left with him a saddle, bridle, and ropes. Ceremonially, the saddle was broken, bridle and ropes cut, and bit mashed with stones. His beads, too, were broken, and rents made in his clothes. Thus the thought that went into the making of all these things would go with him, and his favorite horse was stoned to death so that he might ride it on his longest journey.

The expedition descended the rock stairway attributed to Hoskinini. Judd reports the horses had a rough time of it: "Two of them, trembling with fear and seeking better footing, left the stone-pecked trail, slipped and slid to the bottom, pack and all. Neither was seriously hurt. Both accumulated bruises and left patches of bloody hide on the abrasive sandstone." After twisting through a couple of tight rock throats, the expedition emerged onto a wide place in the canyon with grass for the stock and scrub oak fringing the cliffs. The pilgrims gratefully called it Surprise Valley.

Here, apparently, Douglas' guide, Mike's Boy, and Cummings' wrangler, Dogeye-begay, confessed to Wetherill that they were thoroughly lost. They wanted to turn back. Judd comments: "There is no escape from these infernal gorges." Wetherill, thoroughly the explorer, was determined to press on. Cummings, a diminutive, white-haired, balding professor given to wearing suspenders on the trail, was a man of determination and great energy. He, too, was ready to move out next dawn into the unknown. As the expedition debated over the evening campfire, Noshja-begay, son of old Noshja, rode into camp and said another half-day would bring them to the bridge. The following day he brought them there.

Douglas and Cummings, although they had passed days of hardship together upon the trail, once again became intense rivals when the 309-foot span of the bridge was sighted. To both men, in their own circles, it was extremely important who should reach the bridge first, ride under it; history would not be interested in the second person at the bridge. Wetherill, the guide, sensing this, spurred his horse ahead of both Douglas and Cummings, and passed under the span before the men who had jointly "discovered Rainbow Bridge." Thus both of them could equally share the credit.

The One-Eyed Man of the Salt Clan had told Louisa Wetherill that religious songs were once sung beneath the Rock-Rainbow-that-Spans-the-Canyon, before important parts of this prayer were forgotten. The 1909 expedition of Wetherill, Douglas, and Cummings found what appeared to be a small altar nestled against one arm of the rock span, and surrounding rock surfaces were blackened as if by the smoke of many ancient fires.

Rainbow Bridge, known to the Navajo as the Rock Rainbow That Spans the Canyon.

And so the first white men to come to Rainbow Bridge passed over a hard trail to get there. Although photographs of the arch soon began to appear in magazines and Rainbow Bridge National Monument was created, only a few hundred people ever stood beneath the bridge in the decades between the Cummings-Douglas expedition and the construction of Glen Canyon Dam. True, landmarks had been established, and later there were trails of a sort. Yet to reach the bridge one had to negotiate at least sixteen miles across some of the most gloriously wild and rugged slickrock canyons, baldheads, and whalebacks to be found anywhere.

In 1958 Karl Kernberger and I picked up some groceries at Shonto Trading Post, a stone building under shade trees, and headed north on a winding dirt road. For thirty-one miles the road dropped in and out of ravines and snaked its way along ridges. Here and there wagon tracks led off to distant hogans. Ahead the deep blue turtleback of Navajo Mountain dominated the skyline. The road forked. The more traveled route, to the right, led to Navajo Mountain Trading Post, six miles away. We continued down the left fork, which became rougher with each mile. About seven miles from the fork we arrived at Rainbow Lodge, the end of the road.

Next morning we started down the sixteen-mile trail to the bridge. After a few miles of packing down, into, and out of deep trenches like Horse Canyon, we finally emerged at the head of Cliff Canyon, a gap on the shoulder of Navajo Mountain. The canyon is well named. Massive cliffs wedge the canyon bottom, more than two thousand feet below. Beyond lies a vast stone sea of slickrock, whose swells and crests give little hint of the deep and meandering canyons that are there. In contrast to the massive, soaring cliffs of the upper canyon, where flanks of the mountain itself are open to the sky, the slickrock is a hidden world; there are countless canyons, washes, and cracks where there is as much shade as sun, and almost every place is much deeper than it is wide. Perhaps three miles down Cliff Canyon the trail veered up into a fissure in the sandstone—the entrance to Redbud Pass. As I recall, there was a juniper log corral of sorts there. Foolishly we were toting in enough food to have offset rice-crop failure in a minor Chinese province, and so we cached a good deal of it near the corral, figuring to camp there and eat well when we came out from the bridge in a day or two.

We pushed on. Up through the deep, narrow, and beautiful cleft named Redbud Pass. Then down the tight bends of Bridge Canyon to the bridge itself. We camped near it, rappelled down onto it from a ledge, walked across it, and were delighted. J. B. Priestley, who could not know the forgotten Navajo song of the bridge, nevertheless was able to speak best of it in terms most modern visitors can relate to: "How do we know that Rainbow Bridge is not itself a kind of symphony, no more to be completely explained by geology than Beethoven is by acoustics?"

Karl and I did not talk of that around our campfire near the bridge; we simply heated some stew, for we were hungry. We warmed ourselves before crawling into sleeping bags, as it was turning bitterly cold, and felt good, for it was beautiful to be there. Next day we hiked down to the Colorado through the tight and twisting folds of Forbidding Canyon. From the river the entrance to the canyon was concealed and mysterious. We had thought to swim, but it was chill, overcast, and all we did was take off our boots, splash about in the shallows a while, and skip some stones. By the time we got back to the bridge, a light snow was falling. *Bound to pass by morning,* we thought. *Sleep here tonight and see the bridge with snow upon it before heading back.* The only problem was that nearly all of our food was cached on the other side of Redbud Pass. No matter. We had a box of raisins. . . . It would be supper and breakfast. Tomorrow, at the corral, we would feast before hauling up the 2000 feet of switchbacks to the head of Cliff Canyon.

Snow fell during the night. In the morning we started up through the twists of sandstone, boots crunching upon powder of the night's storm. Except for the sounds of our breathing and walking, it was a soundless world of red cliff overhangs, white slopes. Close to the summit of Redbud Pass a raven, wings flapping blue-black against a drift, hopped around and croaked some raven-message before flapping off into a side arroyo. In places where a wan sun had struck overhead, melt had started to trickle into the defile, forming icicles that dangled inches below the lip of shade.

All of this created a grand sense of wilderness. No one else was moving down *our* trail.

Nevertheless, the inner wolf was chewing at our ribs by the time we once again came to the corral, very hungry and rather cold. Karl gathered piñon and started a fire while I went to retrieve the groceries. I confidently

Forbidding Canyon, on the trail to Rainbow Bridge.

waded through the snow to our cache, plunged my hands into the soil through about two feet of snow, and came up with nothing. Wrong place, obviously. Karl tried. After a while, the area around the corral was a series of holes sunk into the snow with accompanying white mounds of excavation. We might as well have been digging for pirate treasure.

We finally gave up and headed up-canyon to the switchbacks, nibbling the last of the raisins. Trudging up a mountain on a long-empty stomach soon turns the legs a bit watery. Nevertheless, the view from the top of Cliff Canyon was even more dramatic than before—the colors glowed. The first sight of Rainbow Lodge was most welcome, and the steak and baked potatoes that came soon after were sensational.

The wild country that John and Louisa Wetherill came to as traders has changed a bit since then. Monument Valley is no longer a lonely place. U.S. Highway 163 passes down the length of it. Lots of cars, motor homes, and even motorbikes whiz over the blacktop, pausing at pull-offs. Kayenta, where the Wetherills established a post after deciding to move south from Oljato, now has several motels, half a dozen gas stations and a supermarket. Much of the valley is now encompassed by Monument Valley Tribal Park.

Yet there is still a sense of lonely beauty to these gigantic spires and buttes, especially if one walks away from the highway, out of sight of it. There is a powerful presence to these massive stone shapes. After a few days and nights among them, it is not hard to consider the possibility that they are themselves living entities whose thoughts and shifting of mass are infinitely slower than that of man. The coming and going of man may seem to them as transient and trivial as the jiggle of insects is to us.

Oljato Trading Post, ten miles beyond Goulding's Lodge on a spur road to the outback, is still a tranquil place—a stone building with salt cedars growing against it. There is usually a pickup or two out in front, perhaps a wagon with the horse dozing in the traces as its owner leisurely considers buying or selling while consuming soda pop and Twinkies, both favorites on the reservation. The original Wetherill post was about two miles to the south; it was burned by Utes after the Wetherills moved south to Kayenta.

The road from Kayenta to the turnoff for Navajo National Monument follows Laguna Creek to the mouth of Tsegi Canyon, which is at Marsh Pass. Here there are deeply cut arroyos which quickly carry away any runoff, and the names Laguna (Lake) and Marsh seem strange until one learns that prior to 1884 there were numerous ponds and lakes here. Many kinds of wildlife, including waterfowl, were drawn to the area. But the land had been badly overgrazed. A year of heavy rains brought floods, which carved arroyos where there had formerly been flat bottomlands; arroyos whose headwalls and tributaries are still cutting back even today.

The Navajos speak of the floods differently. An old man who had practiced sorcery lived near Kayenta. When the creek would be dry near his hogan, which happened often, he was angry that the lakes up-canyon should hold back the water. He knew many spells. One day he walked up into Tsegi Canyon and all the way up into Floating Reed Canyon, where the Water God lived. He caused the water to spurt out of the earth twice a day, causing the creek to flow evenly. Then, quite suddenly, great storm clouds covered the sky. Rain fell in torrents. The lakes broke and the flood rushed down through the redrock canyons and out onto the lowlands. Dineh, scrambling to high ground, looked back at the flood, and in the churning waters there were entire trees and old phosphorescent logs. That night they saw the Water God pass by, breathing fire. The lakes and meadows were gone now; where they had been was dry sand. The sorcerer was put to death.

A ten-mile paved road leads to Navajo National Monument head-quarters from U.S. Highway 160. From there it is an easy walk out to a canyon rim overlooking Betatakin Ruin. A trail winds down to the floor of the canyon, where it passes through groves of quaking aspen, Douglas fir, scrub oak and box elder before reaching the cliff dwelling itself. It is still a magic place, even with a gaggle of tourists during the summer months, and a squad of rangers hired to keep the campfires going and people from falling off cliffs or carving their initials upon the ruins. Inscription House has been closed to the public since a Boy Scout troop marched in on a winter's day and got snowed on. Their resourceful leader decided the ruins would be a cozy place to hole up, and he and his charges began prying out what wood was close at hand, some of it Anasazi roof beams that were hundreds of years old. It all went into a cheery blaze, and park officials are still trying to shore up the damage.

The cliff city of Keet Seel is reached by an eight-mile trail which drops down off a ridge into the Tsegi Canyon complex and then crosses and recrosses a stream before the city is reached. Keet Seel seems as though it might have been abandoned seven years ago—not seven hundred. A ladder leads to the shelf from which the ancient buildings rise. Inside the rooms themselves miniature corncobs and scraps of squash rind are scattered about. Loops of yucca fiber hang from roof beams. The Anasazi suspended their possessions—clothing, feathers, ceremonial objects—from them. *Manos* and *metates,* stone rollers and troughs for the grinding of corn, sit in their appointed places as if merely left idle for a day's outing rather than for centuries. Keet Seel is a beautiful place to walk to.

White Mesa, southwest of Inscription House, contains a huge natural arch, strange and wonderful pinnacles, and some deep and rarely visited canyons. White Mesa Natural Bridge can be reached by very rough dirt roads which head into backcountry from the vicinities of either Cow

Springs or Kaibito Trading Post. Where the dirt roads fray out and rugged terrain blocks even jeep passage, a backpacker can head into a fine chunk of country that is seldom visited. Make local inquiries.

Navajo country has many such places—the spectacular erosions of Coal Canyon east of Moenkopi; the milky fangs of Toelani that rise hard against Salina Trading Post; the great ruins of Pancho House in a lonely bend of Chinle Creek; the Alpine ponds ringed by aspen and ponderosa pine in the high country of the Chuska Mountains, most of which is roadless. And there is Redrock Valley, west of Shiprock, where spires and buttes lift hundreds of feet from the sandy floor, and a person's feet or a sturdy horse will bring them to Anasazi Ruins and the Royal Natural Arch, which rivals Rainbow Bridge in height.

Although flocks of folks can now buzz across Lake Powell in power-boats to within an easy stroll of Rainbow Bridge, most simply whip up for a few Kodachrome shots and then return to their boats and veer away to the next scenic attraction or a good catfishing hole. The trail down to the bridge from the site of Rainbow Lodge, which has burned, is infrequently used now, as is the trail around the north side of Navajo Mountain to the bridge. The hike completely around Navajo Mountain from Navajo Mountain Trading Post to the site of Rainbow Lodge is one of the finest trips in all of the Southwest. Topographical maps, enough water, and a reverence for a sacred mountain are essential. Some Navajo songs might also be helpful. This is the wildest section of Navajo country—there are still places where white men, and perhaps even Indians, have never been. The country is a scrimshaw of sandstone—a world of rock, hidden ruins, springs, cottonwood groves, grottoes softly lit by the glow of the sun upon opposite walls, places where seeps have created green hanging gardens upon vivid red cliffs. . . .

The songs of the Dineh, or Navajo, are matched in beauty by Dinetah, the land that stretches between sacred mountains which are fastened to the Earth by a sunbeam, a flint knife, a rainbow, and a bolt of lightning.

Guide Notes for NAVAJO COUNTRY

LOCATION—Although the largest portion of Navajo country lies in north-eastern Arizona, sections of it lie in southeastern Utah and northwestern New Mexico, and a bit of southwestern Colorado.

ACCESS—Although the Navajo Nation is as large as many states, and, indeed, some of its leaders have talked about petitioning Congress for statehood, few major highways cross the region. Interstate 40 skirts the southern edge of the Navajo Reservation. Other important routes are U.S. Highway 160, which runs out of Colorado across the Four Corners and passes over the northern part of Navajo country before ending at U.S. 89 near Tuba City; U.S. 163, which heads north from 160 near Kayenta, passing through Monument Valley *en route* to Blanding and Monticello; U.S. 666, connecting Gallup, New Mexico, with Monticello, Utah, by way of Cortez, Colorado; State Highway 264, which passes through Window Rock, Ganado, and the Hopi villages before joining 160 at Tuba City; State Highway 12, connecting 264 and 160 by way of Lukachukia and Round Rock; State Highway 63, which connects Chambers and Round Rock by way of Ganado and Chinle.

GETTING AROUND—Outside of the highways mentioned above, there are a number of paved spur roads and some gravel routes. Navajos do not tend to cluster and most of their hogans are strung out on pickup trails. Navajos have taken to the white man's pickup as enthusiastically as they welcomed the Spaniard's horses. This is a sandy country, with arroyos that tend to flash-flood and often contain quicksand. Whether in a pickup or a four-wheel drive, be sure to stash plenty of water and provisions, as well as shovels and some burlap bags for getting under way when bogged down.

    Many of the most beautiful places in Navajo country can be reached only by horseback or afoot. I have touched upon some of these in the text of the chapter; there are many, many others. There is a vast amount of wild country here, but it is not the sort of wilderness where the only people who you may meet will be, as yourselves, transient, passing through. All of this land is the sacred home of the Navajos, and should be respected as such.

    In the wilder sections the topography can be confusing, and it is surprisingly easy to get thoroughly lost. Springs and running streams are widely scattered. Best let someone know where you are going.

CAMPING—Parts of Navajo country may be dry indeed. Check locally as to availability of water and be sure to pack enough in to cover the possibility of sitting out a sprained ankle in a dry camp or missing a planned-upon spring in the dusk. A small backpacking stove or sterno cans are good for regions where fuel might be sparse or nonexistent. In most areas off the beaten path, there will be enough fuel for a cookfire. Scrub oak or piñon is preferable to cottonwood, which burns rapidly and is smoky. Here, as in most of the Southwest, where precipitation is slight, tents are just so much useless bulk and weight. The region can get very cold in late fall and winter, so outfit accordingly. There are also a number of developed campsites in the Chuska Mountains, as well as single campgrounds at Canyon de Chelly, Navajo National Monument, Monument Valley, and other scattered locations.

SUPPLIES—The bulk of one's supplies, especially dehydrated meals for backpacking, should be picked up at the larger towns outside the reservation, such as Gallup, New Mexico; Flagstaff, Arizona; or Durango, Colorado. Canned goods, beans, fresh meat, eggs, and vegetables can be picked up at any of the numerous trading posts in Navajo country.

SPECIAL FEATURES—Wildly dissected slickrock country, deep and narrow canyons, spectacular rock formations, Anasazi ruins, the Navajo culture itself.

INFORMATION SOURCES—Maps are important here. In addition to obtaining appropriate topographical maps from the United States Geological Service, one should try to get hold of the map called "Indian Country," which is put out by the Automobile Club of Southern California (check with your local AAA office). Also, one should write to the Superintendent, Canyon de Chelly National Monument, Box 588, Chinle, Arizona 86503; Superintendent, Navajo National Monument, Tonalea, Arizona 86044; Superintendent, Hubbell Trading Post National Historic Site, Box 388, Ganado, Arizona 86505; Parks and Recreation Department, Navajo Tribe, Window Rock, Arizona 86515.

TWO

The High Lonesome
(Southwestern Colorado)

Southwestern Colorado is often referred to as the Switzerland of America, with some justification, as it is an alpine region of towering peaks, clear streams, and grassy meadows. There are differences, however. Instead of thatched mountain cottages on the high slopes, here one finds the sun-bleached frame buildings and log cabins of abandoned mining towns, and the animals grazing nearby are a good deal more likely to be elk than dairy cattle. Indeed, game wardens in the High Lonesome, as some people call this part of Colorado, are plagued with complaints about elk and deer getting into their hay barns, not to mention beaver gnawing at trees in their orchards. Not that there are all that many folks to complain; Hinsdale County, for example, one of the larger counties of the High Lonesome, has only about two hundred permanent residents. Much of the High Lonesome has been designated as wilderness or primitive areas.

The mountains of the High Lonesome are magnificent. Thirteen of them crest at better than fourteen thousand feet and numerous peaks approach that level. There are gentle summits such as Redcloud Peak (14,034 alt.), which can and have been conquered by little old ladies in tennis shoes. There are also great fangs of rock, such as Lizard Head (13,156 alt.), that challenge even expert climbers. A trail of sorts twists up the south ridge of Uncompahgre Peak (14,309 alt.), but the north face appears to have been struck cleanly with some heavenly hatchet; it is a vertical wall dropping several thousand feet. The rock is crumbling, rotten, and serious climbers doubt it will ever be climbed.

Detailed maps of the High Lonesome show a number of passes where jeep-tracks or foot-trails zigzag up almost impossible walls to top low gaps of eleven thousand feet or so, or squiggle through notches well above thirteen thousand feet where the snow never completely melts on north slopes or in deep gullies. Recently I made a jeep trip over thirteen-thousand-foot Engineer Mountain Pass in early fall. After reaching the saddle, the jeep-road curls around the cone of the peak itself before precipitously descending into the upper reaches of the Animas River Valley. The route over the shoulder of the final summit was barely axle-wide and covered, for perhaps three hundred yards, with loose, fresh snow over an icy base. It got a bit spooky.

A four-wheel-drive vehicle can, I am convinced, all but track up the side of a skyscraper. Yet here there was nothing substantial for the tires to grip, and the jeep repeatedly slipped to the outside, crowding the edge of the road. The drop was not sheer, yet it was certainly tilted enough to have scattered doors, engine parts, and people over a long slope of scenic Colorado landscape. Driving slowly—very slowly—we crawled up to the summit, where the road was dry once more. Occasionally someone does take a fatal tumble off a jeep-trail. We were told, after leaving Engineer Mountain and dropping down into Ouray, that two jeeps had gone over the edge of the Black Bear Pass road that summer.

The valleys which radiate out from the San Juan Mountains were the home of several bands of Ute Indians, most of whom were united under Chief Ouray. As ranchers and prospectors began pushing into Ute homelands, other Ute chiefs, such as Colorow and Captain Jack, led armed attacks upon the newcomers. Ouray, however, was a peaceful man, though no patsy at the treaty table. At a council held at the Los Pinos Indian Agency in 1872, he eloquently demolished the programs and arguments of the commissioners, who "fell back to Washington in anything but good order." A year later Ouray signed the modified Brunot treaty, which yielded the high San Juans to the hordes of prospectors who were already there anyway, and granted the Utes fifteen and a half million acres on the Western Slope.

Yet Ouray the statesman in the end fared no better than warrior chiefs elsewhere. The white man took the land he most desired, and the Southern Ute wound up with a small, semiarid reservation in the southwestern corner of the state.

In autumn of 1873 a group of prospectors in a Provo, Utah, boardinghouse discussed the possibilities of heading to Breckenridge, Colorado, where they hoped to improve their luck. Alfred Packer, a man with long, black hair and chin-whiskers similar to those of Buffalo Bill Cody, professed to know the country and offered to guide the party in exchange for a grubstake. They started out in early November. Two months later they had covered only 250 miles and were low on provisions. A band of Utes invited them to the camp of Chief Ouray, near the present site of Montrose, and

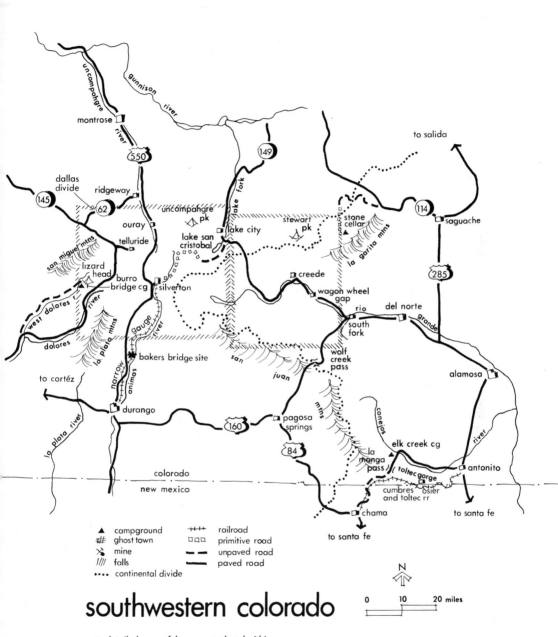

▲ campground   +++ railroad
ghost town   □□□ primitive road
⚒ mine   – – unpaved road
//// falls   —— paved road
•••• continental divide

N

southwestern colorado

0   10   20 miles

note detailed maps of the areas enclosed within
shaded borders will be found on later pages

Ouray urged the exhausted men to stay at his camp until spring. It was a harsh winter in the high country, with frequent blizzards, subzero temperatures, and a scarcity of game.

By now it should have been obvious that Packer knew little or nothing about the rough country for which he had been hired as guide. Yet he convinced five men to push on with him to the Los Pinos Indian Agency, about fifty miles from Ouray's camp. From there they could head north to Breckenridge and start scratching around for fortunes while the rest of the party was still holed up.

Sixty-six days later a hollow-eyed man stumbled into the Los Pinos Agency on half-frozen feet wrapped in strips of blanket. He carried only a Winchester rifle, a skinning knife, and a coffee pot containing some live coals. It was Alfred Packer. His first request was for whiskey. Packer said the party had been struck by a mountain blizzard. Their six-day stock of provisions was soon exhausted and they wandered, lost and starving, eating wild rose pods stuck out of the snow and sharing an occasional rabbit. Eventually they boiled and ate their moccasins. When Packer became lame and snow-blind his companions left him to seek game. They did not return, and so he somehow managed to struggle through the mountains to Los Pinos.

After a remarkably short recovery Packer moved on to the town of Saguache, where he held forth at Larry Dolan's saloon, playing high-stake poker, buying drinks for the house, and otherwise besporting himself. He bought a horse for seventy dollars. At about this time other members of the original party began to drift into Saguache from Chief Ouray's camp. They were suspicious of Packer's free-spending ways, since he had been all but destitute when they had grubstaked him to guide them. He had not owned a Winchester rifle, although two of his missing companions had.

An Indian arrived at the agency with strips of human flesh he had picked up on the trail Packer had taken.

General Charles Adams, the Indian agent at Los Pinos, decided to bring Packer back from Saguache for questioning. *En route* they encountered Frenchy Cabezon, one of the prospectors who had stayed at Ouray's camp. Cabezon, who had heard Packer's story at Los Pinos and disbelieved it, called him a liar.

"You've given me reason enough to kill you. I promise I'll do it next time we meet!" Packer shouted.

Back at Los Pinos, Packer admitted that he knew more about the deaths of his companions than his earlier stories had indicated. Trapped by storm and mountain walls, he stated, he and the prospectors began to starve to death. Winds shrieked off unknown peaks and the snow fell thickly and silently for days. The oldest man in the party died and, after a time, other prospectors ate his flesh to keep alive. Three more of the party died subsequently from hunger and exposure, until only Packer and a man named Bell were left. Bell, Packer stated, finally went berserk and Packer killed him in self-defense.

General Adams placed Packer in the Saguache jail under suspicion of murder.

In August bodies of the missing men were found up Lake Fork of the Gunnison River. Four were lying close together, their skulls split by what was guessed to be an ax or hatchet. It was assumed they were slain as they slept. The fifth prospector, Bell, was found a short distance away, hit by at least two rifle bullets. Although the corpses had been scavenged by wild animals, there were indications that flesh had been peeled away from all of them with a knife.

Alfred Packer escaped from the Saguache jail the night the bodies were discovered.

As the event became past history, the story was told around campfires or in mining-camp saloons. While the drama itself was often embellished, the details of how Alfred Packer looked, how his voice sounded, were

A jeep trip over 13,000-foot Engineer Mountain Pass is likely to have its tense moments.

mostly forgotten. Quite possibly Packer could have rewalked the trail of his own sinister legend after a time and not been recognized. Yet at least one man had marked well Packer's peculiar, high-pitched voice, the look of his eyes, and the shape of his face. He was Frenchy Cabezon, whom Packer had threatened to kill.

Nine years after Packer had cut loose from the Saguache jail, Cabezon was at a roadhouse on La Prele Creek in Wyoming when he heard a high-pitched voice he remembered well. When he talked to the owner of the voice, who called himself John Swartze, the eyes brought him back to the trail encounter with Albert Packer, although "Swartze" showed no recognition of Cabezon. The sheriff of Converse County was notified, and Packer was returned to Colorado. The trial took place in Lake City, a mining camp which had sprung up only three miles from the site of the massacre. Packer was charged with killing Israel Swan, the old man who was the first who had died. During the trial he again admitted killing Bell, but disclaimed knowledge of the other deaths.

Larry Dolan, the saloon-keeper from Saguache, testified to Packer's free-spending ways that came so soon after his ordeal. The jury found Packer guilty. The judge pronounced sentence.

Dolan eased out of the courtroom and gusted into the nearest saloon. "They're gonna hang Al Packer," he proclaimed. He was instantly surrounded by customers, some of whom had more than a passing interest in such judicial affairs, having killed a few folks in the course of promoting or protecting their enterprises, although none had been accused of cannibalism.

The Saguache barkeep described the trial: "The judge, he says, 'Stand up, you man-eatin' sonofabitch. Stand up.' Pointin' his arm at him and his face red as a beet, he says, 'There was seven Democrats in Hinsdale County and you et five of 'em, damn you. I sentence you to be hanged by the neck until you're dead.' "

The actual transcript of the judge's sentencing is almost as colorful. He spoke eloquently of the incongruity of evil and horror in such a beautiful place:

> Your every surrounding was calculated to impress upon your heart and nature the omnipotence of the deity and the helplessness of your own feeble life. In this godly favored spot you conceived your murderous design . . . you, Alfred Packer, sowed the wind; you must now reap the whirlwind . . . I sentence you, Alfred Packer, to be hanged by the neck until you are dead, dead, dead, and may God have mercy on your soul.

As it turned out, Packer did not hang, although he did spend seventeen years in the Colorado State Penitentiary at Canon City. Paroled by the governor at age fifty-nine, he puttered around the green hills near his cabin outside of Denver with the incredulity and suspicion of a man who has lived for years to the rhythm of opening and closing steel slats. He did not live long thereafter.

The Packer party, although principally made up of prospectors, was trying to get through the San Juan Mountains, and entertained little thought that those mountains might contain minerals. Thirteen years before their tragic trek Charles Baker deliberately headed into the San Juans with six companions; he had heard from Indians that they contained gold. They prowled the upper Animas River until the first snows came, and then holed up in crude shelters of logs and boughs. Their encampment was over ten thousand feet high, bitterly cold, and surrounded by hulking peaks. In the spring, joined by other prospectors, the party retreated from the high country to construct a log settlement below where the deep and narrow Animas River Gorge opened into a broader valley through which the river gently meandered. Baker's Bridge, it was named. Unfortunately, this first mining settlement in a region that would produce millions of dollars worth of minerals was a bust. No strikes were made and within a year the inhabitants had drifted out of the San Juans.

Baker learned of the Civil War when he reached Fort Garland in southcentral Colorado. He promptly headed east to join the Confederate Army. He returned to the San Juans after the war, now Captain Baker, exploring the canyons of the Gunnison, Animas, and La Plata rivers. As on his searches before the war, there seemed to be little gold, and once again he spent as much energy pumping optimism into discouraged companions as he did in actually chipping rock samples. The Indians, he insisted, must have been telling the truth about gold in the San Juans.

His fellow fortune hunters pulled out, heading for a bracer of civilization after a spell in these lonely, high, tangled mountains that any fool could plainly see were not constructed to contain gold. Baker himself finally started to trek out. He was killed by Indians.

Other prospectors were now beginning to slip up the high river valleys and canyons, surreptitiously panning sandbars and staking ledges, since this was Ute land by treaty. They were looking for gold but finding silver, often right against the sky, on precipitous slopes over twelve and even thirteen thousand feet high.

The Brunot Treaty with the Utes was signed in 1873. By this time hundreds of prospectors had worked their way into the San Juans. As word of the treaty spread the action became feverish. Claims were recorded, bought, and sold. The echoes of blasting reverberated in narrow canyons as mining commenced. Towns sprang up: Silverton, Howardsville, Eureka, Animas Forks, and Mineral Point on the Animas River; Lake City, below the long and beautiful Lake San Cristobal; Ouray, nestled in a cup of cliffs. Within a decade there were over thirty mining camps in the once lonely and remote San Juans. Del Norte, a raw frontier town of frame false-fronts and log cabins on the Rio Grande River, billed itself as the "Gateway to the San Juan." For several years the only bank in southwestern Colorado was located here, handling the accounts of all the San Juan mining camps, much of it by mail. Freight wagons rolled down the dusty main street, as well as stagecoaches filled with men and women headed for the silver camps, aiming to get rich in a hurry.

As newspapers as far away as New York began running stories on the silver strikes, covered wagons began to stream through Del Norte, many with "San Juan or Bust" painted upon their canvas sides. Most wagons were left at a meadow above Wagon Wheel Gap and their contents packed onto strings of burros. The route led up the grassy valley of the Rio Grande to where it pinched into steep, tight canyons. Some of these were bypassed, but in general the trail led to the headwaters of the river, crossing the divide at 12,588-foot high Stony Pass. The descent down the other side into Cunningham Gulch was precipitous, dropping 2,300 feet in the first two miles. One woman gave birth just after crossing the pass and her husband hastily rigged up a shelter made from wagon canvas and pine boughs, where she rested until able to travel once again.

Most of the silver-seekers had no specific destination in mind—they

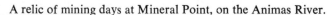

A relic of mining days at Mineral Point, on the Animas River.

the silverton region, southwestern colorado

149
lake city
argenta falls
henson
uncompahgre pk 14,309
nellie creek
matterhorn pk 13,589
wetterhorn
matterhorn
capitol city
henson creek
horsethief trail
american flats
engineer mtn
rose's cabin
denver pass 12,880
whitecross
engineer pass 12,230
mineral point
engineer creek
bear creek
ouray
uncompahgre river
canyon creek
mt sneffels 14,150
camp bird mine
blue lakes
governor basin
marshall basin
sneffels cr
san miguel
telluride
145
san miguel river
ophir
ophir needles
prospect basin
yankee boy basin
imogene pass 13,366
red mtn pass 11,018
three needles
grays basin
bridal veil falls
bridal veil basin
blue lake
waterfall basin
ophir pass 11,743
san bernardo pk
trout lake
lizard head pass 10,222
lizard head 13,113
black face 12,147
wilson pk 14,017
wilson 14,246
elk basin
to rico
lake hope
bandora mine
south mineral creek cg
million dollar highway
gladstone
silverton
animas river
animas forks
cinnamon pass 12,620
eureka
howardsville
cunningham cr
highland mary mine
stony pass 12,588
rio grande
red cloud pk 14,034
sunshine pk
black wonder mine
sherman
lake san cristobal
williams creek cg
gunnison river
yellowjacket gulch
carson
cataract lake
lost trail fork
rio grande reservoir
bear town
bear creek
hunchback mtn
hunchback pass 12,487
grenadier range
elk creek
animas r
silverton
animas gorge
elk park
350
molas divide 10,910
needleton
narrow gauge rr
vestal
needle creek
pigeon pk
mt eolus 14,087
windom mtn 14,087
sunlight pk
chicago basin
columbine pass
needle creek

N

0   2   4 miles

▲ campground
ghost town
⚒ mine
falls
····· trail

railroad
primitive road
unpaved road
paved road

planned to prospect where whim or rumor led them. The two Ennis brothers, however, knew exactly where they were going . . . They had, in fact, paid fifty thousand dollars to a medium in New York City to locate a mine for them in the West. After consultation with the proper spirits she pinpointed a spot on the map where a lake of gold lay hidden in the rocks. That spot, they determined, was high upon King Solomon Mountain near Silverton. They named their mine the Highland Mary and built a ten thousand dollar home with lavish furnishings close to the entrance. The tunnel was cut with specific instructions which the spiritualist sent out from time to time. The tunnel was wildly erratic, with sharp turns and sudden slopes upward or downward. The miners soon learned who was directing the operation and refused to work alone in the shaft. Although several promising silver veins were hit, the brothers did little to develop them, believing the golden pool must be just ahead. By the time the tunnel was nearly a mile into the mountain they went bankrupt, still believers, although they had lost a million dollars in the process.

The subsequent owners of the mine, using more conventional methods, turned it into one of the region's richest silver properties.

The San Juan Range is divided into several subranges such as the La Plata, La Garita, Needle, and San Miguel Mountains, but a quick glance at a map will show they are truly part of the same tangle of mountains: except in the river valleys, towns in southwestern Colorado are generally separated by passes in excess of ten thousand feet high. The majority of the fast, clear streams that tumble out of the High Lonesome find their way into the San Juan, Dolores, or Gunnison rivers, tributaries of the Colorado. On the eastern slope the Continental Divide makes a horseshoe around the headwaters of the Rio Grande, which is America's second longest river.

The Conejos River, just north of the New Mexico border, is one of the Rio Grande's largest tributaries. The Conejos River is large and swift, especially during spring runoff. It meanders its way across grassy meadows of a deep, U-shaped valley where there are several campsites and fishing lodges. The Conejos and its tumbling tributaries are excellent trout streams.

Here, as elsewhere in the southern Rockies, some of the finest early season fishing is to be found in large beaver ponds lying between the nine thousand- and ten thousand-foot level. A spinning lure dropped into deep water near the dam, close to sunken logs or the beaver lodges, will usually soon get a strike from the rainbows and large browns that have been frozen beneath the surface of the pond all winter. One can expect chill weather and snow flurries even after the surface ice is out of the ponds, but a numb reel hand is a small price to pay for hungry lunkers that may run to twenty-four inches or more.

Black bear are common in the Conejos River Canyon. They amble through fishing camps and wander into campgrounds.

One summer evening my wife and I pitched a pair of tents at the Elk Creek Campground—one for us and the other for our three children. While the children and I explored and spun a frisbee, my wife set out with rod and reel to decimate the famed Conejos River trout population. Her luck—a single small rainbow—would have doomed us to pork and beans had not a neighboring camper pulled in the makings of a fine fish fry. As he only liked to catch them, not eat them, we inherited a feast.

We turned in early. Somewhere around the witching hour my wife hissed fiercely into my ear.

"Bear. Do something!"

Sure enough, a dark hulk was rummaging among some provisions we had foolishly left on the picnic table. The bear turned away from the table and started toward a garbage can. I skinned out of my sleeping bag and sprinted in the direction of the car, thinking to drive the beast out of camp by blasting on the car horn. Unexpectedly, the bear turned back to the table, putting us on a collision course.

Beaver pond near Lake City, Colorado.

We did, in fact, collide. It would be pure conjecture to state who was more astonished, but I, not hankering to wrestle the bear, was on my feet sooner and really zoomed to the car.

The horn drove the bear from our camp. We watched it saunter to a nearby campsite and methodically overturn garbage cans there. After pawing through the contents it headed up the line to another camp and more trash receptacles. In its wake we noted a bobcat ghost in out of nowhere to feed on the leavings of the overturned cans.

South of the Conejos River, the Cumbres and Toltec Railroad links Antonito, Colorado, with Chama, New Mexico, by way of the formidable Cumbres Pass (10,022 feet high). From Antonito to the pass, one of the highest rail crossings in the world, the road writhes all over the landscape, passing over the Colorado–New Mexico border twelve times in thirty-two miles. The descent to Chama from the pass is down a steep four percent grade. In one section the huffing steam trains crawl along the bank of a seven hundred-foot precipice rising above Toltec Gorge. A newspaperman, writing of the line in the 1880s, commented that "It is, apparently, a railroad hopelessly gone astray, a sort of knight-errant railway in quest of adventures, a New Columbus, with cars instead of ships, in search of undiscovered realms."

In those days the locomotives had diamond stacks and Russian-iron boiler jackets. They pulled Tuscan-red passenger cars where occupants relaxed upon plush seats. In the soft glow of gas chandeliers miners, ranchers, loggers, drummers (salesmen), Ute and Apache Indians, and other frontier folk conversed or looked out the windows at the high country. The railroad, operated by the Denver and Rio Grande Southern at that time, went all the way to Silverton via Durango.

Today only two segments of the original line are still in use—the Silverton, which runs round trip summer passenger trains from Durango to Silverton, and the Cumbres and Toltec. The combination of antique steam trains and rugged country is highly entertaining, especially if one gets off *en route* to do some backpacking, picking up a return ride on the train a day or two later. The old station at Osier, where the train pauses for passengers to partake of a barbecue lunch, is a takeoff for hiking down in Toltec Gorge; the top of the pass is a good spot to disembark for a skyline hike toward 12,127-foot Chama Peak.

The Rio Grande breaks out of the mountains onto the high, flat San Luis Valley above the town of Del Norte. As during the Gold Rush, the town is still a "gateway to the San Juan," but the red brick buildings of the modest business district, where men in bib overalls stroll, and the neatly painted frame houses on side streets yield the impression that this is a farming community—which it is—rather than what was once referred to as a "rip-snortin', hell-raisin', gold-mad frontier town."

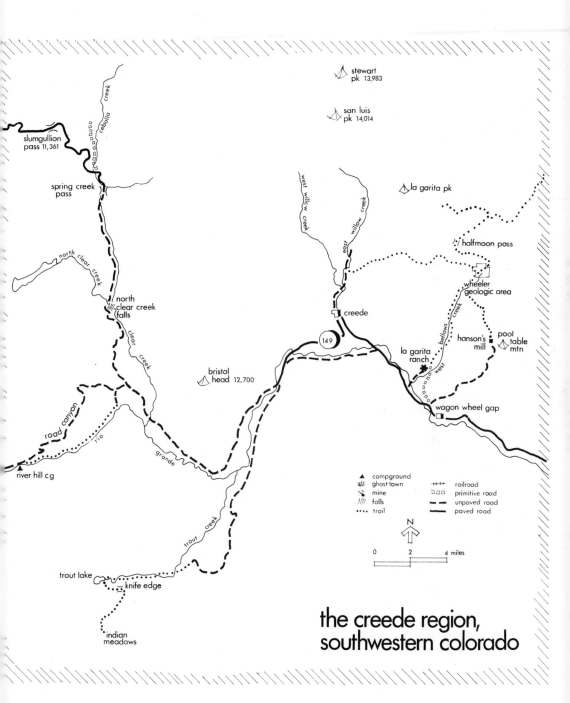

stewart
pk 13,983

san luis
pk 14,014

slumgullion
pass 11,361

cebolla creek

spring creek
pass

west willow creek

east willow creek

la garita pk

halfmoon pass

north clear creek

wheeler
geologic area

north
clear creek
falls

bellows creek

pool
table
mtn

creede

hanson's
mill

clear creek

149

la garita
ranch

bristol
head 12,700

west

road canyon

rio

wagon wheel gap

grande

river hill cg

▲ campground   +++ railroad
ghost town   ▯▯▯ primitive road
⚒ mine   - - - unpaved road
/// falls   —— paved road
···· trail

N
↑

0   2   4 miles

trout creek

trout lake

knife edge

indian
meadows

the creede region,
southwestern colorado

Sixteen miles west of Del Norte, U.S. Highway 160 veers up South Fork toward Wolf Creek Pass while State Highway 149 follows the banks of the Rio Grande itself. North of the road, wooded slopes sweep upward to a skyline dominated by 14,140-foot high San Luis Peak and Stewart and La Garita peaks, both of which are close to fourteen thousand feet high. All of these summits are in the La Garita Wild Area. There are trails into this area from the Rio Grande, as well as trails that wander in from the north out of Stone Cellar Campground.

Wheeler Geologic Area, adjacent to the wild area, contains spectacularly eroded and vividly colored sandstone formations that are scattered through an area of some sixty acres. Between pinnacles and fluted ridges are stands of spruce and pine, as well as meadows that fill with wildflowers in the summer, white mountain daisies, purple asters, star flowers, and goldenrod—a strange and beautiful place. One can hike in from La Garita Ranch, close to Wagon Wheel Gap, and reach the Geologic Area by following West Bellows Creek. This is about a nine-mile trip: for variety, one can return either by walking out to Creede, about twelve miles away, or heading to Hanson's Mill, which is at the head of a rough dirt road that comes off Pool Table Mountain.

The men and women who swarmed beside the Rio Grande during the 1870s and 1880s were in a lather to get over Stony Pass and into the silver country of the high San Juans beyond. Few lingered more than they had to *en route*. In 1889, however, Nicholas C. Creede and George Smith wandered off the beaten path to do a little prospecting up Willow Creek, which empties into the Rio Grande a few miles above Wagon Wheel Gap. Back in the deep canyon of West Willow Creek they found promising silver ore and located the Holy Moses Mine. The following year they sold the property to David Moffat, president of the Denver and Rio Grande Railroad, and a new stampede was under way. New mines were quickly staked and developed—the Ridge, Solomon, Last Chance, Amethyst, and others. Within a year six million dollars worth of silver ore had been shipped from the boom town of Creede.

Tents and then false-front buildings began to line the upper canyon and spill down onto the flatlands below. The population of Creede was increasing at a rate estimated at three hundred people per day during the frenzied summer of 1890. Although there were soon numerous inns ranging from grubby tents with planking upon which one could throw a bedroll to really comfortable hotels, rest was difficult. As one early visitor commented: "I couldn't sleep with all the noise . . . hollering, yelling, horses galloping, wagons chuckling, hammering, pounding, sawing, shouting."

Town lots were being staked in the canyon with the same intensity with which mining claims were being staked on the mountains above. The town lots, just like the mining claims, were occasionally jumped. One

In the mountair
near Creede, Colorad

woman, fearful of just such an occurrence, guarded her property with a pistol while carpenters hurriedly threw up a cabin. "I'll stand here till I am frozen stiff but I'll hold my lot!" The following week she sold it for ten thousand dollars. The pressure for space at the core of the action became wild. Shacks were built upon planks laid across Willow Creek.

When the Denver and Rio Grande Railroad pushed rails into Creede from Wagon Wheel Gap in 1891, Pullman cars upon sidings served as makeshift luxury hotels for a time. Stationary boxcars provided shelter and other offerings. A drape of old blankets divided one car. At one end evangelists held forth, while the other was a crib for women for whom it was always on Sunday, to say the least. The prostitutes complained about the racket of the preaching; one wonders how many miners faced a minor moment of truth in a split-second decision between piety or passion.

By the spring of 1892 there were ten thousand people living in Creede and new hopefuls arrived daily. The first baby being born in the mining camp was an event: townspeople hung around the cabin for days hoping to catch a glimpse of it. The mother was presented with a blue silk dress, a bonnet with an ostrich plume, and a home that contemporary accounts referred to as "palatial," while the father received two suits of clothes, a mining outfit, and a jug of Old Crow. The baby itself was given a silver mine, The Daisy, by Nicholas Creede.

Despite its paternal interest in the infant, the community of Creede also had a more than passing interest in booze, card games, willing women and barrelhouse brawls. As a writer of the time commented: "At night there are no policemen to interfere with the vested right of each citizen to raise as much Cain as he sees fit and . . . three-fourths of the population are of the kind that does see fit." Bob Ford, killer of Jesse James, dealt faro in a Creede saloon for a time, although usually with his back facing the wall and with a nervous eye upon the crowd, for he had achieved his notoriety by placing a bullet through the famed outlaw's back. In an unguarded moment he, in turn, was shot in the back by a one-time marshal named Ed O'Kelly.

Courtly Jefferson "Soapy" Smith wielded considerable influence from his Orleans Club. When public indignation mounted at the number of muggings and other unsportsmanlike means by which citizens were being relieved of their silver, Smith talked the town's respectable elements into hiring Texas gunman John Light as Chief of Police. Unfortunately for law and order, many of the criminals involved were on Smith's payroll, as was Light himself. By the time Creede was aware of Soapy's manipulations, the bunco artist had pulled out for the Klondike, where he was eventually cut down in a gun battle.

Creede was not only a magnet to gunmen but attracted some salty women as well. Calamity Jane Canary drifted in from the Black Hills of the Dakotas dressed in men's garb. No one disputes that she could outdrink most men and could curse with a vigor and imagination to cause trail-hardened bullwhackers to blush. She liked to boast that she had once been thrown out of a bagnio in Bozeman, Montana, for "being a low influence upon the inmates." Although she hung out with many of the roughest men in the frontier West, her own sizable reputation as a quick-draw woman was self-perpetrated—contemporaries claim that even when sober, which was rarely, she would have a hard time hitting the barn, let alone the door. Nevertheless, she was colorful, and bartenders in Creede, as elsewhere, just figured her unpaid liquor bills as part of the overhead.

Her sidekick of the time, Poker Alice, was more businesslike. Born in England, Poker Alice had a way of making men feel guilty to be playing for stakes against such a refined and obviously well-bred lady. She dressed fashionably and never drew a card upon the Sabbath. Nevertheless, count-less cardsharks as well as greenhorns retired from her table with an unchivalrous disposition after being stripped of every penny by that gen-teel, smiling lady. In later years, with white hair and a lined face, she often dealt a deck with a thick cigar jutting cannonlike out of the corner of her mouth. Yet the men still crowded in to be fleeced of their money, though they were cautious of their pride ("with a woman I play just to enjoy her company—I'd never think of cleanin' her out.").

The *Creede Candle* of September 15, 1893, ran the following story after the demise of yet another woman for whom, as a stanza in a popular poem of the time read: "It's day all day in the daytime, And there is no night in Creede."

> Lulu Slain, a frail daughter, laid aside the camelia for the poppy and passed into the beyond early Wednesday morning. She and the Mor-mon Queen had been living in a small cabin in upper Creede but the times grew hard and the means of life came not. They sought relief from life with morphine, the inevitable end of their unfortunate kind, a well-trodden path from Creede. Lulu's dead; the Queen lives.

There were, of course, other amusements in Creede besides whiskey, women and cards. The Keogh Stock Company presented two offerings at the Collins Opera House. *When Women Rule, or* A.D. *2011* and the "Great Labor play"—*By the Sweat of the Brow.* For two bits one could gaze at the mysterious "petrified man" who lay upon a pallet in the Vaughn Hotel, illuminated by a brace of flickering kerosene lamps. Awed spectators were informed that the rigid, chalk-white figure had been discovered in the mud along Farmer's Creek and was believed to have been a member of the Fremont exploration party which passed that way in 1842. After a time even the most gullible rube began to be suspicious of a stone man whose plaster had begun to flake. Even after it was revealed that the figure had been constructed in Denver and hauled in on the railroad prior to being planted in the mud, people still crowded in for a look.

Traveling preachers came to Creede from time to time. They found the Lord's Work an uphill battle in the boisterous mining camp. One Easter Sunday services were held in a large tent. A large supply of fresh eggs had been shipped in to the hotels and cafés, perhaps with the anticipation that men with a good breakfast under their belts would be attentive to the sermon. Most of the eggs, however, quickly wound up in Tom and Jerrys. Although a modest crowd showed up at the service, the same tent was packed that evening for a prize fight.

Parson Tom Uzell delivered a rousing sermon from a pool table in April of 1892. The collection totaled seventy-five dollars, but that evening thieves broke into his hotel room and made off with the money and his pants. It is not recorded if Parson Uzell made any pointed reference to Sodom and Gomorrah in subsequent sermons while at Creede, yet one can safely assume that more than one visiting evangelist warned Creede about the probable consequences of its wicked ways.

In late spring of 1892 a flood roared down Willow Creek, inundating the business district. A few weeks later an early-morning fire broke out in a saloon. Guns were fired into the air, bells rang, and train whistles shrieked. Thus warned, the citizens of Creede were able to flee to safety, but the blaze, leaping from one wooden structure to another, soon consumed most of the business district. Hundreds of people were homeless.

If the flood and fire were divine punishment, the significance was apparently lost on those in greatest need of repentance. As the *Denver Republican* was to report:

> Following the fire, a wild debauch was entered into by all the sots and fast women of the camp. Free liquor was had for the stealing, and many cases of wine, bottles of whiskey, cigars, and such goods were seized and hundreds were drunk before the flames half burned down.

Creede today is a quiet village of 350 people whose economy derives from mining operations and outdoor enthusiasts who flock into the region during the summer months. Ore-trucks of the Emperius Mining Company still rumble through town to a reduction mill, and the Homestake Mining Company employs some seventy men on its Bulldog Mountain property.

West of Creede the highway follows the Rio Grande in a broad sweep around lofty Bristol Head (12,700 alt.). Some twenty miles west of Creede, Highway 149 swings away from the river and climbs toward Spring Creek Pass. The road westward to Stony Pass temporarily leaves the Rio Grande here, winding up Road Canyon to a high terrace above a tight, narrow box of the Rio Grande. Road and river touch again at River Hill Campground. The five- to seven-mile walk back through the gorge to the Spring Creek Pass turnoff (distance depends upon which combination of paths one takes) is one of the most beautiful in all of the High Lonesome. The gravel road continues up to Rio Grande Reservoir, which it skirts. From the reservoir a jeep-trail twists up to Stony Pass, which is on the Continental Divide. A side spur leads up Bear Creek to Beartown, a ghost town dating from the 1890s.

South of the Rio Grande is the Weminuche Wilderness, the most recent area to be so designated. The Weminuche has numerous chill trout streams and lakes as well as sawtooth ranges such as the Needles and Grenadiers. Up around the Continental Divide, which forms the ridgepole of the wilderness, there are some spectacularly steep paths. The trail from Trout Lake to Indian Meadows, for example, runs along the Knife Edge. The view is fine, but it pays to watch where you put your feet. Far below are skeletons of pack mules that didn't. Glen Hinshaw, wildlife management officer for this region, once told me about a rescue effort at Vallecito Lake, which nestles beneath 13,133-foot high Hunchback Peak. A woman hiker had accidentally shot herself. Hinshaw had to put burlap upon the hooves of his pack horse in order for it to negotiate the steep, slippery path to the lake. The woman was picked up off a narrow ledge by helicopter. The chopper blade was barely clearing the rock wall while the rotor hung out in space. The victim survived.

Most visitors, however, leave the Weminuche with warm recollections of their backcountry experiences. There are numerous elk in the high timber, as well as deer, bear, and smaller mammals. Autumn, when the aspens are turning, is an especially beautiful time to prowl the High Lonesome.

The leaves of quaking aspen do indeed quiver in the slightest breeze. A Ute Indian legend tells of a time when the Great God came to Earth on a night of full moon. The people, animals, and plants quivered with anticipation as the deity approached. Only the proud aspen, slender and straight, remained still. God was pleased with the homage shown by His creations; he was angered at the disrespectful aspen. He put a spell on the tree so that its leaves would ever tremble when looked at by mankind.

After leaving the valley of the upper Rio Grande, Highway 149 follows Spring Creek to the pass of the same name (10,901 alt.) on the Continental Divide. Off to the west the crest is jagged, while here the uplands, although ten thousand feet high or better, are more gentle— rounded summits and grassy mesas where Basque and Spanish-American sheepherders graze their flocks in the summer. *En route* to the summit one passes Clear Creek Falls, where the stream, meandering across a brushy meadow, abruptly plunges one hundred feet down into a basalt chasm. The lower section of the falls bursts upon huge knobs of rock, and the water divides into erratic patterns of spray. In the colder months the spray plates surrounding rocks with ice.

Near Spring Creek Pass, on the Continental Divide.

From the crest of Spring Creek Pass, the road dips across the head-waters of Cebolla Creek before topping Slumgullion Pass at an elevation of 11,361 feet. (Slumgullion, in the vernacular of the Rocky Mountain prospectors, was the result of throwing whatever they happened to have on hand into a single pot and cooking it. The ingredients usually were some combination of game or beef, eggs, bacon, potatoes, onions, and beans. Slumgullion, dished up around a campfire after a long day of trekking, and washed down with chill creek water and a hit of whiskey, is still mighty good today.) From the summit the road drops precipitously into the deep valley carved by Lake Fork of the Gunnison. Early-day prospectors, packing up out of the valley, raised the kind of hunger that only a stew as substantial as slumgullion could sate; hence the name.

Hiking or driving Slumgullion Pass, one notes that the western slope has a strange, lumpish quality, and trees slant downhill. About 1270 A.D. the clays underlying a rocky mountain mass gave way, possibly during an earthquake, and millions of tons of stone, clay, and mud plunged down into the valley, plugging Lake Fork. Lake San Cristobal filled the valley behind it—a narrow, long, blue-green body of water that is the largest natural lake in Colorado, and certainly one of the most beautiful. After the initial thunderous slide, viscous clay and mud continued to move slowly by gravity—so slowly that the growth of vegetation was uninterrupted. Conifers that have grown to full maturity—the thick-based and deep-rooted grandfathers—lean to the slope and keep their footing with deep and

102

clutching roots. Geologists feel the original flow has long since stabilized, but that a newer, overlying slide almost two and a half miles long is still active.

Throughout the High Lonesome one sees awesome evidence of avalanches: ten- to three-hundred-yard gaps in the forest where the trees have been swept away by snow that may have been churning at two hundred miles an hour. Scars of landslides are not as common, but are no less spectacular. Yet the Slumgullion Slide is a rare thing; definitely a place to park the car, put on a pack and feel this gritty, lethargic slide under your boots. From the Slumgullion Slide, while the sun is up, you have a view of some of the most spectacular mountains in Colorado. After sundown one can pick out a huddle of lights far below, a single glowworm deep in the folds of dark, hulking mountains. This is Lake City, seat of Hinsdale County.

Hinsdale County is your average-sized American county: about thirty miles wide and fifty miles long. It is all peaks and canyons. Locals claim that if you pulled all those tilts flat, like straightening a blanket, Hinsdale County would be as large as west Texas. Be that as it may, Lake City is the only going town in the county. The map shows places like Carson, Capital City, Henson, White Cross, and Sherman—they are all mining ghosts, sun-warped shells of buildings where, once, hundreds of people lived. Only a couple of hundred people live in Lake City year-round. A recent candidate for the post of county commissioner missed election by a single vote.

Like most of the mining camps in the High Lonesome, Lake City began to boom in 1875 after the Brunot Treaty was signed. Mines were developed with names that could have triggered new religious orders: New Hope, Big Casino, Golden Fleece, Black Wonder, Child of Fortune, Hornet, and Ocean Wave. (Were I to start a new religion, Ocean Wave definitely has the most potential.) The first newspaper to appear upon the western slope of the Rockies went to press in Lake City. The newspaper office was a badly constructed adobe and aspen-pole cabin "which permitted the dirt to sift down upon the editor and his presses in a never-ending shower." There was no post office at that time in Lake City. The nearest agency was some seventy miles away at Saguache, over a rugged trail that could reduce the hardiest mustang to limping. The editor of the *Silver World* editorialized upon this problem:

> Probably no town on the continent similarly situated as we, living on the Pacific slope, are compelled to go to the Atlantic slope to reach the nearest post office. Our mails come in on bull teams. . . .

In contrast to Creede, one of the wildest mining camps, Lake City was a rather staid community, even though it bulged to a population that has been estimated at between two and five thousand people during the

1870s and 1880s. A Presbyterian church was erected in 1876, the first upon the western slope of the Rockies. Soon there were three other churches. Reverend George Darley, the first pastor, often conducted services in gambling halls, with a faro table as altar, until his church was finished. In that building he and a startled congregation watched one Sunday as a deer entered, walked down the aisle, looked casually about, then sauntered out.

In spite of such inconveniences as the eight-foot snows of 1879, which isolated the community, the town steadily grew, and one of its two newspapers, the *Mining Register,* waxed enthusiastic in rather purple prose about the situation. In 1881 it spoke of the San Juans as

> The home of the True Fissure and the Field of the Cloth of Gold and Silver. . . . Our grand mountain canyons echo today with the music of the school and church bell, while the clatter of the busy printing press is heard in every camp and the smoke from the smelters and mills veil the snow-clad summits of our towering mountains and the hot breath from the furnace blast is forging links of silver and gold for the strong chain that binds us to the commerce of the world.

Perhaps delirious from such heady prospects, a miner-turned-lumberman up Henson Creek established Capital City, and for years

Lake City, Colorado.

diligently attempted to convince the Colorado seat of government to transfer there. Today the "governor's mansion" is just some ruined brick walls in a meadow scattered with thick logs of old, decaying cabins—a good base camp for hiking up Matterhorn Creek to the peak of the same name (13,589 alt.) and Wetterhorn Peak (14,017 alt.). Fortunately, smoke from the smelters and mills does no longer "veil the snow-clad summits"— if, indeed, it ever did. The smelters are smokeless, abandoned, and crumbling under the press of seasons.

The *Mining Register,* for all its upbeat approach, also upon occasion reported dark and dire deeds. When Sheriff E. N. Campbell was shot and killed while trying to apprehend two saloon keepers suspected of robbing a vacant but furnished house, a vigilante committee formed. The suspects were jailed. Once the "veil of sweet, mellow moonlight" had given way to darkness, the *Mining Register* reported that:

> . . . a hundred or more unmasked citizens were in waiting at the jail. . . . Then followed the dull thud of sledge hammers against the strong jail lock . . . the prisoners were marched to the bridge . . . a rope was thrown over a cross beam and in less than a minute the two men were swinging. . . . It was now one o'clock. The dark shadows were creeping up the side of the little city . . . the falls under the bridge gurgled and splashed mournfully—silence brooded painfully over the great court and jury and witnesses who stood with upturned faces looking at two figures swinging grimly at the end of the rope of Justice. . . .

A Swedish girl named Huldah came to Lake City in the early days, unattached, and soon made it clear to every lonely miner or tinhorn gambler within a hundred miles that she was *not* entertaining on Bluff Street, Lake City's red light district. For months she worked long hours laundering for miners, saving for the time she could send for her old country lover, Eric. One morning she left upon the eastbound stage with a thousand dollars sewed into the lining of her hat. At the crest of a steep hill, where passengers were told to walk to save the horses, a swoop of wind blew the hat up onto a horn of rock. Huldah pleaded with her fellow passengers to retrieve it, but they told her it would be almost impossible to reach and that they would buy her an even more elegant hat when they arrived at Denver. In tears, she told them of the thousand dollars. A particularly agile man eventually tipped it loose with the driver's buggy whip.

At dusk the stage was held up by three masked bandits. After relieving the passengers of what valuables they carried, the men argued whether or not to take the strongbox, since tampering with the U.S. mails would assuredly incur the wrath of government lawmen. Seeing them hesitate, a passenger named Bennett revealed that Huldah had a small fortune in the brim of the hat. The highwaymen were satisfied with this amount and slipped away, leaving the strongbox unopened. Bennett, as might be assumed, was not a popular man at that moment, and there was talk of stringing him up to a pine limb until he swore that he would repay every penny the girl had lost upon reaching Denver.

The strongbox, it turned out, contained some forty thousand dollars, most of it Bennett's, and at Denver he not only gave Huldah one thousand dollars but bought her a lavish trousseau.

West of Lake City numerous peaks above thirteen thousand feet high cluster on or around the lofty crest that separates the Gunnison Drainage from that of the Animas River. The three principal notches are high and generally passable only in late summer and early autumn. Engineer Mountain Pass (12,250 alt.) and Cinnamon Pass (12,620 alt.) are on jeep trails. Denver Pass (12,250 alt.) is for hikers.

Old mine workings in the gorge of Henson Creek in Colorado's High Lonesome.

The route to Cinnamon Pass follows Lake Fork of the Gunnison in its arc to the south and west. Close to Lake San Cristobal is Argenta Falls, where the river jams and tumbles through a cleft in the rock that a man on a good horse could leap if bullets from behind were tearing through the crown of his hat. Some side tributaries of Lake Fork, such as Williams Creek, have extensive beaver pond systems. One autumn morning, camped near Williams Creek, I strolled through an aspen grove toward the sound of running water, coffee pot in hand. As I started across a small clearing that was covered with brittle red and yellow aspen leaves, I wetly discovered that the clearing was actually a perfectly camouflaged beaver pond.

A couple of miles beyond Williams Creek Campground, a trail heads up Wager Gulch toward Carson, a ghost town which lies partially upon one side of the Continental Divide, partially upon the other. Some of the old buildings lie at twelve thousand feet elevation; others are well down the slopes in stands of white pine. From Sherman, a ghost town on Lake Fork, one can hike up to Cataract Lake to the Black Wonder Mine or ascend Sunshine Peak (14,000 alt.) and Redcloud Peak (14,032 alt.). Neither peak is difficult and they are both usually climbed the same day.

There is high, beautiful, and lonely country all along Lake Fork, as there is along Henson Creek, which leads to Engineer Mountain Pass. Henson Creek joins Lake Fork at Lake City, emerging from the mouth of a deep gorge with ash-gray walls. In places there are gorges within gorges. Old mining equipment and buildings are plastered into nooks and crannies of the verticalities. It is spectacular. At Henson, where ore was pulled from the Ute-Ulay and Hidden Treasure Mines, locusts whir around the oil-stained timbers of deserted mine buildings and rusting ore cars. There is a high old concrete dam here, through which the river has torn a ragged opening. When one opens the wooden door to a mine shaft dating from the 1920s, cold air flows out of the mountain darkness. . . .

North of the Henson Creek road is the Uncompahgre Primitive Area, which contains Uncompahgre Peak. With an elevation of 14,309 feet, this great thrust of rock, which mining men called the "Leaning Tower," commands one of the finest views in all of Colorado. Although the peak is now reckoned to be the sixth highest in Colorado, for a time many considered it the highest. In 1881, after the death of President James Garfield, a band of forty miners placed a flag at half-mast upon the summit in memorium. They had made the ascent during a gathering storm, and once the flag was positioned, a lightning bolt struck in the middle of the group, injuring one of the men. Stoutly, they reraised the flag before making a hasty descent. From Henson Creek, Uncompahgre Peak can be approached by hiking up Nellie Creek (jeeps can be taken as high as timberline) or from Matterhorn Creek.

An improved road follows Henson Creek as far as Rose's Cabin, which in the early days was a stage stop, restaurant, saloon, store, and post office. The large, roofless log building is in a meadow at 11,300 feet elevation. Beyond Rose's Cabin a jeep-trail ascends steep slopes where stands of aspen have been bent or swept away by snowslides, then climbs above timberline into terrain of rocky peaks, wedges of perpetual snow, and tundra vegetation. Even here, at the ridgepole of the Rockies, there are the roofless buildings that once housed the men who dug silver close to the sky. After curling around the head of 13,218-foot Engineer Mountain, the jeep-track plunges precipitously down toward meadows where the Animas River rises. The track here is barely a jeep-width wide: far below are the ruins of Mineral Point and the San Juan Chief Mill.

From the early 1870s, when prospectors began pouring through Stony Pass, until well after the turn of the century, the upper Animas River was a hive of mining activity. Most came looking for gold, yet it was silver that boomed the towns of the area: Mineral Point, Animas Forks, Eureka, Middleton, Howardsville, Gladstone, and Silverton. All are ghost towns today except Silverton, whose income is largely derived from people who have come to enjoy the High Lonesome. Some of the most interesting trails here switchback their way up to old mines, most of which were christened with a flair—Pride of the West, Shenandoah Dives, Royal Tiger, Silver Wing, Mystery, North Star Sultan, Coming Wonder. . . .

Animas Forks took pride in its elevation of 11,300 feet, and pointed out that although Mineral Point might be a little higher, it was definitely smaller. Judge Dyes, justice of the peace at Animas Forks, was outraged when a fellow he had fined for drunkenness refused to pay up since he intended to appeal the case to a higher court.

"There is no such thing," fumed the judge. "This is the highest court in the United States."

The elevation of the Animas River camps and the steepness of the slopes above them caused snowslides to be a common and dreaded occurrence. Cabins and mine buildings were swept away, their occupants buried. An avalanche that roared down Cinnamon Mountain was described as "crossing the Animas River near the Eclipse smelter, ran up the other mountain and then folded over and fell back like an immense wave." On another occasion miner John Haw was puttering around his cabin when he heard an ominous low hum. Suddenly the door burst open and the cabin was filled with powdery snow. Haw clawed out an air-space. Methodically digging, he worked his way out of the doorway and upward through the packed mass of snow. Three hours later he broke out into sunlight.

Al Bernard, over in Eureka Gulch, headed for his mine across snow that was eight feet deep upon the level: it had snowed steadily for a month. A slide caught him and he thrashed frantically to stay near the surface of the churning mass. He was rescued by fellow miners when the snow finally stilled, only bruised, even though he had been carried over the face of a sixty-foot bluff. He was helped to a cabin, where rescuers massaged him with whiskey and cayenne pepper to restore vital functions. Bernard was conscious, but was too numb to tell them where the whiskey would do more good.

Although one promoter attempted to publicize the civilized virtues of the silver camps with pictures of steamboats huffing up the Animas (which here can be waded in most places), most of the early-day newspapers of the area admitted to some rustic edges. The *Ouray Times* of February 7, 1880, commented that:

> Mineral [Point] is held and carefully watched over by Ed Tonkyn, who is Mayor of the city, Street Supervisor, Post Master, proprietor of the Forrest House, and deacon of all the churches. Monday morning he takes up a collection of the poker chips and sweeps out cigar stubs.

The *Silver World* in 1877 described a dance held in a Eureka cabin, where the music was provided by fiddle and banjo. "Soon the damsels began to arrive, some on burros and some on foot . . . the 'iron clads' of the miners began to raise the dust from the floor . . . before long it was impossible to tell what was what." There was a late supper at which "ground hog was the main dish."

The Denver and Rio Grande Railroad constructed a narrow gauge line into Silverton from Durango in 1874, blasting a bed up through the deep cleft of the Animas River Gorge. In some places tracks were laid upon rocky ledges overhanging the cascading water far below. It was—and is—a testimony to the unshakable belief of Rocky Mountain railroad men that they could lay tracks anywhere as long as there was ore to be taken out. By the turn of the century Silverton had a population of 4500. Although there were thirty-seven saloons that never closed, there were also churches, numerous fraternal organizations, and a Dodge City import as town marshal—Bat Masterson.

The current Silverton population is 797. Its setting—a high mountain meadow surrounded by towering peaks—is magnificent. But then so is that of Ouray, twenty-one miles to the north on the Million Dollar Highway, so named because of the value of the gravels with which it was surfaced. Their worth was not discovered until after the project was completed, when a curious geologist ascertained that the gravel was actually high-grade silver ore. The road follows the route of a toll road constructed by Otto Mears in the early 1880s. A typical freight outfit of the times consisted of three spans of mules pulling two large wagons. The highway twists its way over Red Mountain Pass (11,018 alt.) before descending sharply to Ouray on the Uncompahgre River. As throughout the High Lonesome, old mining camps are scattered everywhere and jeep- and foot-trails wind off toward timberline.

Ouray (population 785) is at the head of the Uncompahgre River Valley, with high, rugged peaks lifting on three sides. Where the Million Dollar Highway switchbacks its way down into town, a truck once lost a wheel and tumbled down the slope to smash through the roof of a house. Ouray is a fine base for many backcountry rambles. To the east is the vast Ouray State Game Refuge. Elk and other animals often wander into town to browse in the citizens' vegetable gardens. The refuge is thickly wooded, with numerous small clearings and a network of trails. One of the more interesting routes is the Horsethief Trail, over which stolen stock was driven back and forth to Utah. The trail winds up through timbered country, then crosses the Gate of Heaven, a hogback ridge that drops off two thousand feet to canyons on either side. The path then leads above timberline into American Flats, the site of much early-day mining activity. One can return by way of Bear Creek to the trail's junction with the Million Dollar Highway (a distance of eighteen miles), or continue on the Horsethief Trail to Lake City.

Mines high upon the mountains and old buildings in town are existing remnants of Ouray's silver-mining days. The Beaumont Hotel, an ornate three-story structure of white brick, was constructed in 1886. One evening a little girl skated up beside me as I strolled past the darkened hulk.

"Walk me home, mister?" she pleaded. "I just live a couple of blocks away." She was an earnest, dark-haired child with glasses that made her seem owlish. "I'm scared to walk by the hotel by myself."

"How come?"

"The old woman. The ghost. She lives around the back. All the kids see her at the windows."

Once past the hotel she became more relaxed and skated ahead of me with short, quick strides. She wheeled neatly at an overturned trash can.

"Skunks. Knock 'em all over ever since they bulldozed the dump."

After she waved from the safety of her brightly lit porch, and as I once again passed the hotel, there did momentarily seem to be a faint glow deep in one of the rooms, perhaps from a candle.

Like most other mining camps in the High Lonesome, Ouray began as a silver-mining center in the early 1870s. The big discoveries came mostly from canny geological knowledge rather than Lady Luck. The Camp Bird was an exception. Thomas Walsh was operating a pyritic smelter in Silverton in 1895 and needed siliceous ores that could be used for flux. An old fellow named Andy Richardson scoured some mine dumps in the Ouray vicinity for a quantity of the humble substance. A tunnel in the old Gertrude Mine had a lot of loose rock that seemed promising. The last miner in the shaft had not bothered to tote out the rubble from his blasting. He had been spooked by a sudden thaw that caused rock and snow to slide down the almost vertical area of the mine with frightening regularity. Richardson sacked some rubble and brought it down the mountain to Walsh.

Almost as an afterthought, Walsh had the ore assayed. Some of it was quartz shot through with gold—worth as much as three thousand dollars a ton. Walsh bought up and developed the mine, which became known as the Camp Bird, prospector's term for the Canadian jay. It eventually made him a multimillionaire; his wife owned the Hope Diamond for a time.

The Camp Bird and neighboring mines were all close to timberline or above it. Sawtooth peaks crested above them. The slopes upon which buildings clung dropped off into gorges slashed so deep into the rock that sunlight never touched the cascading waters. Snowfall was prodigious. Cabins at the Virginius Mine were often completely buried by blizzards overnight during the winter months, and miners had to "dig their way to daylight," simply to get to work. One of the principal boardinghouses at the Camp Bird Mine was built hard against the tunnel, constructed with such symmetry with the mountain that when avalanches occurred they simply tore off the stovepipe, of which the management had laid in an abundant supply. The *Denver Post* sent a reporter to the boardinghouse who filed a story that ran in the issue of February 7, 1904:

> At times, the roof sustains the weight of ten to eighteen feet of well-packed snow. Entrance from the surface in the winter is gained by going down an opening in the snow like a ground-hog. The track from the mouth of the tunnel to the waste dump is covered by a shed. Every winter, for from two to four months, the only air which penetrates the building finds its way through this tunnel.

Perhaps to offset the rather unreal conditions outside, Camp Bird bunkhouses would have put many of the best hotels of the area and era to shame. Among other things, they boasted porcelain bath tubs, steam heat, electric lights, and libraries stocked with the leading magazines and newspapers of the day. A dinner at one of the boardinghouses, it was reported, began with oyster soup and finished with fruitcake and cheese. There were platters of roast beef, boiled ham, and fried chicken, as well as sliced cucumbers, young onions, lettuce salad, new peas, lemon and apple pie, snow pudding, coffee, and milk.

The Camp Bird Mine is five miles southwest of Ouray on a gravel road that is both narrow and steep as it ascends the deep gorge of Canyon Creek. Beyond the pitched, red-roofed buildings of Camp Bird, the road becomes rougher and steeper. For a mile or so it follows a narrow ledge high above Sneffels Creek and then climbs up through a steep valley above the timberline. One passes the abandoned mill and three-story boardinghouse of the Atlas Mine before arriving at Yankee Boy Basin, where scattered mine buildings lie beneath soaring, sawtoothed peaks. This is a great place to set up a base camp for hiking or climbing. Mount Sneffels, 14,150 feet high, rears out of a magnificent massif where no less than thirteen peaks approach the fourteen-thousand-foot level. Some climbs are strenuous walkups; others are technical climbs requiring a high degree of proficiency. Mount Sneffels itself was first ascended in 1874. After expending great effort to reach the steep summit, its conqueror discovered signs that he had been preceded by a grizzly bear. Blue Lakes, reached by a trail that switchbacks over a spur of Mount Sneffels, makes for a lovely high-country jaunt.

Timid drivers should be advised that the jeep-trail into the Yankee Boy Basin mining sites has aptly been described as one of the most frightening mountain rides in the entire state.

In airline distance Yankee Boy Basin is only four miles from the old mining camp of Telluride. By road it is more than fifty miles—back down to Ouray, out the Uncompahgre River Valley to Ridgeway, and over the Dallas Divide. The most interesting way to get to Telluride, however, is to hike up over high rock saddles on one of the old mining trails. Some of the most interesting routes are over Imogene Pass, approached from Camp Bird, or the trail connecting Governor Basin with Marshall Basin. Local inquiries should be made as to trail conditions and exact routing.

From the crest, one looks down the steep rock walls of the mountains to the rooftops of Telluride over three thousand feet below. The historic mining town lies at the head of a green valley that dead-ends against a mountain face down which water cascades in the spring. The town itself has scores of old buildings dating from the era of the San Juan silver boom. Some of them have been converted into restaurants, craft shops, and the like. The town rather reminds me of Aspen some thirty years ago, before skiing became a big business there.

In the summer of 1975 Telluride was the site of a national hang-gliding (or sky-soaring) competition. Spectacular flights were achieved from the high peaks above the town. Although no one was injured in the actual contest, one participant was killed on a practice flight when he sailed into a church steeple.

Telluride was no rougher than any other High Lonesome mining camp in the 1880s, but the considerable amount of wealth coming out of mines like the Smuggler, Mendota, and Cimarron attracted the interest of Butch Cassidy and the Wild Bunch. Their principal commerce with the citizens was to sell them horses stolen over in Utah. On June 24, 1889, they went after bigger stakes. On that morning a teller was alone in the San Miguel Valley Bank when Butch and Matt Warner, wearing masks and well-

Hang gliding at Telluride, Colorado.

armed, ambled in and demanded money. The teller scooped up the contents of the cage—$21,000—and gave it to them.

The robbers leaped onto horses that were being held outside by a third gang member and galloped down the valley. Three men urging their horses full-tilt attracted some attention, especially as one of them was imprudent enough to snap off an ineffectual shot at a bystander. A posse was soon formed and pounded after them. One posse member, who possessed a superb saddle horse, soon found himself well ahead of his companions and drawing uncomfortably close to the desperados. He reined up and dismounted. He later explained he had been forced to answer a call of nature, a story that provoked a good deal of mirth around the Telluride watering holes and barbershops for some time to come.

The Wild Bunch, as was their custom, had another gang member waiting with fresh mounts at a rendezvous on top of Keystone Hill and, thus supplied, were able to outdistance the winded horses of the posse and escape back into the mountains near Rico.

There are numerous interesting trails radiating out of Telluride, most of which eventually lead to mines above timberline. The routes to Prospect, Lena, Bridal Veil, and Grey's Basin fall into this category. The trail into Blue Lake, beneath the Three Needles, is a beauty. A forest trail follows the contours of the mountain mass immediately north of Telluride for several miles, mostly above the ten-thousand-foot level.

Telluride is beginning to attract a number of ski-touring and snow-shoeing enthusiasts during the winter months. Equipment can be rented in town.

Four miles west of Telluride State Highway 145 winds above the south fork of the San Miguel River to Trout Lake and Lizard Head Pass. The river valley is wedged between the La Plata Spur of the San Juans to the west, in which there are few notches lower than twelve thousand feet, and the sky-pushing peaks of the San Miguel Range to the east. The road moves up through ranching country with split rail fences, winds through stands of aspen and across meadows before reaching the Ophir Loop, twelve miles from Telluride. Here a hundred-foot-high wooden trestle marks a spectacular example of the kind of engineering it took for Otto Mears to push his Rio Grande Southern Railroad over the mountains. The Loop, in the form of a great horseshoe, had the tracks all but overlap themselves.

The town of Ophir has dwindled since the closing of the railroad, but the station and a few other structures still huddle beneath the high, gray fangs of Ophir Needles (12,100 alt.). About two miles from Ophir the large, deep-blue expanse of Trout Lake is cupped by wooded slopes.

Trout Lake is the hub for a number of excellent trails. The Lake Hope trail winds its way up to where the lake fills a high rock basin, then crosses the crest of the La Platas at 12,445 feet elevation and drops down to the Bandora Mine on the south fork of Mineral Creek. One can come out at South Mineral Campground, which is on a dirt road reached from the Million Dollar Highway. The Lizard Head Trail is a sky-climber. It switchbacks its way up onto the saddle between San Bernardo Mountain, which resembles the Matterhorn from some angles, and the long crest of Black Face. The long, high (12,147 alt.) spine of Black Face leads to the base of Lizard Head, a volcanic neck that is one of Colorado's more challenging pinnacles.

A 1932 U.S. Geological report spoke of it thusly: "Near Mount Wilson is Lizard Head . . . in its upper four hundred feet a sheer rock spine, absolutely insurmountable unless steps are artificially cut in the bare rock walls." Actually Lizard Head had already been conquered by two human flies, Albert Ellingwood and Barton Hoag, twelve years before. They had packed into Bilk Basin from Lizard Head Station on the Rio Grande Southern Railroad with eighty-pound packs that included one

The jeep trail over Ophir Pass.

hundred feet of climbing rope and three "long, thick spikes somewhat like those used for steps on telephone poles"—primitive pitons, probably among the first used in Colorado. The adventurers soon realized they would need something special for this tower.

> It was apparent when we reached the Head that there was nasty work before us. A rottener mass of rock is inconceivable. The core may be solid, but the surrounding tuffs are seeking a lower level in large quantities. . . . In many places one could with one hand pull down hundreds of pounds of fragments, and occasionally we could hear the crashing of small avalanches that fell without human prompting. . . .

Ellingwood finally started up a shallow chimney. After scaling a "rather open stretch practically vertical and with exiguous holds about the size of a thimble," the lead climber eventually reached a three-inch ledge

115

which would support one boot while the other hung over space. With a
hand hooked over a rock at arm's length and the other manipulating the
rope, he belayed, if one can call it that, his partner up the ninety-foot pitch.
Ellingwood continued his unprotected lead up vertical slabs and chimneys
until a "sheer, smooth cliff" blocked the way.

> Finally I decided to try to reach a crack that lay near the south end of
> the wall and appeared to lead through to the arête above. The first
> eight or nine feet was an overhanging pocket or alcove, and above
> this the wall was vertical and unbroken save for the narrow end of
> the crack to which we aspire. . . . Standing on Hoag's shoulders,
> I probed all things within reach for what must have seemed an in-
> terminable time to him. At last I found holds at arm's length, but it
> was a strenuous pull to reach the crack. . . . At the extreme limit of
> the rope I reached a large safe anchor rock at the south end of the
> summit arête, and saw that we had won.

Beyond Lizard Head the trail drops into Bilk Basin, where there are
good campsites, several waterfalls, and great peaks on all sides. From the
basin one can ascend rugged Mount Wilson (14,246 alt.), Wilson Peak
(14,017 alt.), or El Diente (14,159 alt.), which European climbers com-
pare favorably with some of their favorite Alpine summits. Silver Pick
Basin, the site of a great deal of mining activity in the early days, is another
excellent base camp for hikers and climbers. The Navajo Lake Trail, which
heads out of Burro Bridge Campground, is also a fine approach to this
magnificent cluster of peaks. Burro Bridge Campground is on a gravel road
that follows the west Dolores River.

Early-day travelers could enter the San Juans in style on steam trains
of the Rio Grande Southern, which offered Pullman service as well as
scenery unsurpassed by that traversed by railroads anywhere. My first clear
childhood memory is of a family outing to Trout Lake on the Galloping
Goose. I was three, going on four, yet in my mind's eye I can still climb
aboard a silver car with a snowplow and whoosh off down railroad tracks
as if it were yesterday.

By the 1930s the Rio Grande Southern was facing a dilemma common to most railroads that had been constructed to serve mines whose
production was assumed to be eternal. Prices for minerals had dropped, the
best veins had pinched out, and these railroads were subsisting upon their
contracts with the U.S. Postal Service. In 1931 the Rio Grande Southern
concocted a lovely rail beast whose hood and front portion were that of a
Buick, the rear the flatbed of a stake truck, all of it mounted upon railroad
wheels. This remarkably efficient unit was soon dubbed the Galloping
Goose, and it was followed by several other models, usually employing six-
cylinder Pierce Arrows as the vehicles and Wayne bus bodies, to carry the

mail. Driving over one of the highest rail passes in America in a Pierce Arrow boggles the mind. Unfortunately, in the early 1950s the rails were pried up and the Geese are now grounded.

While the Rio Grande Southern may have offered one of the most beautiful train rides in the country, working on the railroad was not always so much fun. In November of 1920 a cattle train left Rico at seven A.M., bound for Dolores. Shortly after noon some cars derailed. While the crew laboriously heaved them back onto the tracks with camel-back frogs (grooved flanges designed for this purpose), Conductor Crum inspected the roadbed. It had softened after heavy rains. This factor, in combination with the extreme curvature of the tracks and rigid side bearings on the cattle cars, had caused the derailment.

The telephone was out of order so the conductor trudged two miles to the station at Millwood to report the cause of delay. He returned to find the cars rerailed, and the train started off again. More cars derailed and were placed back upon the tracks, only to jump them again at the next sharp bend.

It was 9:30 P.M. when the train finally reached Millwood. The crew had now been working for fourteen and a half hours, the latter part by the flickering light of kerosene lanterns. Conductor Crum asked permission to leave the train at Millwood and take the exhausted crew into Mancos. Permission was refused. Dourly Crum told them to send out a wrecker and then pushed on. In the next five miles they had three additional derailments. A rear car overturned. Crum was out on the tracks appraising the situation when he looked up to see cattle from the smashed car stampeding in his direction. There was no time to run; nothing to hide behind. So he stood his ground, yelling and waving his lantern, as the frenzied animals streamed by on either side.

When the train finally reached its final destination, Conductor Crum was reprimanded for not making out accident reports on all the derailments. The exasperated trainman replied that he had used up all of his report sheets in the course of twenty-five derailments in an eleven-mile stretch.

As he was later to recall, "that was the worst trip I ever made."

It has been a good many years since conductors have been bedeviled by hordes of derailed cattle on the dismantled Rio Grande Southern, or Galloping Geese pulled through the heart of icy mountains. Yet only some twenty miles to the east as the crow flies, a steam train still chugs up through some wildly vertical country. The narrow-gauge line from Durango to Silverton is laid over ledges that are high above the Animas River Gorge, as well as beside the Animas as it brawls its way downward. There are no roads in the gorge: one is dazzled by the engineering feat of putting a railroad there.

During the summer months an excursion train, the Silverton, makes the scenic run from Durango to Silverton. After allowing the passengers time to have lunch and see the sights, the train returns to Durango. Schedules and information can be obtained from the Durango Chamber of Commerce.

The narrow-gauge line is a fine way to get back into some of the most rugged mountains of the High Lonesome—the Grenadier Range and the Needle Mountains. One can request to be put off at a selected departure point, head into the high country, and then flag the train down when you wish to return to civilization. Getting out at Elk Park, for example, one can hike up Elk Creek, which is the watershed immediately to the north of the Grenadier Range. This trail eventually crosses the Continental Divide and leads to the ghost mining camp of Beartown.

Sudden, violent summer thunderstorms are common in the High Lonesome and many early-day surveyors, prospectors, and miners have recorded close calls with lightning. A few years ago a man named Bill Hughs and I were very nearly skewered by lightning on Windom Peak (14,087 alt.), which looms above Chicago Basin. We had swung off the steam train at Needleton, an abandoned mining town and stage stop, and hiked up a trail beside Needle Creek. It is some six miles into the Basin—a broad, grassy meadow encircled by jagged peaks. After camping in the Basin, Bill and I started up Windom Peak. Bill, a soft-spoken, middle-aged man with intense brown eyes, had been a mathematics professor at a midwestern university. One summer he resigned, sold his house and car, and started walking—he walked down the length of the Appalachian Trail, rambled throughout the mountain west and trekked all the way to Guatamala. An expert at foraging for wild edible plants, he managed to live on a dollar a day!

Windom is not a particularly difficult climb, but there is a knife-edge close to the summit with a lot of space off to either side. As we were approaching the top, the dark mass of a thunderhead was approaching our mountain, blotting out the sun. By the time we had started back down the knife-edge, hail was gusting down and our hair crackled with electricity. Several lightning strokes had hit neighboring peaks by the time we reached the saddle. We looked longingly at the shelter of the forest far below. We started across a large patch of snow that had been firm enough to bear our weight on the ascent. It had softened in the afternoon sun, and we found ourselves plunging through the crust. The lightning was striking the ridge close to us now. Wallowing out of waist-deep snow is tedious at any time: it is a nightmare when trying to hustle off a mountain with lightning whacking all around. The rocks were so charged with electricity that they gave off a steady sound—rather like bacon frying. We had just broken free of the last large snowpatch when a bolt hit so close that I was knocked off my feet and momentarily blacked out. We came down the mountain like gazelles, leaping and sliding down wet slopes. We finally reached a grove of trees, drenched and very happy to be there.

There are two other fourteen-thousand-foot peaks rising above Chicago Basin—Sunlight and Eolus. While they are only moderately difficult, other crags in the area, such as Pidgeon Peak (13,961 alt.), are a challenge to experienced climbers. East of Chicago Basin is Columbine Pass (12,600 alt.). A trail leads over it to the Vallecito River and then up the river to its head at Hunchback Pass (12,487 alt.). One can loop back down Elk Creek to pick up the train at Elk Park.

Most of the High Lonesome has been designated as wilderness or primitive areas. It is one of the most beautiful areas in America, rich in history, a feast for those who love the high and lonely places.

Guide Notes for the HIGH LONESOME

LOCATION—Southwestern Colorado.

ACCESS—This is one of the most mountainous regions in America, and all of the roads through it cross high passes. U.S. Highway 550 tops Molas Divide (10,910 alt.) between Durango and Silverton and then twists over Red Mountain Pass (11,018 alt.) *en route* to Ouray. State Highway 145 follows the Dolores River into the mountains, crossing Lizard Head Pass (10,222 alt.) *en route* to Telluride. State Highway 149 follows the upper Rio Grande River past Creede before swinging over Spring Creek Pass (10,901 alt.) and Slumgullion Pass (11,361 alt.) and then dropping down into Lake City. U.S. Highway 160 connects Del Norte with Pagosa Springs and Durango by way of Wolf Creek Pass (10,850 alt.).

GETTING AROUND—In addition to the highways mentioned above, there are a few spur roads, paved and unpaved. Except in the wilderness and primitive areas, the entire region is laced with jeep-trails, most of which follow wagon roads that were created during the mining boom before the turn of the century. Motorists are required to stay on established jeep-trails, some of which are hazardous. Black Bear Pass, for example, switchbacks down a two-thousand-foot escarpment in its descent to Telluride. The water of Bridal Veil Falls sprays down this cliff and the hairpin turns are tough for even highly skilled operators of four-wheel-drive vehicles. Information is available from jeep rental agencies in Lake City, Silverton, Ouray, and Telluride.

Two narrow-gauge railroads, the Denver and Rio Grande Western and the Cumbres and Toltec, offer a delightful way to get into the backcountry on the excursion steam trains they run in the summer months. The Denver and Rio Grande Western run can be boarded at either Silverton or Durango, although the day-long round trip begins at Durango. The day-long trip on the Cumbres and Toltec may be started at either Antonito, Colorado, or Chama, New Mexico, with the return by motor coach over La Manga Pass.

There are numerous trails throughout the High Lonesome, many of them in wilderness or primitive areas. Unless you are ski-touring, the best time to hike the high country is from late July, when most of the snow is out, until deer- and elk-hunting season in October, when the cold settles in and legions of hunters are blasting up the woods. It is pleasant at the lower elevations from late spring until mid-autumn.

CAMPING—There are a number of developed campsites in the High Lonesome, and innumerable primitive sites. One is never far from chill, clear mountain water. Campfire permits can be obtained from any of several ranger stations located in what few towns there are, as well as in the outback. Campers should be prepared for extremes of weather, as snow flurries can and sometimes do occur even in midsummer.

SUPPLIES—Freeze-dried foods and other backpacking paraphernalia can be obtained at Durango, Creede, Telluride, Silverton, Lake City, and Ouray. It is good to remember that most of the other towns in the area are ghosts. The region is a rich larder of natural foods—trout and many edible plants. A book on edible plants is a worthwhile investment.

SPECIAL FEATURES—One of the highest and most rugged mountain clusters in the continental United States. A number of ghost towns with mines high on slopes above them. The unique rock formations of the Wheeler Geologic Area. Two narrow-gauge railroads where steam trains still huff along dizzy ledges during the summer.

SOURCES OF INFORMATION—Forest Supervisor, San Juan National Forest, Olinger Building, P. O. Box 341, Durango, Colorado 81301; Forest Supervisor, Rio Grande National Forest, Route 3, P. O. Box 21, Monte Vista, Colorado 81144; Forest Supervisor, Uncompahgre National Forest, 11th and Main Street, Delta, Colorado 81416; Silverton Chamber of Commerce, P. O. Box 656, Silverton, Colorado 81433; Tourist Division, New Mexico Department of Development, 113 Washington Avenue, Santa Fe, New Mexico 87501 (for information on the Cumbres and Toltec Railroad); chambers of commerce at Durango, Creede, Lake City, Antonito (Conejos River information), Telluride, and Ouray.

THREE

Pecos Wilderness
(New Mexico)

The Sangre de Cristo Mountains form the southernmost spur of that great, complex and rugged wall of western America, the Rockies. The range formally begins at Poncha Pass at the head of Colorado's San Luis Valley, a single crest of towering peaks that is breached by only one gap, La Veta Pass, in the first 120 miles. The Sangre de Cristos, which mean "blood of Christ" in Spanish, push another 75 miles to the south before falling away to a country of grassy, rolling plains and piñon-studded mesas near Santa Fe. The mountains end at what was once the Santa Fe Trail, over which General Stephen Watts Kearney marched his troops to effect the bloodless acquisition of New Mexico from Mexico. The final, sharp summits cradle the headwaters of the Pecos River. To be sure, there are mountains—high ones—yet to the south, but they are isolated and not connected to the Rocky Mountain chain.

As elsewhere along the great range, a person coming in off the prairies to the east is usually dazzled by the abruptness of the Sangre de Cristos. Coming out from Oklahoma or the upper Texas panhandle, one passes through vast rangelands of gentle horizons and frequent small ponds, winding up through an occasional cedar break cliff—Hereford and antelope country. Ahead, quite suddenly it always seems, the mountains loom, a barrier of blue that becomes greener as one gets closer, crested with snow much of the year.

For pioneers of a century ago the mountains were a landmark signifying the great plains had been crossed; Santa Fe was near at hand. Some families, recalling burned-out wagons seen along the way, would kneel together in quiet prayer of thanksgiving; trappers and bull-whackers were more likely to break out a jug of whiskey, if they had it, and try to outshout the coyotes after a few hefty pulls.

Sections of Santa Fe have changed little over the past hundred years; Pueblo Indians sell jewelry and pottery beside the plaza and new coats of adobe are slapped onto the ancient walls of homes up side streets. From almost any point in the old section of town, a short walk brings one onto ridges that sweep up into the mountains. Bear and other wildlife sometimes wander down into the narrow, winding streets of the city. A child, whose elementary school is only a few blocks from the state capitol building recently startled his teacher by commenting that there was a bear on the playground. "All black. Like a big dog." The child was right, and game and fish officials captured the animal, then released it far back in the mountains.

Santa Fe, almost seven thousand feet high and nudging the mountains, is a city, albeit a small and remote one. At the time of writing this state capital is served by no commercial airline flights—which is a burden or a blessing, depending upon your point of view. Most approaches to the southern Sangre de Cristos, however, take one through villages where there is a scattering of mud houses, a church, a store, a post office—high-country Spanish settlements that were taking shape long before children whose grandparents voyaged west on the *Mayflower* ever laid blue eyes upon the broad Mississippi. A typical village house might have strings of red chili peppers (a staple food) hanging down the walls, a couple of junked cars in the yard, a broom-swept dirt yard, and a rounded adobe bread oven. The people of these villages are poor by economic standards; New Mexico has the third lowest per capita income in the nation. Yet one almost never sees a thin baby. These are a proud, self-sufficient people who have learned to work with the cycles of land and weather over the generations. Usually they own land, no matter how few in acres or niggardly in crop. One feels few segments of society would be better equipped for survival should the economic systems falter.

Like many rural people with a strong ethnic identity, they have developed numerous folk sayings and proverbs. *A pan duro, diente agudo* means "sharp teeth for a hard loaf of bread," or, set a thief to catch a thief; *pisar el sapo,* "step on toads," or, be fearful of consequences; *ser lo mismo que el sol puesto,* "as useless as the sun which has set." In some villages folk beliefs are still strong. Instead of placing a lost tooth under the pillow for the tooth fairy, a traditional village child throws the tooth toward the sun and recites: "Sun, sun, take this tooth, and give me one better."

Thunderstorms are frequent in the Sangre de Cristos. Although it is believed lightning will never strike an innocent child, a prudent old person may spread ashes upon the cover of a pot, draw a cross with a finger, and then place the utensil outside for protection for the household.

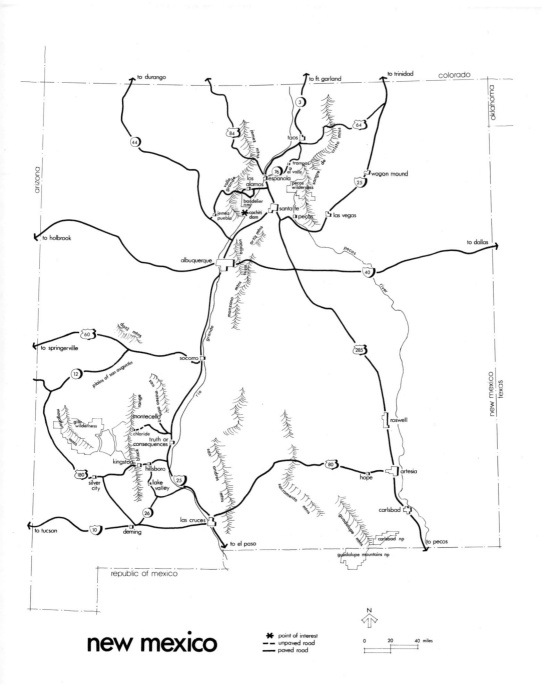

new mexico

* point of interest
-- unpaved road
— paved road

N

0   20   40 miles

Every mountain village has its own stories of La Llorona, the wailing woman. Most agree she is seen dressed in black, wandering the night and crying in anguish in an endless search for a child that has been murdered—usually, it is thought, by herself. In many stories she was a young bride whose husband died before the birth of the child. When the child came, she killed it in a spasm of grief, and then was unable to take her own life as intended. Thus she must lament and seek fruitlessly the body of her murdered offspring for eternity . . . back in the deep pine groves, across darkened fields of stubble corn . . . sometimes shrieking in the voice of the baby itself: *"No tengo dientes!"* "I have no teeth!"

The villagers of the Sangre de Cristos, like most hill people, tend to be insular and somewhat suspicious of strangers from the outside. Until recently all the inhabitants of one village had the same surname. Like their city brethren, the mountain people are sometimes a bit eccentric. A few years back I made a visit to an old Spanish gentleman who lived in a steep canyon of the foothills. When I reached his small adobe home, it had begun to rain. Coffee cans had been set out all around the living room floor, each melodiously catching a leak. The dripping water, he explained, was coming through bullet holes. His neighbors downcanyon, it seemed, took potshots at his house from a nearby ridge; this was why he vigilantly wore a pair of ancient opera glasses around his neck. Looking more closely, I saw they were without lenses, and later, observing the angle of the bulletholes and the position of the ridge, I concluded the old fellow had done all of the shooting from inside.

Aside from his fantasy of being under siege from time to time, he proved to be a lovely, gentle man, who upon subsequent visits always stoked up his wood stove to warm coffee and tortillas for me.

A more serious form of gunplay occurred many years ago in a nearby village. Two families (whose names I have altered for the sake of surviving descendants) had been feuding for some time. A Protestant medical missionary moved into the area and was welcomed by the Luceros, who had been converted to that faith. The Archuleta family, staunch Catholics, would have nothing to do with him until one of their women was having problems with childbirth. Since the midwife was away, they sent for the medical missionary. Somehow he arrived before any men of the family had returned, and delivered the child without serious complications. Unwittingly he had broken one of the strongest taboos of that time and place—no man, even a doctor, should ever be with a woman giving birth unless a male member of the immediate family is present.

The Archuleta men, incensed at this transgression, jumped the doctor as he was returning to his home and beat him so badly that he was crippled for life.

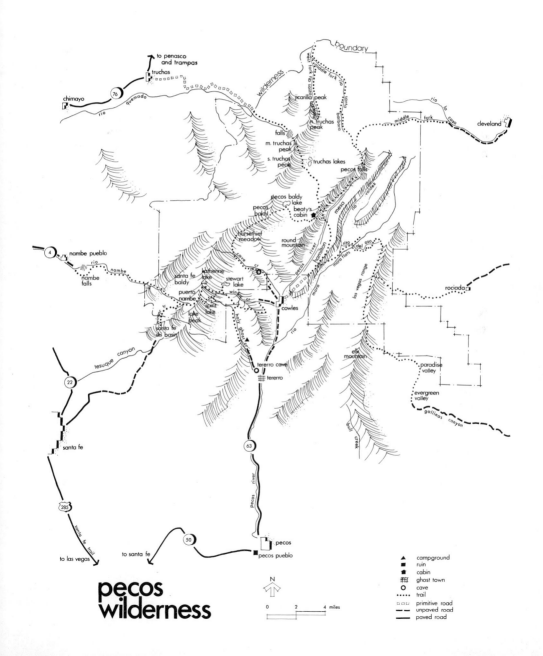

to penasco
and trampas

truchas

chimayo

76

quemado

rio

wilderness

boundary

west fork rio santa

middle fork

rio santa barbara

jicarilla peak

n. truchas peak

falls

m. truchas peak

s. truchas peak

truchas lakes

pecos falls

middle fork

rio la casa

cleveland

rio

mesa

rio osha

pecos baldy lake

beaty's cabin

pecos baldy

horsethief meadow

round mountain

pecos river

hamilton mesa

rio del oso

mora flats

nambe pueblo

4

rio

nambe

nambe falls

santa fe baldy

katherine lake

stewart lake

cave cr

rio mora

las vegas range

rociada

puerto nambe

lost lake

win cr

santa fe ski basin

lake peak

holy ghost cr

cowles

rio mora

elk mountain

paradise valley

tesuque canyon

22

tererro cave

tererro

evergreen valley

gallinas canyon

bull creek

santa fe

pecos river

63

285

santa fe trail

50

to las vegas

to santa fe

pecos

pecos pueblo

▲ campground
■ ruin
🏠 cabin
⊞ ghost town
○ cave
•••• trail
▫▫▫ primitive road
— — — unpaved road
———— paved road

N

pecos
wilderness

0   2   4 miles

The Luceros, hearing of the attack, planned their revenge. There was soon a wedding in the Archuleta family, and the men, by custom, gathered in a small *cantina* to toast the event. Lucero men, from rooftops and nearby cover, picked off several of the Archuletas as they emerged from the *cantina*. The windowless ruins of the weathered building, walls pocked with bulletholes, remain to this day.

The mountain villages and the roads connecting them encircle 167,416 acres of the Pecos Wilderness. The crest forming the eastern boundary of the wilderness is more rounded and not as high as the line of peaks forming the western boundary. From the dominant western summits such as Truchas Peaks, Santa Fe Baldy and Lake Peak, one can look out over the entire Pecos River headwaters and, on a clear day, see over the eastern ridge to where the Great Plains begin their long sweep to the Mississippi River.

The Truchas ("trout" in Spanish) Peaks are the highest in the wilderness, and among the most beautiful in the entire Sangre de Cristo range. From the Española Valley the slab face of Middle Truchas (13,000 alt.) appears to be the principal summit, yet South Truchas is actually 100 feet higher. North Truchas, which for a time was considered the highest summit in New Mexico, is actually 13,110 feet high. One can climb all three in a single energetic day without technical skills or equipment.

From Española one drives east on State Highway 76 through the Chimayo Valley—orchards and small settlements, at least one of which, Santa Cruz, is more than three hundred years old. Near the head of the valley the road twists its way up a series of ridges to the village of Truchas. This huddle of dark mud adobe dwellings is perched upon a high shelf of the mountains and commands one of the finest views in the state. Continue eastward through the village and out into pasturelands on a dirt road that is all but impassable when muddy. There are actually a number of roads along here that fork only to come back together again, or veer off to dwellings and logging sites. Consult a topographic map and aim for the place where the North Fork of the Rio Quemado emerges from the wilderness area—a good trailhead. Although the setting is beautiful, cars left overnight here have been vandalized and I would suggest you get someone to drop you off and arrange a pickup.

A couple of miles into the wilderness, the stream plunges over a waterfall. I usually make base camp in this vicinity. Here one is in a cirque with the walls of Middle Peak looming to the south. A steep grassy shaft leads up to the shoulder of the mountain, from which one can scramble up the face of the summit. It is an easy walk from the top of Middle Peak across the saddle to South Peak. One can then descend into the Pecos River drainage to Truchas Lakes. North Peak is a walk-up from this side,

Middle Truchas Peak, one of the most beauti
in the Sangre de Cristo Ran

and one can return to base camp by the trail which crosses a pass between the peaks.

The Truchas Peaks are bighorn sheep country. Two major herds roam the high rocky ridges between the Truchas and Pecos Baldy, a 12,600-foot mountain. They are descendants of animals introduced in the 1960s—white bighorns brought in from Banff National Park in Canada and bighorn sheep from the Sandia Mountains near Albuquerque that are a light chocolate color. Stalking the glue-footed beasts with a camera or simply to observe them is great fun. Best take good binoculars—their vision is better than yours even when you are lamping them with eight-power field glasses. Sometimes the herds are very elusive; yet I have a friend, Cradoc Bagshaw, who has managed to ghost so slowly and quietly toward them they have taken potato chips from his hands. Another friend, a wildlife photographer who has spent many days in this bighorn turf, recounts only one episode of belligerence. While shooting close to a herd he shifted his tripod, and immediately a large ram lowered his curl and charged. The animal braked a few feet from the alarmed lensman, snorted and pawed a bit, and then returned to the herd. Possibly the ram took the raised outside leg of the tripod to be a rifle being aimed.

When climbing above timberline, as in the Truchas, it is good to get an early start. From dawn until early afternoon it is generally warm, sunny, and thoroughly delightful. From July through early September a violent thunderstorm in the waning hours of the afternoon is more likely than not. If thunderheads begin to build up above you, start looking down for the closest patch of thick timber.

West Couglin, a friend and a fine climber, had his own problems with the weather during an attempted winter ascent of the Truchas Peaks. West, his brother Jay, and two other companions set out from the village of El Valle on snowshoes. On the second day out the party trekked up the ridge to the top of Jicarilla Peak, a wind-blown ascent of three thousand vertical feet. The following day they probed their way along the series of summits that lead to North Truchas Peak. On one knife ridge a climber peeled out and slid some fifty feet before arresting his fall with an ice-ax. After an arduous ascent of the approach ridge, progress was finally blocked by cliffs only fifty feet from the summit. "With pitons we could have made it. No way without them," West later commented. The group descended into the cirque valley and camped.

Although the next morning was clear, windless, and promised fine climbing, one climber started back down the valley toward Truchas, exhausted from the efforts of the day before. The other three began the ascent of Middle Peak, crampons (icespikes) lashed to snowshoes. High altitude snow and ice ascents are physically demanding. One climber chose to wait

Cross-country skiing in the Pecos Wilderness. (*Cradoc Bagshaw Photo*)

at the summit of Middle Peak while West and Jay continued on toward South Truchas. On the way up West had stumbled over a spur of rock. He cursed at it impatiently. Jay spoke with concern. "Never talk to a mountain that way; some terrible things have happened after that." Clouds had been gathering with astonishing rapidity during the ascent of Middle Peak. Now, midway between the peaks, the storm struck the ridge with fury. There was lightning and West's hair was crackling with static electricity. As he recalls it: "By the time we got onto the knife ridge the weather had deteriorated. Wind ripped my face mask off—that's when the frostbite started. We reached the summit in an almost total whiteout." To the climbers it looked like the end of the earth—black rocks and cornices of crusted snow hanging over a white, windy void.

Struggling back to Middle Peak, they discovered their companion was gone—whether staggering around in the swirling snow or over some precipice it was impossible to tell. Gale winds snatched away their shouts. Cornices were huge. One of Jay's boots broke through an overhanging cornice; beneath the hole was gusting snow and an abrupt dropoff. By some kind of crazy luck or an eerie sense of sightless direction, Jay managed to grope his way out onto the narrow ridge that leads back down to the valley, tapping his ice-ax before him like a blind man's cane.

Somehow they made the descent and got out to safety, as did their missing companion, who had managed to navigate down another spur in total whiteout, using his compass and topographic map.

All had some frostbite, but no extremities were lost.

U.S. Highway 84, which tops a crest just north of Santa Fe and then casually drops its way into the Española Valley, is a delight to drive. There are virtually no billboards beside the highway for a good many miles because esthetic vigilantes with chainsaws—or torches for metal poles— keep knocking them down.

Just beyond the Nambe River bridge a state road, Highway 4, swings off to meander east through cottonwoods, chamisa, and tall cedar-pole fences hiding homes built—and built well—while Chicago was still a sod village and a few tattered tents. A short distance off this road is Nambe Pueblo, and beyond, Nambe Falls. There are actually four large drops, the highest being about one hundred feet, set in a deep cleft where there are tangles of oak brush and wild grape vines; ancient cedars lean from crannies, roots gripping the rock as if for balance, and in the twilight the appearance of a troll would not seem astonishing.

In the pueblo people sometimes speak of a sacred cave whose opening, long since obliterated by landslide, lies close to the falls. At one time, they assert, the cave passed completely beneath the entire range, emerging some twelve miles away on the Pecos River. It is said that before the landslide Spanish soldiers cached some armor and weapons in the cave. To handle these things, the cacique—the shaman—warned, would bring ill fortune. Moreover, entering the cave was taboo except for religious ritual, as the guardian serpent of the pueblo was thought to reside there. In spite of this, a young man ventured into the cavern, planning to gather up the Spanish artifacts and sell or trade them at a distant pueblo. He carried a large knife, and when a huge snake lunged at him from a dim corner he lopped off its head. Immediately there was a grinding roar, as if the mountain were devouring itself in agony. The chamber swayed, great slabs falling from the roof. The terrified young man sprinted out of the entrance and had reached the stream when the side of the mountain pulled loose, sealing the cave.

For the next few years things were bad in the pueblo. Winters were harsh, summers dry; crops struggled in flaky dust and game was nowhere to be found. The right arm of the man who killed the serpent turned black and hung useless at his side. After a time the climate softened, and there was corn once more in the storage bins, deer on the hillsides, and rabbits and doves by the stream. Yet until he died at a very old age, children would scamper away in fright and older people avert their eyes upon meeting the man with the blackened arm.

Above Nambe Falls the trail follows the creek to its headwaters at Puerto Nambe, some eight miles away. Puerto Nambe, a high grassy meadow, lies beneath 12,622-foot high Santa Fe Baldy and 12,402-foot high Lake Peak. Both mountains are heavily forested with conifers to timberline, yet upon the western slopes there are several massive areas of aspen or open areas which, from a distance, look as if they were bare. One of the largest of these areas, upon Baldy Peak, resembles the shape of a thunderbird. Many Indians of the valley, and Spanish-speaking farmers as well, schedule their spring planting for the moment when the last snow has gone from the thunderbird.

These vast clearings are the scars of old forest fires. The largest on record is a conflagration that started in Tesuque Canyon in May of 1887. It was soon burning across the slopes of Lake Peak and then Santa Fe Baldy, but as no settlements were threatened, no effort was made to fight it. The fire steadily burned its way into the Pecos drainage, jumping the river north of Cowles, and gradually moved across the Las Vegas Range. The fire was finally halted by a crew cutting railroad ties northwest of Wagon Mound, over fifty miles from the point of origin. Although it had burned out of control for two months, the fire was given scant notice by the press.

From Puerto Nambe one can switchback over a pass to Katherine Lake, from which trails lead to Cowles and Holy Ghost Campground, the most popular portals to the Pecos Wilderness. Southward, the gently contoured Windsor Trail winds like a balcony above the Española Valley to terminate at Santa Fe Ski Basin (10,500 alt.).

Many early-day travelers approached the Sangre de Cristos from Las Vegas, New Mexico, which is on the Santa Fe Railroad. In Gallinas Canyon, six miles west of town, Fred Harvey constructed one of the most elegant hotels of the frontier West—the Montezuma. A spur line routed all first-class passenger trains to the imposing red castle upon a hill. Refrigerated cars were also pulled up the spur, filled with fresh fruit, meat, seafood, and vegetables. Yaqui Indians in Mexico had a contract to provide live green turtles from the Gulf of California. The turtles were fattened at a pool near the hotel until needed for the table. The fare was served with great pomp and ceremony in a dining room that could seat five hundred—a vast chamber finished in quarter-sawed oak, magnificent chandeliers, and a variety of stained glass windows. Water from a nearby hot spring was piped into the hotel through redwood ducts. Among the guests who enjoyed such amenities were General Ulysses S. Grant, President Rutherford B. Hayes, President Theodore Roosevelt, and Emperor Hirohito. Jim Flynn sparred in the hotel casino while training for his world heavyweight championship bout with Jack Johnson.

But as the El Tovar hotel at Grand Canyon and other places in the area became fashionable, the prestige of the Montezuma declined. Some years after the hotel closed, it became a seminary for Mexican priests.

Lake Peak in the Pecos Wilderness.

Today the magnificent structure is unused, its oak corridors prowled by a solitary caretaker.

Folks getting off the train at Las Vegas who yearned for a more rustic setting were able to take a carriage or wagon twenty-one miles back into the mountains. Here, at the foot of a steep gradient, they mounted horses or burros for a seven-mile ride up through the timber to Paradise Valley, a log cabin resort. Infants and toddlers were placed in two pack boxes which were secured upon Old Reuben, a docile and sure-footed burro. If there was only one child, balance would be struck by filling the other pack box with supplies of approximately the child's weight. The resort, abandoned now for many years, lies some two and a half miles northwest of Evergreen Valley and is a summer pasture for cattle.

When the *conquistador* Francisco Vasquez de Coronado marched eastward in quest of the mythical kingdom of Quivera, he camped at Pecos Pueblo. Since his historian spoke of it as "a village of five hundred warriors who are feared throughout the country," a total population estimate of two thousand does not seem unreasonable.

Today, when approaching the Pecos Wilderness from the south, one passes the high adobe walls of a mission church built in the early eighteenth century. On the mesa around it lie the broken remains of what was the largest southwestern pueblo of its time—roofless stone rooms and great mounds of unexcavated ruins. Pecos Pueblo declined gradually. Raiding Comanches plundered and destroyed crops, frequently killing warriors. From time to time epidemics swept through the pueblo. Slightly less than three hundred years after Coronado viewed the pueblo in its full glory, only a handful of people lived in what was rapidly falling into vast ruin. When there were only seventeen of them left, tradition tells us, they abandoned the pueblo and made their way to Jemez Pueblo, where they found the people to be friendly.

Fifteen miles upriver a few blisters of rock rubble, slate-colored among evergreens, and some concrete foundations mark the site of another abandoned place—the former mining camp of Terrero. Whereas the warriors of Pecos were nearly always out-of-doors—hunting, in the fields, or skirmishing with raiding bands of Plains Indians—most of the men of Terrero spent much of their time deep under the soil, digging out high-grade zinc and lead. Terrero flourished during the decade of the Great Depression, with a payroll of seven hundred men. Then, ironically, as times were getting better across the nation, the mines closed and the town was completely dismantled.

Close by, at the mouth of Holy Ghost Canyon, is the opening of the cave which, legendarily, once ran all the way to Nambe Pueblo before a landslide sealed the other end. I have followed it back for perhaps the better part of a mile before giving up at a tight crawlway partially filled with water.

The resort and summer-home village of Cowles is the major portal to the wilderness area. From here trails fan out through the backcountry. One can begin at Cowles and arrange to be picked up at a number of roadheads: Truchas, Nambe, or Santa Fe Ski Basin on the western side; Evergreen Valley, Rociada, or Rio La Casa on the eastern slope; and Rio Santa Barbara to the north, among others. The Windsor Trail heads westward toward Puerto Nambe.

Three lakes on this trail—Spirit, Stewart, and Katherine—are noted for fine trout fishing. Another trail heads toward Horsethief Meadows via Cave Creek. The meadows, a fine, grassy opening, have been used in the past as pasture for rustled horses, a number of which, it is said, were brought there by members of the Las Vegas gang known as Vicente Silva and his Forty Thieves. Silva, a truly genuine badhat, eventually came to grief over a lady other than his wife. The woman insisted that the child resulting from their dalliance carry the name of Silva. Whether out of some sort of code of honor with regard to his legal, childless wife, or just plain cussedness, Vicente murdered his mistress. His gang collectively had a great deal of blood on their hands, though none of it was feminine. They claimed they then killed their chief in chivalristic outrage, although his heavy money belt may have had something to do with it.

True to its name, much of the water of Cave Creek drains off into two openings in a limestone cliff. The caves extend back for quite a distance, but exploring them is a dampening experience.

It was on Cave Creek that Miguel Lamy, a Navajo who had been raised by Archbishop Juan Bautista Lamy, was chewed on by a black bear. He was standing next to a boulder one late afternoon when a cub tumbled around the corner of the rock. Lamy shot it, then looked up to see its charging mother. He tried to reload but the cartridge stuck. His back against the rock, he threw up his left arm to protect his face and throat as the bear, upright, snapping and clawing, lunged against him. While the bear's teeth ripped through the flesh, exposing bone, Miguel drew his knife with his right hand and slashed at the animal's neck. The bear, in rage, continued to bite into the man's shoulder, apparently oblivious to the pain of her own opening throat. The man, in desperation, continued to slash at the bear's throat, unaware of the pain of separating muscle and snapping tendons. The bear finally collapsed at his feet, head almost severed from its body. Bleeding from various wounds, Lamy managed to make his way to a ranch some eight miles away.

For the rest of his life Lamy bore the scars proudly, for how many men have fought an enraged bear and lived to tell of it?

There were, at one time, many grizzly bears in the Pecos high country. Professor L. L. Dyche, a highly respected naturalist who collected specimens in the Pecos during the 1880s, reported seeing *seven* of them at one time, plodding between his exposed position and the forest. Since there was a vertical drop at his back, he simply watched the procession with horrified fascination. Professor Dyche had killed grizzly bears with the heavy Sharp's rifle he then carried—but it had been on a one-to-one basis. Seven, he felt, would have been a bit too much for even a good marksman with a Sharp's or any other rifle.

There are no more grizzlies in the Pecos. The men that shot them and tried to eat the meat said it was tough, strong, and a curse upon the tongue. Yet they continued to blast away at every grizzly they could find—for sport. And, often as not, if we are to believe the journals left us, it might better be called sadism than sport. A good many of the bears dropped by intrepid hunters expired as they lunged with a leg inescapably seized by a forty two pound bear trap.

The sizable elk herds that once roamed the Pecos were an important source of food for the grizzlies. But settlers, prospectors, and market hunters soon learned to take advantage of the elk's instinct to bunch together in open, fairly accessible places for the winter, and by the 1880s there were no more elk. Cattle moved into the pastures elk formerly browsed, and the grizzlies acquired a taste for beef, which hastened their demise.

Unlike the grizzly, elk have made a comeback, with transplanted herds gradually expanding through careful game management. Mule deer are the commonest large game seen in the Pecos country, and today one also may see bighorn sheep, mountain lion, black bear, and a number of smaller animals.

There are a great many fine hiking trails in the Pecos Wilderness, which contains fifteen fishing lakes, some of the highest peaks in the state, and seven major streams. A detailed description of even a small portion of these trails would, and does, fill a volume of its own (see Bibliography: *Trail Guide to the Upper Pecos*).

Most extensive trips into the wilderness eventually will pass by the site of Beatty's Cabin, which was a two-room log hut built by a prospector and hunter named George Beatty around 1870. Beatty apparently found little

Mountain sheep, Pecos Wilderness. (*Cradoc Bagshaw Photo*)

gold, but had many a yarn to spin about encounters with grizzlies. He was fond of displaying his brace of foot-long knives, which he figured were capable of reaching a bear's heart. All that remains of the original cabin today is a mound of fallen bricks from the fireplace. Close to the site are two more recent cabins belonging to the Forest Service and the Fish and Wildlife Service.

One of the most popular trails in the Pecos Wilderness runs north from Cowles along Hamilton Mesa. The first supervisor of the Pecos River Forest Preserve headed up that trail in 1897 for an inspection trip. Both he and his ranger were political appointees from Kentucky, and their wrangler noted with amusement that instead of slickers each man had an umbrella tied behind his saddle. On top of the mesa it began to rain. The supervisor popped open his umbrella. His skitterish horse, unaccustomed to such gadgets, bucked furiously. The supervisor made a grand arc through the air and landed in a strawberry bush, still clutching the open umbrella.

A trail 4.7 miles out of Cowles leads down into the valley of the Mora River. Mora Flats, where the Mora River, Rito del Oso, and Rio Valdez come together, is a good fishing spot—but not what it used to be. Elliot Barker, whose book, *Beatty's Cabin,* recalls years of experience in the upper Pecos country as forest ranger, rancher, and outdoor enthusiast, had a fishing contest at Mora Flats with two companions when he was a teenager. The youths fished from 8 A.M. to 2 P.M., and between them landed 438 trout.

If one continues along the mesa trail, another fork is encountered three miles beyond the Mora River trail, the left-hand route dropping down to Beatty's Cabin on the Pecos River and the right-hand route leading to Pecos Falls, a series of drops and cataracts of more than fifty vertical feet. In the Pecos, as in other wilderness areas, the majority of people hike the major trails to camp beside the principal lakes or in frequented meadows. Many fine side trails offer solitude, especially on weekdays and in the autumn. This is a subtle country, well deserving of a leisurely pace.

Varieties of mushrooms may spring up after summer rains. There are a number of limestone ledges that are nubby with fossils—brachiopods, gastropods, and corals. There are forests of Engelmann's spruce, corkbark fir, and here and there a bristlecone pine—among the oldest of all living things on earth. Especially at twilight, walk softly. You may happen across deer who stand motionless, regarding you with large, liquid eyes before gliding away in a series of short, supple leaps.

If you are lucky, you may share a campfire with Rufus McShannon, a red-bearded giant with a headful of stories. He recalls a rainfall so lethargic that a man could dodge the drops in his sleep, and a curious winter storm where the snow lifted off the slopes and drifted back up into clouds. Mosquitoes, he insists, used to be bigger in the old days. One day, break-

Camping in the Pecos Wilderness, the author puts a kettle on the campfire. (*Cradoc Bagshaw Photo*)

fasting on Bull Creek, he was watching with amusement as a baby mosquito ineffectually attempted to lift off with an egg. Hearing a scraping noise, he whirled around to see its parents fly off with the skillet.

Rufus modestly asserts that in his younger days he was considered the finest climber in the West. He loped up Truchas Peak one afternoon when there was a massive thundercloud rising above it. Without pausing at the summit, he dug his hands into the cloud and started hauling himself up the side of it. He reached the top, he claims, using pitons on only one pitch ("Good solid thunderhead—not flaky."). And then took a fast slide back to the rock on a thunderbolt.

Generally speaking, no matter who is on the other side of the campfire, whether backpacking in summer or ski-touring and snowshoeing in winter, Pecos Wilderness is a fine place to go.

137

Guide Notes for the PECOS WILDERNESS

LOCATION—Northcentral New Mexico. The 167,416-acre Pecos Wilderness of Sante Fe National Forest is at the southern end of the Sangre de Cristo Range.

ACCESS—Most access roads to the edge of the Pecos Wilderness lead out of mountain villages to the northeast of Santa Fe, such as Cowles, Truchas, and Las Trampas. Santa Fe Ski Basin, at 10,300 feet elevation, is a popular road-head with backpackers.

GETTING AROUND—There are a thousand miles of mapped trails in the Santa Fe National Forest, many of them in the Pecos Wilderness. From Memorial Day through Labor Day a great many backpackers, having discovered the delights of the Pecos Wilderness, stride along the major trails, sharing them with an increasing number of equestrian parties. If you like solitude, I suggest you route mostly along lesser-used trails during this period (most rangers can help you plot this), or, better yet, travel the wilderness in spring or fall when traffic is relatively light, or cross-country ski and snowshoe in winter, when traffic is almost nonexistent.

SUPPLIES—Santa Fe has sporting goods stores that specialize in backpacking, and everything anybody could need can be purchased here. Cross-country skis and snowshoes can be rented. Last-minute sardine and V-8 juice purchases can be made in any of the villages that ring the Pecos Wilderness.

SPECIAL FEATURES—Fine trout fishing; some thirteen-thousand-foot rugged peaks that have fairly easy routes, but also some rock faces to challenge the most intrepid piton or chock technician. There are old Spanish villages as well as Indian pueblos on the rim of the Pecos Wilderness.

INFORMATION SOURCE—Santa Fe National Forest, P.O. Box 1689, Santa Fe, New Mexico 87501.

FOUR

Bandelier Backcountry
(New Mexico)

The backcountry of Bandelier National Monument may not have every-thing—no oceans, for example—but within the forty-six square miles of the monument a hiker can find a variety of wilderness delights. There are cliff dwellings, pueblo ruins, tall forests of ponderosa and other conifers, mesas with bunchgrass, cedars and piñon, spectacular waterfalls, weird rock formations, and a cave covered with exquisite pictographs. Some sixty miles of maintained trails follow the streams of canyons such as Frijoles and Capulin, or switchback in and out of other steep-sided gorges.

Eons before there was man to see or hear it, a gigantic volcano blew its top, blotting out the sun with volcanic ash and pouring rivers and sheets of molten rock across the Bandelier country. The caldera, or collapsed cone of the volcano, is what we now call Valle Grande, one of the largest in the world; its rims are the principal summits of the Jemez Mountains. The ash became compressed into tuff, a rock so soft that some of it can be grooved with a strong finger. The fiery rock, mostly overlying the ash, gradually cooled and hardened into basalt. Streams, cutting into the easily eroded rock, then carved the deep canyons of the region.

The late thirteenth century was a time of extended drought in the Southwest. Many large Indian pueblos were abandoned, and no one really knows where all the people went or what happened to them. A number settled in Frijoles Canyon and its vicinity. The stream, although not large, flows year-round. Squash, beans, and corn were grown above the rimrock as well as in the canyons. Using harder stone, Indians gouged numerous cliff rooms out of the tuff, building external rooms out of masonry.

139

Adolph Bandelier, the Swiss-American scholar who studied prehistoric sites in the Santa Fe region in the 1880s, commented that the numerous man-made caves "appear like so many pigeons' nests in the solid rock from a distance."

A great many large pueblos were also built in the region, one of which, Tyuonyi, is one of the most impressive ruins in the Rio Grande drainage. Encircling a central plaza, the building once had more than four hundred rooms.

There is only one developed campground in Bandelier, located on the rim of Frijoles Canyon overlooking Tyuonyi Ruin and the Visitor Center. Don't let the pay phone at the campground or the presence of motor homes and other highway monstrosities disturb you—only two short twigs of asphalt poke into the National Monument, the one to the campground and one to the Visitor Center. The rest is trail country.

Backpackers are required to register at the Visitor Center, where there is an outstanding new museum. There is an interesting loop trail to Tyuonyi and some other ruins that takes about an hour at a leisurely saunter, but if you are itching for some backcountry, I would suggest you save this one for a Sunday afternoon fried chicken picnic with grandma and the toddlers.

One of the most enjoyable weekend jaunts anywhere involves hiking out to the Shrine of the Stone Lions, down Capulin Canyon to the Rio Grande, then back to your car—twenty to twenty-two miles, depending upon whether one reads the Bandelier brochure or adds up trail mileage markers—a fairly rugged twenty or twenty-two miles, I might add, especially in the heat of summer. From June through August the sun really booms off all that volcanic rock, and when the sun is not there you have thunderheads that can dump a lot of water in a hurry. On the whole, I think Bandelier is most comfortably backpacked in the spring or fall.

From the Visitor Center a trail cuts up the south wall of Frijoles Canyon, reaching the rim at a point opposite Ceremonial Cave, where there is a restored *kiva,* a subterranean chamber where religious rituals were practiced. Here the trail swings sharply to the south, dipping in and out of Lummis Canyon. Small ruins are on every hand, and bright shards of pottery and chips of black obsidian are scattered between twisted piñons.

Alamo Canyon, slashed four hundred feet into ancient rock, is magnificent if you're still stepping lively, a baleful cleft if you have a big pack, couldn't figure what to leave out, and so just put it *all* in—gold pan, twenty pounds of C rations, and *Prescott's Conquest of Mexico* in two volumes. One zigs down four hundred vertical feet and does the reverse upon hauling out. There are curious rock formations galore—conical witches' hats;

On the trail between the Rio Grande and the Visitor Center, Frijoles Canyon, Bandelier National Monument.

leaning gargoyles; smooth, white walls perforated like swiss cheese. Alamo Canyon is usually dry at this point—carry enough water to take you over to Capulin Canyon, some seven miles from the Visitor Center.

Sometimes from the rim of deep canyons such as Alamo it sounds as though there is a great tumbling river down at their bottoms. Actually the canyons are dry, or host streams so narrow a wildcat could easily spring over them; the sound is that of wind raking through tall ponderosa pines.

Occasionally a bemused backpacker will tell a ranger he or she spotted a rabbit peering down from the branches of a ponderosa. The ranger, rather than checking the person's pulse or rummaging his pack for empty tequila bottles, explains that he has seen an Abert squirrel, whose great tufted ears do indeed give him the appearance of a rabbit at certain times of the year. Curiously, the Abert squirrel is a selective beast, and will only live in ponderosas. There are more than 130 species of birds that live in Bandelier, as well as black bears, mule deer, skunks, raccoons, porcupines, badgers, foxes, and coyotes. On rare occasions a mountain lion is seen, usually when driven from cover by a forest fire.

Backcountry Bandelier trails are usually free of litter, yet beside the trail between Alamo Canyon and the ruins of Yapashi I once noticed a broken-off woman's purple spike heel. Carried in as a gag? Or had some woman actually attempted the trail in high heels? (I see her in silk dress, nylons, wearing a floppy flowered hat and carrying a Japanese fan.)

Yapashi itself is a vast ruin, rubble and a few low stone walls overgrown with cactus. It is a quiet, distant place, where the call of a single bird is so sharp as to be startling. I first saw these ruins at sunset, and was overwhelmed by the setting. To the northeast the snowy Sangre de Cristos poked at the horizon, dead ahead the Rio Grande slashed through basaltic cliffs of White Rock Canyon; southeastward, yellowed grasslands ran out to the Ortiz Mountains, the Sandias, and beyond. This broken city, mysteriously abandoned, commands one of the finest views in all America. At our backs the sun was sinking behind the dark horn of Boundary Peak, floating out that soft luminous glow so often associated with treasure.

A half-mile up the ridge is the Shrine of the Stone Lions, a brace of ancient, fashioned rocks. A circle of upturned stones surrounds the shrine, broken by the single tilt-slabbed entrance, and a huge piñon, which leans over the eroded lions, branches spreading as if in benediction. Deer antlers have been placed around the rock rim and there is a flat stone covered with bright prehistoric pottery shards and chips of obsidian. In this rock circle men worshipped long before the Spaniards arrived.

This is not merely a historic relic: Indians of Cochiti Pueblo still venerate and use the shrine.

Just beyond the shrine the trail forks: the right-hand branch leads to Alamo Crossing and the upper reaches of Frijoles Canyon, the left fork descends abruptly into Capulin Canyon. This is a deep and lovely gorge, where ponderosa pines crowd a clear and chill creek. There are a number of fine camping spots, as well as scattered ruins.

At such a camp, to waken in the middle of the night as the wind is gusting and look up to see the towering trees swaying above you, seemingly supple as grass against moon or starlight, is an awesome, scary and beautiful sight.

Both in Capulin Canyon and along the Rio Grande one is likely to see wild burros. Rather than braying, some of them announce their presence with a curious woofing sound—sort of a cross between a hiss and a snort. The burros are subtle torture for a photographer without a telephoto lens. They stand watching you, perhaps thirty yards away, just out of good camera range. If you move ten feet toward them, they retreat ten feet. If you, scrambling over boulders and, ripping your shirt upon a piñon stub, manage to advance twenty feet, they have receded twenty feet, watching and woofing at you with what may be amusement. Best just to enjoy them from a distance.

Painted Cave lies about midway between where the trail down from Stone Lions Shrine reaches the creek and where Capulin Canyon opens into the Rio Grande. It is a large alcove on the southwest wall of the

Alamo Canyon, a vast chasm in the ancient rock.

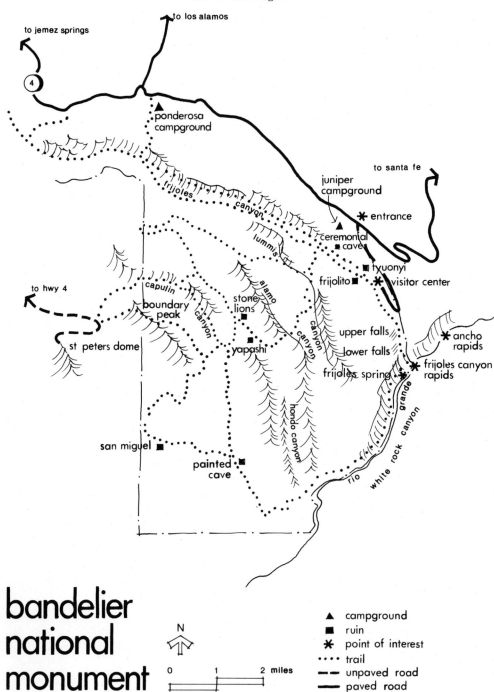

to los alamos

to jemez springs

④

ponderosa
campground

to santa fe

juniper
campground

✳ entrance

frijoles canyon

ceremonial
cave

lummis

tyuonyi

frijolito ✳ visitor center

capulin

to hwy 4

boundary
peak

stone
lions

alamo canyon

canyon

capulin
canyon

upper falls

st peters dome

yapashi

lower falls

✳ ancho
rapids

frijoles spring ✳ frijoles canyon
rapids

san miguel

painted
cave

hondo canyon

grande

rio

white rock canyon

bandelier
national
monument

N

0   1   2 miles

▲ campground
■ ruin
✳ point of interest
••• trail
– – unpaved road
—— paved road

canyon; the pictographs are easily visible from the main trail, which is on the other side of the creek.

It is hard to miss. The Park Service, in fact, has made it all but impossible to miss unless you are sleepwalking. There is a sign, "PAINTED CAVE," right under the curved rock wall of pictographs. One looks about apprehensively to see if a nearby juniper has a sign, "JUNI-PER," on it, or if a cliff swallow wears a tiny rustic placard about its neck saying "SWALLOW." This sort of thing is proper and commendable on the self-guiding nature trail near monument headquarters. Yet much of what is enjoyable about backcountry travel is that everything is not spelled out—one hauls out a topographic map to try to determine natural features and debates with a companion whether yonder tree is a ponderosa or sugar pine. Clear trail markers with mileages are indeed appreciated, but unnecessary signs are a clutter.

Needless signs aside, the cave is a memorable sight. Although the curved overhang is shallow, it is some fifty feet long and covered with dozens of paintings. The artists worked from a ledge that can be reached only by clawing up a cliff pocked with ancient hand- and foot-holds. All but experienced rock climbers will probably want to view the paintings

Wild burros roam Capulin Canyon and along the Rio Grande in Bandelier National Monument.

Indian pictographs in Painted Cave, Capulin Canyon.

from below, as the pocks are marginal and it is a lonely place to break a leg.

The paintings are mostly done in red or black and white. There is a Zia sun symbol, masked dancers, the mystical plumed serpent that is a theme of prehistoric art as far south as Central America, cloud and rain symbols, animals, and other designs. Some of the most ancient paintings are badly faded and later artists have superimposed their own designs over them. A few were done after the arrival of the Spanish *conquistadores*— there is a man on horseback as well as a church surmounted by a cross. Rising out of the other paintings, dominating them, is a monstrous, snarling red beast.

Below Painted Cave the vegetation becomes more sparse and thorny; the creek dwindles and finally disappears into sand except during storms. The lower end of the canyon is on private land, and so the main trail swings up across a pair of rocky ridges and crosses Hondo Canyon before reaching the Rio Grande. Fill your canteens where the trail leaves the creek, since Rio Grande water is not considered potable. The next good water is at the mouth of Frijoles Canyon, some six miles away.

The walk beside the Rio Grande is one of the most enjoyable in all of Bandelier backcountry. The sharply sliced cliffs of White Rock Canyon wedge the river, whose colors range from metallic blue to *cafe con leche,* depending on the season. Hawks and buzzards glide on thermals high overhead. During the hot months it is mightily refreshing to peel off pack and clothes and take a dip.

146

In the spring and summer one is apt to see a raft or two, or perhaps some kayaks, swinging along with the river's brisk current. The river is a popular route for getting into Bandelier backcountry. Most boaters put in at Otowi Bridge and take out at Cochiti Dam, a long single day's run, or a more leisurely overnight trip. There are several tough rapids on this stretch, and many a boater, including the author, have taken unplanned swims in the likes of Frijoles Canyon Rapids or Ancho Rapids during high water of the spring runoff. Some foolhardies, neglecting to wear life preservers, have been drowned in these rapids.

Close to the mouth of Frijoles Canyon one passes Frijoles Spring. There was once a small lagoon here, separated from the river by sand dunes and a tangle of scrub trees and brush. The lagoon dried up several years ago, but the spring still pushes out a clear flow. This is a tranquil spot, with the muffled roar of Frijoles Canyon Rapids in the background and canyon wrens, robins, grosbeaks, hermit thrushes and other songbirds trilling close at hand—not, we are now told, so much out of exuberance as to define territories.

Lower Frijoles Canyon has places of thick, almost junglelike growth —willows and cottonwoods festooned with wild grape vines. The sheer canyon walls are monumental, especially when viewed on a night of the full

The Rio Grande in White Rock Canyon, Bandelier National Monument.

The Upper Falls on Frijoles Creek in Bandelier National Monument.

moon. It is two and a half miles from the river back to monument headquarters, a climb of seven hundred feet. The steepest parts of the trail switchback to the top of Lower Frijoles Canyon Falls, forty feet high, and Upper Frijoles Canyon Falls, eighty feet high. A side trail leads into a cul-de-sac beneath the upper falls, a gorge so deep and narrow that a claustrophobic might well wonder if it will snap shut, pinching out the sky altogether—a journey-to-the-center-of-the-earth sort of path that crosses and recrosses the creek. Figure on getting your feet a little wet, and watch out for falling rocks.

Another fine backcountry trail follows Frijoles Creek up past Ceremonial Cave and into the upper canyons. Here the intermediate life zone, where ponderosa predominates, changes to the Canadian zone, and the

148

forest is now mostly large firs and spruces. Rainbow and brook trout lure fishermen onto this stretch, and there are several beaver dams. From Upper Frijoles Crossing one can return to the Visitor Center on the rim trail or head over to Upper Alamo Canyon, where there is water. Beyond lie trails to the Shrine of the Stone Lions, Saint Peter's Dome via Capulin Canyon, and the Painted Cave. The variations are numerous.

Like all recreation areas, the Bandelier backcountry is beginning to feel the press of population. The biggest threat is Cochiti Dam, south of the national monument. The backup is now inundating some 274 acres of the monument, allowing motorboats to invade part of White Rock Canyon and its tributaries. Land speculators are rubbing their hands with glee, predicting that a city of forty thousand will rise up beside the reservoir. Hopefully this figure will prove to be a pipe dream, but no one doubts that a good many folks will flock there in an attempt to savor southwestern patio living.

Partially because of the Cochiti development, at time of writing a bill has been introduced into both the United States Senate and the House of Representatives that would designate some seventy acres of Bandelier National Monument as a wilderness area—a commendable piece of proposed legislation.

Guide Notes for BANDELIER

LOCATION—Northcentral New Mexico.

ACCESS—Bandelier National Monument Headquarters is reached off a spur road which drops into Frijoles Canyon after veering away from State Highway 4.

GETTING AROUND—Most of the forty-six square miles of the monument are accessible only by good trails. The Rio Grande River forms the eastern perimeter of the monument. This section, White Rock Canyon, offers whitewater challenges and superb scenery, although the lower end is inundated by backup from Cochiti Dam.

SUPPLIES—Backcountry equipment and supplies are available in Santa Fe and Los Alamos. There is no grocery store at the monument itself. Frijoles and Capulin canyons have streams that run throughout the year, but other water sources are seasonal. Check with Park Service employees before heading out into the backcountry.

SPECIAL FEATURES—Spectacular canyon and mesa country. Several ruins of ancient Indian pueblos.

INFORMATION SOURCE—Bandelier National Park, Los Alamos, New Mexico 87544.

FIVE

The Great Reef
(New Mexico and Texas)

The Guadalupe Mountains of southcentral New Mexico and adjoining Texas rise sharply out of desert country, where hawks hover for prey over gently rolling hills that are spiky with slender columns of sotol, tentacles of ocatillo, and cactus lying close to the ground—prickly pear, cholla, and Devil's head. Massive, angular ramparts loom over vast salt flats, usually dry, that become lakes after infrequent and violent storms, shallow sheets of water where a man might wade for miles. There is a sense of immensity, of clarity, here that carried a sense of vague menace to some early-day travelers. From the slopes of the mountains the dry and dissected swells, dotted with creosote bushes, stretch to the horizon.

The Guadalupes, an exposed section of what may be the largest organic fossil reef on earth, are subtle and secretive. Hidden from travelers upon the parched desert floor are tall stands of fir and pine; deep canyons where cactus and oak trees grow from the same ledges, and bigtooth maple trees shade pools where trout glide. And most wondrous and camouflaged of all are the caves—hundreds of them—that lie in darkness beneath the rock.

The rugged Guadalupes have never encouraged permanent settlement. A forlorn brick chimney marks the site of Queen, the only village established in the mountains. It lasted, after a fashion, from 1905 to 1922, and then faded away. The town of Hope, in the foothills of the range, still has a small population that is a far cry from the great agricultural and trading center projected by its founders. Hope's dreams were struck down from every side. The lively little river which was to irrigate the farms went dry and the wealthy Englishman who planned to build a railroad to the settlement was drowned when the *Titanic* sank.

Although Indians roamed the Guadalupes as long as twelve thousand years ago, there were no permanent settlements; they were scattered bands of nomads. Mescal, a species of agave cactus, was a principal food. Remains of mescal cooking pits, as well as pictographs, are scattered throughout the range. In more recent times the Apaches dominated the mountains, where they hunted elk, deer, bighorn sheep, wild turkey, and other game. Their unbenign presence, as well as the aridity of the lower slopes of the range, were no doubt responsible for deflecting the interest of Spanish and Yankee frontier people until the middle of the last century.

As cattlemen began moving herds into the Pecos Valley from Texas and throwing up rough dwellings, Indians took to raiding the ranches for horses. Mostly they were able to elude pursuing posses with the ease of rain slipping through mesquite. When they drove off a herd of ponies from Fort Stanton in the late 1850s, however, the cavalry pursued the band for almost 150 miles. Near Devil's Den, an alcove in the western cliffs of the Guadalupes where there is a spring, the Apache encampment was attacked. Although most of the Indians were able to escape back into the mountains, the horses were recovered and the ramada burned.

Mid-nineteenth-century Americans were in a lather to get to the golden shores washed by the Pacific, where it appeared a prospector, a farmer, a high-spirited and comely girl, or even a blacksmith might soon work themselves into a fortune. The problem was how to get there. Clipper ships around Cape Horn took time, money, and generally were over-crowded and miserable. One could tempt the fates (principally malaria and bandits) by crossing Panama upon a mule's or native's back. More direct routes also had drawbacks—most of the trails necessitated crossing high passes where poor seasonal timing or a freak snowstorm might result in the sort of horror that had the Donner party devouring each other. On the routes that skirted to the south of the great swells of rock, through southern New Mexico, Arizona and California, unless the guide knew what he was about (as many did not), the "Golden Shore Adventure" ended with Apache arrows, stock collapsing from starvation, and dry waterholes where swollen tongues had become too thick to articulate anguish.

The Butterfield Stage Line, which briefly ran big Concord coaches from St. Louis to San Francisco and back, opted for the southern route, waterhole to waterhole through hundreds of miles of mirage and lumpy burned mountains. The first coaches leaving from both terminals met at Guadalupe Pass. Not far from the pass a stage station was built at Pine Springs. Lack of reliable water sources for their relay stations, Indian raids, and other problems plagued the line, and the Pine Springs station was abandoned after a year. Stone ruins now mark the site.

The Guadalupe Mountains from the northeast.

Several expeditions visited the Guadalupes around the middle of the last century. John Ford of the Texas Rangers and Major Robert Neighbors, the federal Indian agent for Texas, led one of the first documented expeditions into the region in 1849. After killing and eating a "panther" they somewhat cryptically noted that it had "a peculiar fresh taste." A rather more detailed and eloquent account of the mountains was given by John Bartlett, commissioner of the Mexican boundary survey. Visiting the Guadalupes a year after Ford and Neighbors, Bartlett wrote that:

> No sunrise at sea or from the mountain's summit could equal in grandeur that which we now beheld, when the first rays struck the snowclad mountain. The projecting cliffs . . . stood out . . . against the azure sky, while the crevices and gorges, filled with snow, showed their inequalities with a wonderful distinctness. . . .

Like most remote ranges in western America, the Guadalupes were prowled by a number of prospectors. Ben Sublett was a widower who lived

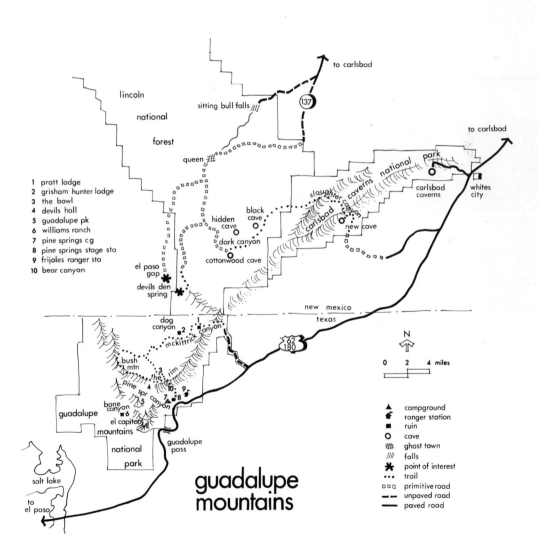

1 pratt lodge
2 grisham hunter lodge
3 the bowl
4 devils hall
5 guadalupe pk
6 williams ranch
7 pine springs cg
8 pine springs stage sta
9 frijoles ranger sta
10 bear canyon

lincoln

national

forest

to carlsbad

sitting bull falls ////

137

to carlsbad

queen #

hidden cave

black cave

slaughter c caverns national park

carlsbad c canyon

new cave

carlsbad caverns

whites city

dark canyon

cottonwood cave

el paso gap

devils den spring

new mexico

texas

dog canyon

2 1

mckittrick canyon

62 180

bush mtn

the rim

3

pine spr canyon

10 9

7 8

guadalupe

bone canyon

6

5

el capitan

mountains

guadalupe pass

national

park

salt lake

to el paso

guadalupe mountains

N

0   2   4 miles

▲ campground
🚩 ranger station
■ ruin
O cave
ghost town
//// falls
✳ point of interest
••• trail
□□□ primitive road
– – unpaved road
— paved road

Ruins of the old Pine Springs Station of the Butterfield Stage Line.

in the railroad construction camp of Odessa, Texas, in the 1880s. While his children took in washing and performed odd jobs around the tent town, Ben turned to more visionary pursuits such as witching for water with a forked stick and prospecting. One afternoon he reined up his rig in front of Odessa's only saloon, stalked inside to announce he had struck it rich, and proceeded to buy rounds for the house. Thereafter, whenever he ran low on money he would head back to the Guadalupes and return a few days later with his poke bulging with gold. Naturally, men tried to follow him back to his lode, but Old Ben would simply ghost away from them in the foothills. He died in 1892 without revealing the location of his bonanza—making it, in other words, your classic lost mine.

Since the limestone, shales, and other sedimentary formations of the Guadalupes are not likely to be associated with gold deposits, subsequent prospectors all had theories as to the source: it had been hidden by Spanish *conquistadores;* it had been gathered, through trading, by Indians, and then stolen by Spaniards, who hid it; it had been mined by Spaniards and stolen by Indians, who hid it; and so forth.

In 1912 Ed Long, foreman for a company mining bat guano, discovered a partially buried Wells Fargo redwood express box in Pine Spring Canyon. It contained gold bullion. Possibly Ben Sublett had discovered the same loot a couple of decades before, but in any case Long saw no merit in taking away the treasure piecemeal. He shipped the bullion, ninety-thousand-dollars-worth of it, to the West Coast, and was seen no more around the guano deposits of the Guadalupes.

Wells Fargo investigators, never complacent about missing express boxes, especially those containing gold, eventually found the empty box in Pine Canyon and traced Long to a cattle ranch in Oregon. Although the investigators could scarcely be pleased at Long's "finders keepers" attitude, several years had elapsed since the discovery and the money from the bullion was long since spent. After deciding that Long had not placed the express box in the canyon but merely removed its contents, they dropped the matter. The express box itself wound up in that great storehouse of Americana, the Smithsonian Institution.

It is ironic that while the largest amount of precious metals taken from the Guadalupes was by a former guano miner, the only mining operations of any consequence in the range were for guano. In 1885 a homesteader, Ned Shattuck, was seeking a lost cow when what he described as a black whirlwind rose out of the ridge ahead of him. It was millions of bats emerging from the mouth of Carlsbad Caverns on their nightly quest for insects.

Several companies tried their hands at guano mining in Carlsbad and other Guadalupe caverns. The guano, an accumulation of centuries, was hauled out and shipped away for use as fertilizer. Although one hundred thousand tons of guano was taken from Carlsbad Caverns alone, it was lean going. Mining and transportation costs were too high for any substantial profits.

For most of the guano miners, it was a job; a dirty and dark one at that. But one miner, Jim White, was curious about what lay beyond the next bend of the corridor. During his off-hours he probed deeper and deeper into Carlsbad Caverns. When he told fellow miners of the wonders he had seen they figured too much time underground had addled his brains, causing hallucinations. After a time, however, a few people took him seriously enough to look for themselves, and were overwhelmed by what they saw. As a result, the caverns were declared a national monument in 1923. A year later *National Geographic* published a story on the caverns, and so seemingly unreal were the formations that when one photograph was accidentally published upside down only a handful of people caught the error. The area is now a national park.

Today, of course, much of the cave is lighted. By elevator, one can drop into the heart of the cavern and stroll asphalt paths to view the lighted formations. Boxed chicken dinners and soft drinks are served more than seven hundred feet underground, and recording devices passed out to visitors describe the features in English, Spanish, and for children. All of

The Guadalupe Mountains, looking east from near Dell City, Texas.

which is very fine, I suppose, but places Carlsbad Caverns well out of the design of this book except as a historical reference.

New Cave, also within Carlsbad Caverns National Park, is something else again. From Whites City, turnoff for Carlsbad Caverns whose only street is lined with overpriced motels and sleazy curio shops, it is a five-mile drive down Highway 180 to the Rattlesnake Springs road. From this junction an eleven-mile road leads up into Slaughter Canyon to the parking area below the cave. Much of the road is unpaved, but presents no problem for passenger cars. The mouth of New Cave, some five hundred feet above the bone-white bed of the canyon, is reached by a short but steep trail. In the heat of midsummer it seems the longest, steepest path in the world.

This is an undeveloped cave. At certain times (check at park head-quarters) a ranger or two will guide parties through the cavern. Although the rangers tote lanterns, each person should carry a flashlight and wear hiking boots or sneakers.

New Cave, while actually not as vast as Carlsbad, seems much larger when picking your way through it with a flashlight. The formations are spectacular. The Monarch is a giant stalagmite rising almost one hundred feet above the cavern floor. Klansman is a curious hulk of white and buff that resembles a sinister robed figure. It was used as a native god in the filming of *King Solomon's Mines*. Some of the more delicate formations are the most engrossing, such as the Great Wall of China, a scalloped barrier only inches high that runs for some three hundred feet and has several offshoots. Most of the natural wonders of New Cave are not named, or, if they are, the rangers say little about them, and there are no identifying plaques. You can enjoy things for themselves without having to crane your neck to see if this or that formation really does look like a duck, the Queen's Hatpin, an ice cream cone, the Baby's Behind, or whatever.

In the 1930s a guano miner named Tom Tucker heard some goats bleating but could find no goats until he almost fell into the entrance of New Cave. Although an outfit called the Ogle Mining Company soon began to mine the fertilizer, it appears Tucker received little more than the recovery of his goats for the discovery. Although the company built a tramway up the sidehill and installed a tractor and other machinery inside the cave, apparently it did little better. A considerable amount of guano was taken out, but overhead held down profits. Though the mining stopped some sixteen years ago, tractor treads in the cave seem as fresh as if made yesterday, accenting the fragile ecology of the underground worlds.

There are several mysterious things about New Cave. Despite extensive beds of guano in parts of the cave, no bats have roosted in it for at least 17,500 years. Why did they leave? Fire, caused by spontaneous combustion of guano, is a possibility. Bones present other puzzles. Thousands of bat bones have been found in the cave—wing, rib, pelvis, leg—but only two skulls. In a section known as Fossil Alley lie the bones of numerous extinct animals such as the Pleistocene camel, deer, and bison. How did they get there? Did they wander into the cave to die deep in the darkness? Were the bones washed into the cavern through an ancient, now-sealed entrance or entrances? A riddle for paleontologists.

There are a few pictographs in the cave: one of them poses other problems. The painting could be that of a horse or a camel. Yet archeologists identify it as being made by the early basketmaker cultures—who flourished long after camels were extinct in the Guadalupes and a few centuries before the Spaniards brought horses into the New World. Perhaps it was done by an old sage who simply dreamed his paintings.

Sitting motionless for any length of time with lights off in New Cave or other undeveloped caverns is a strange experience. After a time the only movement seems to be your own blood, and later you may see visions from the inner eye of imagination. The only sound is one of infinite slowness—the measured splatting of water droplets, heartbeats of the dark world.

Yet there is life—harvestmen, or daddy longlegs, cave crickets, and blind brown cave beetles. In New Cave the beetles feed upon cricket eggs;

when there were bats, they feasted upon sick, dead, and baby bats. Infant bats were left by their mothers in a sheltered "nursery" area of the cave, usually thousands of them in a given place. The mothers, who, like all mammals, suckle their young, had but the remotest possibility of locating their own offspring. And so, following the ancient drive to nourish, to perpetuate, they nursed whichever tiny bat they alit close to. When the mothers were gone seeking insects in the darkened world outside, the babies would often lose their grips upon the cavern ceiling and fall to the floor. Within minutes they would be attacked and devoured by blind cave beetles, crickets, and other scavengers that waited in the guano.

Bats, an odd evolution of mammals, have long been associated with mystery and magic. In Shakespeare's *Macbeth* crones cackle around a boiling pot of witchery as they intone:

> Fillet of fenny snake
> In the cauldron boil and bake
> Eye of newt and toe of frog
> Wool of bat, and tongue of dog

Throughout centuries, Egyptians have rubbed bat blood against the skin of a newly born female to prevent unseemly growth of hair. A long-enduring myth, perhaps spiced with occasional success, tells us that one can ward off evil by wheeling around a room three times with the body of a bat and then nailing it over a window head downward. And although Halloween, All Saints' Day, spans a gap from the burning of presumed witches centuries ago to modern psychopaths who tuck razor blades into apples, the image of Halloween is mainly that of black bats and orange moons cut out of composition paper and pasted upon school windows everywhere in America.

Bats are an ancient species, having evolved into their present form more than fifty million years ago. They are descendants of tree shrews. Like the shrews, their diet is varied and voracious. Some species favor fruit, some insects, and the vampire bat gently sips blood from sleeping warm-blooded animals. In some places bats eat fish. To balance things off, in some places fish eat bats. Bats appear to have no widespread taboos about eating other bats.

These night-fliers have an extremely high metabolic rate. They may literally consume their own weight in insects during a single dusk-to-dawn feeding. It is estimated that there are some one hundred million Mexican freetail bats in the United States. Calculator buffs figure the bats' yearly consumption of insects could fill 340,000 one-ton trucks—not to speak of the other thirty-one species of insect-feeding bats found in this country. We would do a lot more neck-slapping and fanning of flies off watermelon without them.

Physically, bats have some remarkable properties. Their wing membranes are so thin one can read a newspaper through them. When roosting in caves during daylight hours, they cling to the cave roof and walls with claws so sharp that the animals have been known to hang from slight imperfections in lightbulbs and window panes. Sleeping freetail bats fold up so compactly that 250 to 300 bats may be roosting within a square foot of a cavern ceiling.

In the jungles of the Far East, where bats often live in ancient, abandoned temples, a legend is told that the small mammals were once birds who came to the shrines to pray that they might become men. After a time they were given some human characteristics such as the ability to suckle their young; they grew teeth, lost their feathers for hair, their faces became more humanoid—like tiny simians with huge ears. Somewhere along the line the prayers lost their meaning and the process of change was arrested. Shamed to be in the company of other birds because of their grotesque failure, the bats only emerged at night, returning every dawn to the temples to supplicate the gods to make them birds again.

Regardless of the bats' mythical evolution, the species has developed a sonar system that weighs no more than a single gram—yet is as effective as sonar apparatus devised by man that can weigh several pounds. It appears that almost all living creatures have some sense of sonar—the bouncing of sound off unseen things to determine by echo their shape, size, density, and thus potentialities as foe, friend, or supper. The average human, relying mostly upon sight, is usually unaware of this sense unless blind for a period of time.

Bats make most of their sonar soundings with an acoustical pitch so high as to be inaudible to the human ear, and can instantly respond to the echo from their own probes while thousands of other bats may be making similar soundings. A remarkable beast indeed.

As one emerges from the magnificence of New Cave, the fact that better than two hundred caves have been explored in the Guadalupes takes on a heightened significance. Rarely does a year pass but what spelunkers discover yet more caverns. Geologists estimate there may be more than three hundred additional caves in this enigmatic range, their entrances concealed by brush or sealed from the surface altogether.

The Guadalupe Mountains, hollow with caves, are an exposed part of the Capitan Reef, which encircles a vast basin with arms four hundred miles long. Some 250 million years ago minute lime-secreting algae began to thrive in the shallow waters of the sea which then filled the basin. The lime, deposited upon the sea floor over spans of time so great as to be all but impossible to grasp with the mind, slowly built upward. Lying off the shore much as the Great Barrier Reef of Australia does today, the limestone reef became gigantic—several hundred feet high and at least a mile across.

Millions of suns arced over the sea and upon millions of nights starlight reflected off wet pockets of the reef as the waters gradually became more saline, while channels to the sea gradually silted off. Finally the basin was dry, the now "dead" reef deeply buried. Perhaps sixty million years ago the earth buckled and parts of it thrust skyward, not in monstrous cataclysm, but with the patient metabolism of rock—inches of faulting over centuries, up and down. At the south end of the Guadalupes four thousand vertical feet of Permian limestone are exposed.

Cave building began while the reef was still buried. Hairline cracks in the limestone admitted groundwater which had picked up a weak acid content from surface humus and the rock through which it passed. The acid, over millions of years, ate its way into the limestone, creating cavities, until much of the ancient reef was like a vast water-filled sponge. As the water level slowly dropped and the cavities dried, sections of delicate

Marine fossil in the Guadalupe Mountains limestone.

honeycombing collapsed of their own weight, creating vast chambers. A bubble of water emerging upon a chamber roof would lose its carbon dioxide to the air, and then could no longer carry the limestone in suspension. Drop by drop the limestone was deposited upon the ceiling as stalagtites and upon the floor as stalagmites. As the variations of seepage and the minerals it picks up are endless, so are the shapes and colors of cave formations created.

There is a healthy conspiracy of silence about the location of the caves: spelunkers deflect the casual question; maps rarely pinpoint the entrances. It takes a vandal seconds to destroy the work of centuries. In the past numerous delicate formations have been broken off as souvenirs or sold in curio shops. Some of the more famous caves of the Guadalupes, such as Black and Hidden, may be visited by qualified spelunkers with a special permit. Hells Below Cave requires not only a permit but climbing equipment to descend into it. People interested in exploring these caves as well as numerous others in the Guadalupes should investigate joining a speleological society. Equipment is important. The author, in wriggling through a long slot in one of these wild caves aptly called Crystal Crawl, would have bumped his head to a pulp on the low roof without the protection of a hard hat. The squirm was more than worth the effort, as the carbide lamp attached to the hat picked out innumerable slender needles that gleamed in the light, and later, when the roof lifted up to form a high chamber, great flows of rock that resembled robes of rich velvet.

Cottonwood Cave, which is shown on the maps, is reached by driving back into the mountains on State Highway 137 north of Carlsbad. A spur road off this leads to Sitting Bull Falls, an enticing glade in spite of a rather cryptic name. Probably the famous Sioux chief never came within a hundred horizons of the Guadalupes: perhaps someone once came upon a bull there, sitting upon its hindquarters sniffing a wildflower like Ferdinand. Some thirty-eight miles from the beginning of Highway 137 one passes the site of Queen. About six miles beyond that you can leave your car in the bottom of Dark Canyon and hike three miles up to the cave. For perhaps a thousand feet back from the entrance the cave is open to the public, although the back section, containing many magnificent formations, has been sealed off to protect it from vandalism.

For those who prefer the sky to a cavern roof, no matter how beautifully decorated by nature, there is lots of fine backcountry to explore aboveground.

The Guadalupes are essentially a narrow plateau dissected by several deep canyons, which culminate in Guadalupe Peak, which at 8751 feet is the highest in Texas. Most of the range is in Lincoln National Forest and Carlsbad Caverns National Park. The southern end is the newest and least developed addition to the national park system, Guadalupe Mountains

National Park. Guadalupe Peak and the magnificent limestone prow of the adjacent El Capitan are a steep scramble rather than a rockclimb if one takes off from the vicinity of Guadalupe Pass or by ascending the ridge beyond Devil's Hall up Pine Springs Canyon. Across Pine Springs Canyon, the site of many a treasure tale, is the main plateau. The flanks are mostly dry, with desert plants, but on top there are fine stands of Douglas fir, ponderosa pine, and limber pine.

Bear Canyon offers an abrupt trail up to the rim. The trail begins near the old Pine Springs stage station. Winding up past Upper Pine Springs, it begins a series of switchbacks, crossing and recrossing the usually dry stream several times. Beside, over, and under the trail are long sections of rusted pipe, mementos of an era when ranchers grazed stock in meadows of the high country. The pipe was originally hauled up the gentler Dog Canyon Trail to the north, and then maneuvered into place from the rim by burros. Water from Pine Springs was pumped up to the top under high

Guadalupe Peak.

pressure; pressure which, indeed, was so high that the pipe repeatedly ruptured and the ambitious gesture against gravity was abandoned. Since most springs are far below the rim in cactus country, one should pack in plenty of water for camp needs when prowling the piney highlands.

I began my first trip up Bear Canyon on a hot, cloudless November day. Basking in a hot, dry breeze at Pine Springs and regarding the parched slopes above us, water seemed much more relevant to my companion and me than warmth. We left our winter gear—heavy parkas, mittens, and the like, in the trunk of our car. Our packs were bulging with juice and water bottles filled with chill spring water obtained from the hose behind nearby Frijoles Ranger Station. I expect we could have trekked halfway across the Sahara.

The trail ducks through oak thickets, around huge boulders, and occasionally passes the red-barked madrone tree—climbing, always climbing. More and more gently rolling plains open up, dropping along the New Mexico–Texas border over the Phantom and Paduca Breaks. We reached the rim just after sunset to face a herd of several elk, frozen in twilight under tall Douglas firs. For a few minutes we all simply gazed at each other. Finally the lead bull started loping up the hillside with that peculiar elk gait which is sort of like horses choreographed to move as if they were deer.

A short distance along the trail was a grassy campsite. After a supper of steak and chili we talked a bit, looked out at Carlsbad's yellow cluster of lights below and in the distance. I went to sleep under the sharp glitter of a skyful of stars. Later I awakened briefly and noted that some stars had dimmed and others had disappeared altogether. *Might be cloudy tomorrow,* I thought, *maybe a little cooler,* and promptly went back to sleep.

By the first morning light it was snowing heavily. Not big, drifting flakes that put a thick layer upon the ground, but hard, stinging pellets that gusts of wind whipped everywhere—down the necks of our sleeping bags, into our faces, and onto our sterno stove (open fires are prohibited in the high country). The sterno would flare briefly, then either the wind or a cluster of snowflakes would put it out. A thickening circle of burned and futile matchsticks formed the inner eye of despair: coffee and hot soup, oatmeal—all seemed out of the question.

Once my companion had crawled out of his ice-crusted bag, we hurriedly packed and headed out, toting all those unused, now frozen, water bottles. Less than an hour later we were back at our car, mustaches full of ice, somewhat wiser as to the unpredictability of the Guadalupes.

There are a number of interesting trail routes in the Guadalupes. A brisk one-day hike or a leisurely overnight can be made up Pine Springs Canyon to The Rim with a return via Bear Canyon. From the campground near Pine Springs the trail winds upcanyon past alligator juniper, scrub oak, sotol, yucca, and patches of prickly pear and cholla cactus. It is an easy amble for the first mile until the trail, swinging into a side draw, switchbacks its way determinedly to the top—a steep, long 1.3 miles if one has been taking too many elevators instead of stairs or has overburdened one's pack. The trail forks on top of The Rim, the left-hand fork skirting Pine Springs Canyon to Bush Mountain and along Blue Ridge, the right fork leading along the high western crest into The Bowl. From The Bowl one can return to the starting point by way of Bear Canyon. The round trip is some seven miles, much of it very up or very down.

There are nine designated campsites in the high country of Guadalupe Mountains National Park. As mentioned, all are dry camps where wood-fires are prohibited. To balance things off, perhaps, most of them are in lovely, sheltered settings only a stone's throw from where mountains fall sharply away to desert far below.

From Pine Springs to McKittrick Canyon is a fine two- or three-day jaunt. Instead of turning right toward The Bowl at the top of The Rim, one follows the edge of Pine Springs Canyon to Bush Mountain (8,676 alt.) and then along Blue Ridge. The view off this, the western escarpment, is even more abrupt than that of the eastern side. There are three campsites along this section. From Blue Ridge the trail heads westward and to the north, crossing the interior of the plateau before winding along the south rim of McKittrick Canyon. Close to where the trail drops into the canyon there is a campsite. Camping, for valid reasons, is forbidden in the canyon itself.

McKittrick is a canyon where desert and mountain plant life subtly blend, where there are some species found nowhere else on earth, and whose parched mouth gives no hint of the cool stream and pools that lie deeper back in the mountains. It is the kind of place you walk through hoping few others know of its existence, and only speak of to close friends. Since the Guadalupe Mountains are now a national park, however, McKittrick Canyon is featured in various brochures and booklets, and its cover, one might say, has already been blown. One can only hope visitors will respect the fragility of its environment.

From The Rim the trail works down a ridge, where tall ponderosa pines spike upward and there are scattered bigtooth maples, chinquapin oaks, and Texas madrones. The rim country is great for watching buzzards and hawks gliding on the air currents, and that occasional whistling whoosh is probably not a misplaced radio-wave sound effect from Super-man doing his "faster than a speeding bullet"—just a swift world's fastest bird, hurtling about his business. Down in the canyon, if it is spring, dragonflies and butterflies jiggle over the water, resting upon willowy banks where there are drapes of resurrection fern. Bird life at all times of the year is varied and profuse. A short distance below the site of the Grisham

Hunter lodge, a limestone overhang exposes stalactites and stalagmites, hinting at the hidden caves that exist in this canyon like most others that drain the Guadalupe plateau. A mile beyond is another abandoned lodge, the Pratt, an unusual stone building whose roof is made of rocks. The canyon becomes progressively drier—pools smaller, stream dwindling—until a little more than a mile from the roadhead the water has been totally lost to sand. Yucca, sotol, grasses, and juniper line the bed.

A road leads to the mouth of McKittrick Canyon from U.S. Highway 62. It crosses private land *en route,* and most of the year a key for the locked gate must be obtained from ranger headquarters at Frijoles Ranch Ranger Station close to Pine Springs. During the summer months a shuttle bus brings day hikers to the mouth of the canyon. Either way, if you have left your car at Pine Springs, beginning of the loop just described, you are bound to be able to hook a ride back to point of origin.

The Guadalupes are a grandly undeveloped thrust of mountains bearing a unique and fragile ecosystem. If the Park Service will refrain from "development," they may remain so for quite some time.

Guide Notes for the GREAT REEF

LOCATION—Southcentral New Mexico and an adjoining region in Texas. While the largest portion of the Guadalupes is contained within Lincoln National Forest (New Mexico), 46,753 acres of the range and its foothills comprise Carlsbad Caverns National Park. Guadalupe Mountains National Park, America's newest, has 77,500 acres on the Texas side.

ACCESS—U.S. Highways 62 and 180 bring one across the edge of Guadalupe Mountains National Park, as well as close to Carlsbad Caverns National Park. From this highway, spur roads, either paved or improved, lead to the mouth of Carlsbad Caverns, the mouth of Slaughter Canyon (trailhead for New Cave), McKittrick Canyon, Frijoles Ranger Station, and Pine Springs Campground. The road into McKittrick Canyon crosses private land, and therefore prior permission and a key for a locked gate must be obtained at Frijoles Ranger Station. Ten miles north of Carlsbad, State Highway 137 winds back toward the Guadalupes. Twenty miles from the turnoff, the road forks. To the right is Sitting Bull Falls; to the left, an improved forest road that passes through the site of Queen and then hugs the western rim of the mountains to El Paso Gap. Side roads lead south into Dark Canyon and north along the crest of the range.

GETTING AROUND—There are fifty-five miles of developed trails in Guadalupe Mountains National Park, as well as a number of rugged paths and game trails. These trails connect to a network of routes in Carlsbad Caverns National Park and Lincoln National Forest. Trails above the rim, as well as into McKittrick, Slaughter, Dark, and Dog canyons, will get one into beautiful country.

CAMPING—In Guadalupe Mountains National Park only the primitive campground in Pine Springs Canyon can be reached by vehicle. Otherwise, camping is permitted only at designated backcountry sites. These places do not have water; open fires are not permitted. Carlsbad Caverns National Park and Lincoln National Forest are also cautious about ecological damage; current policies for camping in either area should be checked by writing the appropriate agencies before planning a trip.

SUPPLIES—All one will need in the way of grub can be obtained in Carlsbad. Most grocery stores carry sterno, in case you do not have another sort of backpack stove unit. Or maybe you would just like to truck in to the backcountry with pockets full of oranges and jerky, a highly satisfying way to travel. Plan to carry lots of water. The springs of the Guadalupes are lovely, but rarely where you need them when you need them.

SPECIAL FEATURES—Rugged mountains and lovely canyons. Caves. Carlsbad is magnificent, but hardly wild. It might be the beautifully decorated pedestrian subway of some future city. New Cave, which the average person has to huff a bit to climb to, and where one might readily turn an ankle in lantern-light upon a slippery section, is an interesting bridge between the wild and the tame cave. Portions of Cottonwood Cave, which is undeveloped, are open to the public. Most Guadalupe caves are wild and permits to visit them are given out sparingly to prevent vandalism. Probably the best way to gain access to these magnificent caves is by joining speleological organizations.

There are a number of interesting historical sites, including Pine Springs Station, Williams Ranch in Bone Canyon, and the settlement of Queen.

INFORMATION SOURCES—Speleological societies; Guadalupe Mountains and Carlsbad Caverns National Parks, P. O. Box 1598, Carlsbad, New Mexico 88220; Lincoln National Forest, Federal Building, Alamagordo, New Mexico 88310.

SIX

The Gila (New Mexico)

The Gila is, perhaps, a state of mind as much as an actual place—an enormous outdoor set for every kind of frontier drama ever played. Indians were growing corn and making brown pottery there shortly after the time of Christ. The army of Coronado brushed the edge of Gila country eighty years before the Pilgrims landed at Plymouth Rock. Coronado's men plodded northward seeking treasure—cities where the roofs were tiled with solid gold and where there were entire streets of silversmiths. The mountains that cradle the headwaters of the Gila River—the Mogollons, Pinos Altos, and Black ranges—were veined with lodes of gold, silver, and other minerals. Had the *conquistadores* veered eastward into the Gila country, they might have found an ancient cliff city with sealed baskets containing what the Indians most prized—feathers, turquoise, and other ceremonial objects. Yet the gold and silver were there, too, often right on the surface of the ground. Later, a drunk would pillow his reeling head upon a rock of almost pure silver; a man would pick up a chunk of gold ore to throw at a straying cow.

Coronado continued to the north instead. By the time other treasure seekers, as well as beaver trappers, ranchers, and sod breakers, had started to filter into the Gila, it was a stronghold of the Apaches, who continued to fight the intruders long after every other tribe in America had laid down its arms. The Apaches had a passion for freedom, not of the oratorical variety, but of the kind having to do with space and game, the right to move from one waterhole or creek to another without crossing fences or roads.

The Gila is the large, sparsely populated corner of southwestern New Mexico. At its heart is the high, piney country of the Gila Wilderness

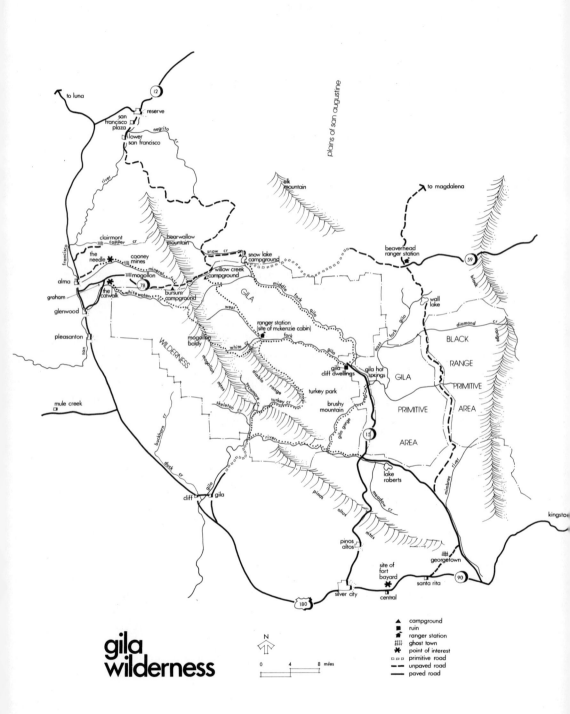

**gila
wilderness**

N

0   4   8 miles

▲ campground
■ ruin
🏠 ranger station
▦ ghost town
✳ point of interest
▯▯▯ primitive road
— — — unpaved road
——— paved road

Area, the first such area to be so designated in the United States. Next to the Gila Wilderness are the Gila and Black Range primitive areas, and all three are contained in the Gila National Forest. To the north the high mountains drop away into grassy rangelands; to the south the landscape is dry and largely flat, although stark desert mountains loom above alkali beds where lakes and strange visions jiggle in the mirages of summer.

Throughout the mountains are ancient, sagging cabins, many with gunslots cut for defense against Indian attacks. Around the edges of the high country are a score of ghost towns and mining campsites—shells of vanished sound and movement. The remains of an adobe fort are slowly eroding away, its location so obscure that only a handful of ranchers in the immediate area knows of its colorful past. Lying next to a splashing stream reached only by rough game trails, and hearing wild turkey gobble and shift in nearby trees, it is easy to peel away a century of concrete, traffic jams, and people pressing at each elbow.

The Gila seems to begrudge change. In thinking about trips there over the last few years, I remember filling up with gas from an antique pump at the village of Alma. To make conversation, I asked the grinning, gap-toothed youth at the pump handle if he got into Silver City often.

"Oncet," he replied.

I recall a false-front saloon next to rusted railroad tracks where men gravely played stud poker under the skull of a two-headed calf. And in another old frame saloon in a dried-up hamlet, I can still hear the bar-maid's indignation as she reached for the .38 pistol a sheepish miner was handing to her.

"Dammit, Harry, how many times I got to tell you guys—*no guns allowed in the bar!* Next thing you know, they'll be a shootin', they'll close me up, 'n' you guys'll have to drive all the way to Silver for a beer.

"Coors, you say?"

In 1969 the police chief of Silver City made an attempt to get the government to preserve the old home of Judge McComas, who, with his wife, was killed by Apaches in 1883. Since the current occupants of the historic place were in the business of selling sexual favors, the chief's efforts drew unexpected national publicity. The media's gleeful interpretation—police chief tries to get local bordello recognized as national monument—mostly amused or puzzled the residents. Like all frontier institutions, the bordello does not die easily in the Gila.

A while back I shared a campfire and some bacon on Whitewater Creek with a fellow who had come out of the canyon with three tail-wagging dogs. Although he was a friendly and warm man, his voice had that odd sense of tone and emphasis one associates with deaf people who never hear themselves. Turned out that my companion and I were the first people he had spoken to in several weeks. He had been up in the Gila, prospecting and wandering. Later he was arrested for alleged cattle rustling.

Silver City, an old mining town of 7700 population, is the commercial hub of the Gila country. Other once-thriving gold and silver camps on the edges of the Gila—Carlisle, Mogollon, Pinos Altos, Georgetown, Kingston, Chloride, Hillsboro, and Lake Valley—have become ghost towns or the next thing to it. State Highway 15 climbs back into the mountains north of Silver City. Six miles out is Pinos Altos, where a number of old buildings still line dirt streets from the boom days, including the well-preserved Buckhorn Saloon, which is noted for good whiskey, country music, and the Uncle Remus Special—a beef, mushroom, and wine concoction. Thirty miles beyond, at Gila Cliff Dwellings National Monument, is the end of the road. From here numerous trails lead into backcountry. The West and Middle forks of the Gila River have carved deep canyons where rock pinnacles tower above the trails. The East, Middle, and West forks join at Gila Hot Springs, close to the National Monument. The forty miles down

On the West Fork of the Gila River.

Gila Cliff Dwellings.

the Gila Gorge from the Hot Springs to Turkey Creek are a delight, whether hiking or on horseback. Side creeks have carved intricate chambers into rock walls that in places drop sharply into lush river bottoms.

During spring runoff (late March or April) the Gila River can be canoed. One should write or call the national monument headquarters for information on water level. Several unhappy souls, not heeding this precaution, have ended up dragging their canoes for much of the distance.

The early Mogollon people lived in pit houses and were hunters and gatherers of wild plants. They also grew corn and beans. At first they made simple brown pottery; later they made patterns that were varied and exquisite. Some thousand years ago they moved up into cliffs above the river and built sturdy, interconnected chambers that stand to this day. Using red and orange pigments crushed from hematite, they decorated granite and sandstone slabs with stick figures, animals, zigzags, and other markings. About four hundred years later they, like most cliff dwellers of the southwest, abruptly left their homes forever.

James McKenna and Jason Baxter, who at the time were supplying wild turkey and venison to meat markets in Silver City and Pinos Altos, unearthed a mummy at the cliff dwellings in 1884. "It lay with knees drawn up and the palms of the hands covering the face. The features were like those of a Chinese child, with high cheekbones and coarse, dark hair," McKenna later recalled. The mummy was displayed in a Silver City store window until a man who called himself Webster showed up and asked to borrow it for a few months for study at the Smithsonian Institution. He was an official of the Smithsonian, he said, displaying appropriate letterheads.

Sixteen years later a prospector named Jack Stockbridge found two mummies and brought them out to the town of Hot Springs (now Truth or Consequences). There they caught the attention of a gentleman who claimed to represent the Academy of Science at San Francisco, and he borrowed them for study.

Since neither institution has any official recollection of receiving said mummies from Gila Cliff Dwellings, one is tempted to speculate that they lie side by side in the same private collection, along with mounds of artifacts gathered by a con man with a carpetbag full of letterheads.

Unlike the Mogollon people, the Apache was a nomadic tribe for whom freedom meant space. The wild highlands of the Gila country were their last stronghold. Even after they had been conquered as a tribe and placed upon reservations, bands under the leadership of Loco, Nane, Victorio, Geronimo, and other chiefs would abruptly leave the reservations and head into the Gila, which they considered their domain. Old newspapers of the area are full of accounts of prospectors and settlers killed by the "red fiends of Hell."

The earliest outsider that the Apaches remember was a trapper named James Johnson who had heard that the governor of Sonora in Mexico would pay one hundred dollars for an Indian scalp, twenty-five dollars for a prisoner. In 1835, near the present settlement of Cliff on the Gila River, Johnson summoned Apache leaders and their families for "trade talks" and gifts—flour, blankets, saddles, and whiskey. As the Indians examined the items Johnson touched off a howitzer loaded with slugs, nails, bits of chain, and other shrapnel. Some twenty Apaches died, women and children among them.

Johnson was never able to collect his reward from the Mexican government, and in retrospect one regrets that he was not captured by the Apaches and stretched over an anthill to die a slow and painful death, like that suffered later by a number of innocent white men and women who came later to the Gila. The principal leader of the Apaches at that time was Mangas Coloradas, who favored negotiating with the outsiders until he heard of Johnson's treachery. After hearing of the massacre he told his people to "shoot anyone who wears a hat" (no Apache of that era wore headgear).

Naturally there are reasons why the Gila became the last stronghold of the Apaches. It is rough, rugged country where the creeks do not always run, and steep-sided canyons have clawed up the topography. Moreover, the substantial mining strikes made in the region were all on the periphery of the central highlands.

There are several hot springs in the Gila. The hot springs close to Gila Cliff Dwellings National Monument have been used for centuries by Indians, and, as James McKenna remarks in his book *Black Range Tales,* "Miners used to go to the springs to boil out during lulls in Indian fighting."

In the 1880s the Silver City *Enterprise* quoted one Uncle Jim Metcalf about the properties of Hudson's Springs in 1849:

> It seems to me that the water of Hudson's Springs was much hotter than it is now. I well remember that we would kill and draw a rabbit, fill it with a little bacon and salt, shove it far down into the spring and in an hour or so it would be well-cooked. The boys never built a fire to make their coffee or tea—the water was hot enough for that. . . . One fellow, who was sort of a wag, suggested that when the country settled up we could come back and organize the "Toro Soup Company." He said it would be such an easy matter to throw in some cattle and then pipe the soup out over the plains. . . ." [*the Gila High Country,* New Mexico, Holiday Issue, 1971]

Game has always been a fascination of the Gila. Bird lovers from all over the world make pilgrimages to the Gila to observe the unique diversity of species found here. Over 170 species have been seen on a single weekend. Bear Mountain Guest Ranch, close to Silver City, is a popular retreat for bird watchers.

The Gila has long been known for its big game. Trapper James Pattie roamed the Gila with a companion in the 1820s. Leaving his companion at the hot springs, Pattie worked his way up a brushy creek. After eating a turkey he had killed, he stoked up his fire and fell asleep against a pile of drift logs. When he awoke the fire had dropped to coals, and a mountain lion lay upon a log not six feet away, regarding him with grave curiosity. Pattie shot the cat, and moments later was surprised to hear a report from the direction of the hot springs. Later it developed that his companion, awakened by the rifle shot, found himself face to face with a silvertip grizzly. He, in turn, fired at it and the animal retreated.

Most old-timers in the Gila managed to get chased by at least one silvertip, by their own accounts; but none had a more harrowing encounter than the recluse known as "Old Bear" Moore. Moore was hunting in the San Mateos in 1892 when he shot a bear cub whose mother suddenly loomed out of the brush and jumped him. Moore fell back over a log, losing his rifle, as the bear mauled him. "The bear got a hold of me and bit me through the jaws and on my forehead and through my arms and clawed me across the breast. That bear just darn near chewed me up and spit me out," he later recalled. After killing the bear with his bowie knife, Moore crawled more than a mile to a cabin and help.

Somehow he eventually survived the severe wounds, but for the rest of his life he wore a heavy beard to cover his ruined face and spoke with an odd slur. He moved into the Gila, keeping to the remote places. Only rarely would he show up at a settlement like Pinos Altos, and then linger only long enough to barter game, hides, or a little gold dust for the meager supplies he found necessary. Moore had a cabin up on the West Fork and also spent periods of time in a cave on Turkey Creek. For some thirty years after the bear attack he lived in the backcountry and probably talked to less than a dozen people in all that time.

Loneliness and pain can do strange things to a man. Hunters who ventured up into the Gila high country occasionally would come upon a log bear-trap. The traps were well-contrived, with logs up to a foot in diameter. They had been built patiently and with immense effort, and yet none of the well-known trappers claimed them.

> Jack Stockbridge, a noted frontiersman of the Gila, was riding through Little Turkey Park when he heard a commotion nearby. "I listened a bit, and it was Bear Moore a-swearing and a-cussing, and an old bear growling and just raising Cain. Between them they made a devil of a noise.
>
> "I rode down and there was Bear Moore with a bowie knife tied onto a stout stick, poking between the logs of a trap at the bear caught in it. All the time he was cussing the bear. He says, 'Oh, you will eat a man up will you!' and then he'd cuss some more. And he kept on until he killed the bear. The bear hide wasn't no good after that—all full of holes. . . . [Elizabeth McFarland, *Wilderness of the Gila,* University of New Mexico Press, 1974.]

Old Bear Moore's body was found in the 1920s on the slopes of Brushy Mountain, which overlooks Turkey Park. Apparently he had been the

Examining one of the
Gila Cliff Dwellings

victim of a sudden snowstorm. Near the corpse, half-buried in a drift of snow, was a pot of congealed tallow and beans, two partially frozen deer carcasses from which steaks had been hacked, a gold pan, and a notebook which the men who buried him described as being about "some little accounts that he had here and there. He was a very educated man and wrote a beautiful hand."

For Nat Straw, to whom grizzly trapping was a business rather than revenge, the Gila provided a livelihood for a number of years. A mellow yet tough, mustachioed man who had been captured by Sioux as a child and later lived with the Navajos as an adult, he preferred to read a book by firelight than jaw or play cards in the kerosene flicker of the settlements. Stockmen paid him to lay waste the sizeable number of silvertips remaining in the Gila.

As he commented: "A bear will travel thirty miles to find a good harvest of acorns; he will graze on clover like a cow, and he will get as fat as a hog on piñon nuts, wild cherries, manzanita berries, and other fruitage, but once let him get the taste of cow or sheep meat and after that he is a confirmed killer."

Straw, during the course of his work, had some very scary things happen to him: being wedged into a tight crevice of rock as an enraged grizzly, inches away, clawed and bit at the rock in an effort to rip him open from hairline to toes, for example. Yet perhaps his most engaging story may drift a few degrees from what is considered authentic history. He trained a bear cub to hackemore and saddle, yet as the bear got larger neither were needed, as Straw would guide him by tugging on the animal's ears. He named the bear Geronimo and found his back was as "soft-cushioned as a rocking chair."

Geronimo was a great tracker. He brought bear-hunter Straw one afternoon into a glade where a huge bear came out flying to "batter and waller with Geronimo." The clearing was a vortex of growls and tearing fur until Straw, fearing the loss of his pet, yelled out, "Geronimo!" The bear, rip-sided and bleeding, came roaring up to him and Straw jumped upon its back.

"We went tearing through oak brush and under scrub juniper and over fallen pine logs as if they were nothing but weeds. It was all I could do to stay on that bear, and not hardly any of my skin was staying on me. I'd a jumped off but that from the sounds going on I judged the other bear was tearing after us."

After a wild ride down a hard-rock canyon that dropped like a giant's staircase with impossible thickets, Straw grabbed at Geronimo's right ear to slow him down. The ear was gone, it was not a new wound, Straw suddenly realized he had been riding the wrong bear. He bailed out, and although

Cooney Canyon.

Geronimo waddled back to camp eventually, Straw never rode him again, figuring it to be bad luck.

The country around the San Francisco River Valley, on the western side of the Mogollon Mountains, is one of the loveliest parts of New Mexico, remote and off the beaten path. A road sign in the ghost town of Mogollon reads: "Next gas 122 miles mtn. road." The valley lies in Catron County, an area larger than Connecticut, whose population (2000) could fit into a couple of large office buildings in Hartford. In 1874 members of the Chavez and other hispanic families drove oxen westward from Socorro across the Plains of San Agustin (then, as now, a vast sea of grass where mountain ranges—San Mateo, Datil, Elk—rise against the horizon like great wooded islands). On the San Francisco River they built a snug village around a central plaza; in time of Indian attack it could be defended like a fort. Soon there were three such pueblos: Upper, Middle, and Lower San Francisco Plazas. Anglo ranchers were also moving into the country, settling near Upper Plaza where Milligan's saloon was the hub of convivial activity, or some twenty miles downriver at a settlement called Alma. Mormon elder William Maxwell founded nearby Pleasanton at about the same time.

Four years before the first roof was raised in San Francisco Plaza and the first beef cooked in chili sauce to celebrate the occasion, Sergeant James Cooney rode through the valley of the San Francisco River on a mapping expedition out of Fort Bayard. Up Mineral Creek, east of where Alma would be established, he discovered some promising ledges of gold ore. His first attempts at mining, after his discharge, were emphatically discouraged by roving bands of Apaches, and he was forced to flee to the comparative safety of Silver City. He returned to the Mineral Creek area in 1878 with two ox-drawn wagons of equipment and supplies and a deter-mined company of miners. They were soon sacking ore from the Silver Bar claim and prospecting Mineral and Silver Creeks from their cabins at Clairmont on Copper Creek.

A year later Indians fired upon some men plowing near Alma. The ranchers gave chase, killing three of the attackers near the present site of Glenwood. For the ranchers it was just the gunning-down of some "fiendish red devils," to use a popular journalistic phrase of the day. One of the dead braves was Torribeo, brother-in-law of Victorio. Had the ranchers known, they would have probably rushed home to barricade their settlement, for Victorio, although he had no use for missionaries, was a firm adherent to the Old Testament adage of "a tooth for a tooth and an eye for an eye."

Generations of Americans nurtured upon pulp books and magazines, movies, and television, tend to regard Cochise, Geronimo and Mangas Coloradas as the greatest Apache leaders of them all. Taking nothing away from these better-known chiefs, many Apaches would nominate Victorio, whose band humiliated units of the U.S. Army Cavalry not once or twice but again and again and again. The press of the era was careful not to accent the fact that the Warm Springs Apache chief was almost always outnumbered in battle, sometimes by as much as fourteen to one, as many jittery miners and ranchers would likely have left southern New Mexico without so much as a backward glance. As with most Apaches, plunder and the killing it often occasioned were simply a means of survival. Yet the death of Torribeo was only one of the violent scores Victorio had to settle.

Apart from their penchant for stealing horses, much of Victorio and Geronimo's struggle with the army had to do with homeland. The Warm Springs Reservation, in the foothills of the Black Range, was familiar ground. When, in the early 1870s, it was decided to move the inhabitants of the Warm Springs Reservation to the distant Tularosa Valley, only 450 of them complied, the rest heading into mountain retreats or joining the Chiricahua Apaches in Arizona. After the Chiricahua reservation was abolished, many of this band returned to Warm Springs, and raids upon ranches and settlements increased. In 1876 troopers visited all the Indian rancherias on the Warm Springs Reservation and told everyone to report to headquarters for a general meeting. Once there, Victorio, Loco, Nane, Geronimo, and all the braves were arrested and marched into the black-smith shop, where irons were shackled onto their wrists and ankles.

It had been decided to move all the Apaches to the San Carlos Reservation in Arizona. *En route* to San Carlos, miners near Silver City fired upon the unarmed, shackled Indians, killing several. The soldiers did nothing; Victorio would not easily forget.

In April of 1880 Victorio led a band of Apache braves in an attack upon the Cooney Mines. Four miners were killed outright. Cooney and James Chick galloped wildly down the canyon to Alma, their horses sliding and almost stumbling upon wet sections of exposed bedrock. Throughout the night women and children huddled in the cabin of a family named Roberts as the men alternately stood watch or worked feverishly to fortify the log building until dawn came. There was no attack. Cooney and Chick decided to ride back up the canyon to look for survivors and survey the damage. A couple of hours later the horses returned, riderless. Around noon settlers from Pleasanton arrived at the Roberts' cabin, followed by the Meader family, who lived on an outlying ranch. Apaches were gaining on their jouncing wagon as they broke into view. A bullet winged through the bonnet of little Agnes Meader and another clipped a shaggy lock from her father's head, but they gained the safety of the cabin.

Women and children crouched behind upturned featherbeds and tables draped with quilts as men fired through gunslots until the room was blue with smoke. The Apaches, quick, patient, and masters at using natural cover, seemed as hard to drop as hallucinations. On the other hand, the cabin had been braced for siege by a couple of hard-bitten frontiersmen who had survived in the wilderness so long that in many respects they were able to think like Indians. Although guns banged throughout a long after-noon and throughout the night, only two incautious souls were actually killed—an Apache who tried to mount and make off with a settler's horse within rifle range, and a defender of the cabin who opened the door a crack for a fatal peek outside.

In the chalky light before dawn the Apaches left. Before heading into the Sierra Madre of Mexico, Victorio and his warriors left a number of settlers and miners sprawled dead next to ransacked and burned cabins in the Gila.

While newspapers of the era chronicled what seemed to be completely random ferocity on the part of Victorio and his warriors, historians later discovered some interesting inconsistencies. Victorio made a solemn pact with the villagers of Monticello in the eastern foothills of the Black Range never to attack them. He killed miners and plundered horses in the surrounding area, yet Monticello was never harmed. Many of the soldiers assigned to the Gila country during the Apache uprisings were blacks—recently freed slaves. Unless they were forced into actual combat, Victorio's people and the black troops generally had warm relationships—perhaps the kinship of those who realized their lands would soon be lost to them with a race that had lost its ancestral places generations before.

After the Apaches had been gone from Alma for a reasonable spell, some men rode up the canyon to find and bury the bodies of Cooney and Chick. Today Alma is a quiet village. A five-mile dirt road leads up to the site of the ambush, marked by a tomb of gold-bearing ore with a marble slab that proclaims: "J. C. Cooney, killed by Victorio's Apaches, April 29, 1880." A little beyond this is the entrance to Cooney Canyon, where the road peters out. Here Mineral Creek breaks out of a narrow canyon of sandstone walls. A trail leads into a deepening canyon. The Needle, a towering spire, and the Needle's Eye, a rock window above it, loom over the creek. The creek itself is small, fast, and snaky, slithering and tumbling down ledges of lichen-stained rock. Deeper into the canyon, abrupt walls fall back into multicolored terraces. One can sense prospector Cooney's excitement at the potential of such a place, as well as Victorio's lack of interest in seeing it civilized. The Apache's ghost, should it walk this canyon now, is probably at peace. The once-ambitious Cooney mines are now but thorn-tangles upon blisters of scraped-out rock, stone foundations of a mill and what may have been a house or store, the barren branches of an abandoned orchard—a good camping place.

If you have a friend who can pick you up or if you possess a lucky thumb for attracting rides on lonely roads, you may want to follow Mineral Creek up past its source to Bursum Campsite on State Highway 78. The campsite lies at an 8500-foot elevation, on the summit of a rough and steep grade out of Mogollon.

Mogollon, on Silver Creek, immediately to the south of Cooney Canyon, is a more substantial ghost town than Cooney. Numerous old buildings and foundations line the creek, and mine hoists rise from hillsides. The great, grey mass of the Little Fanny dump, scarred with erosion, marks the opening of a mine which yielded over a million dollars annually in gold and silver during the boom years. In those days, one of the popular gathering spots in town was a saloon that the owner intended to call the Longhorn. He commissioned a local painter to render a likeness of a steer on the building, but perhaps due in part to liberal liquid encouragement from the proprietor, the finished animal was sway-backed, had a peculiar-looking head, and sides that seemed inflated to bursting. Someone commented that the creature looked more like a bloated goat than a longhorn, and the name stuck.

The Bloated Goat Saloon has long since vanished. One twilight, camped not far from its site, I watched a flock of goats trotting purposefully toward me, led by an immense billy who had, so help me, a sag to his spine and a bulge in the belly. A companion was frying potatoes and bacon at the time, and an open can of beans, some carrots, and other chow were lying on the hood of his jeep. Often goats will mill around a camp, curious, affable, always hungry and mannerly in their fashion. This billy all but bowled me over in lunging to devour the uncooked potatoes beside the fire,

The Cooney tomb near the site of the Apache ambush.

as the rest of the flock did in the beans and carrots. After cleaning out the skillet, despite cuffs from my friend, the billy, eyes rolling in its head, tried to chomp upon the fire itself. After singeing off most of its luxurious beard, the goat snorted, leaped, and then abruptly led the flock down the hill. The camp looked as if a bear had raged through it—scraps of food everywhere, upturned tent, scattered pans and gear. A very ungoatlike performance, even for extremely hungry goats, and this flock appeared well-fed. Out of dozens of nights when I have camped in ghost towns, this is the only instance when I sometimes wonder if there were a demonic spirit from the past.

Many of the miners who lived in Mogollon crossed the ridge each dawn to descend a precipitous trail to Cooney for a ten-hour workday in the mines along Mineral Creek. After an all-night whoop-up in the likes of the Bloated Goat, one miner decided to save his feet from the rocks of the trail by hooking a ride down into Cooney Canyon and climbing into a bucket of the Sheridan Mill tramway. As the wildly swinging iron nest moved out over the almost sheer drop of the gorge, he waved his broad-brimmed hat at friends back on the brink. Moments later, the bucket in front of him tore loose and bounced downward for hundreds of feet, clanging upon each rock ledge. When the miner reached the bottom, quite a while later, he was not only stone sober but swore off strong waters for life.

One can follow the old trail from Mogollon down into Cooney even today, and marvel at the endurance of miners who daily made the round trip just to get their hands upon a pick and shovel. North of Mineral Creek, dirt roads and trails lead to other abandoned diggings—the ruins of Clairmont on Copper Creek, the Wannaman Cabin with triangular loopholes cut through the logs for defense against Apache attack . . . roofless cabins in lonely glades.

As miners poured into the mountains the valley of the San Francisco River was fenced and vast ranches staked out. Butch Cassidy, the Sundance Kid, and other members of the Wild Bunch worked for a time on the WS Ranch near Alma. As adept at driving half-wild cattle as blowing baggage-car strongboxes, they impressed foremen with their cowpunching abilities. WS manager William French later recalled that after a long and arduous trail drive, "they were most decorous. There was no such thing as drinking or gambling or shooting up the town. I was frequently congratulated by the merchants of Magdalena on having such a well-behaved outfit." One surmises that their gentle profile in the Gila country may have been less occasioned by a sudden moral uplift than by the fact that Pinkerton agents were scouring the western mountains with nooses for their necks.

Cabin near the ghost town of Clairmont, New Mexico. (Note triangular cut in log just right of window, used for firing guns during Indian wars.)

Not all residents of the San Francisco Valley were as highly regarded by their neighbors as the Wild Bunch. It was observed that the Hall family, of Pine Cienega, had stock of astonishing fecundity. Within three years their herd of two hundred cattle had grown to over two thousand without additional purchases, and all the while animals were being slaughtered for meat or sold on the hoof. The Halls' original two mares somehow apparently produced nine two-year-old colts the first year.

The Halls' technique was simple and effective—kill someone else's cow or mare that had recently foaled or calved, and put their brand on the offspring. For a time the Halls and their cowhands terrorized the valley, showing up at ranch houses of those who protested with two or more armed men. Then the tables turned—armed men would surround one of

the Hall ranch houses. After some classic shootouts the gang scattered, and
the epilogue was that of drawn-faced Hall women plaintively asking sheriffs, settlers, and ranchers if they knew where their husbands had been slain
so they could go and bury them.

The blizzard winter of '88 killed thousands of cattle. Most of the big
outfits had to lay off a number of hands, some of whom were a bit careless
as to where they slapped their brand. During the dry season that followed
the blizzards, a neighbor approached Montague Stevens, owner of the SU
Ranch, and asked if he could water the cattle he was driving to the
railhead. Since the waterholes were almost dry, the SU foreman was
astonished to hear Stevens give permission. When asked about it, the genial
Englishman is said to have retorted, "Now, really, you don't think I could
turn my own cattle away without water, do you?"

When Epitacio Martinez was twelve Apaches raided his family homestead on Tularosa Creek, killing his father. The boy, although wounded in
the leg, managed to hide out under a log until the Indians left. Some years
later Epitacio was living in San Francisco Plaza. For no particular reason a
group of drunken cowboys had tied Epitacio up and were going to use him
for target practice. He had been hit four times—none of them fatal—when
Elfego Baca interceded. Baca had been kidnapped by Navajos as an infant,
returned to his family four days later, and now, at nineteen, was not a man
given to backing out of a fight. He shot one of the cowboys outright and
decked another. As outraged cowboys milled around Milligan's Saloon,
Baca dodged into a log and mud hut. For thirty-six hours he held off as
many as eighty men. Hundreds of slugs slammed into the hut, but Baca,
slithering about the floor and rationing his own ammunition carefully, held
his attackers at bay. When a deputy sheriff arrived safe conduct for Baca to
the jail in Socorro was negotiated, and Martinez was untied and helped to
safety. A jury found Baca innocent of murdering the cowboy.

Whitewater Creek cuts out of the Mogollon Mountains through a
gorge so precipitous that the "Catwalk," a steel walkway suspended from a
cliff, is the only practical way through its portals. The Catwalk follows the
route of an early-day waterline to the gold mining village of Graham, now
a ghost town. A trail wanders up the scenic canyon and eventually tops
Mogollon Baldy, a 10,770-foot summit where there is a fire lookout—good
country for spotting wild turkey and mule deer. The mouth of Whitewater
Canyon is reached by a five-mile spur road out of Glenwood on U.S.
Highway 180.

The Gila River emerges from the wilderness area at its confluence
with Turkey Creek. There are a number of small caves and ruins of cliff
dwellings or storage rooms above the creek. Prospector Jack Stockbridge
recalls that on a trip up the creek in 1903 he found a willow basket "full of

feathers—some of the prettiest feathers you ever looked at—red bird feathers and all kinds in there!" Where Manzanita Canyon comes into the creek, a hot spring boils up through a fracture in bedrock. According to Stockbridge, all an angler has to do is land a trout in cold currents nearby, clean it, and then dip it into the hot spring to be poached. "Just leave it right on the hook."

Turkey Creek and its tributaries—Skeleton, Sycamore, and Manzanita—are beautiful places to backpack today, yet a number of early wanderers had their appreciation cut balefully short. Skeleton Canyon is said to be named for two prospectors killed by Apaches in the 1860s. Subsequently, four off-duty soldiers from Fort Bayard headed into the region hoping to make a strike. Only one, Sidman by name, returned, bearing a tale of Indian ambush. An army burial detachment was sent out. Sidman, however, seemed vague and disoriented, and nothing was found for proper interment. He soon departed for Missouri.

A good many years later a camper on Turkey Creek was digging a hole for a beanpot when he drove his shovel into a skeleton. Nearby were two others. Since Sidman had returned to the area from time to time during the interim, usually heading back by train to Missouri richer from the sale of high-grade ore, folks wondered if the three soldiers who never returned were indeed victims of Apaches or had simply been cut out of a strike by their partner.

The elusive gold of Turkey Creek seems to have been as cursed as any pirate treasure-trove. A young surveyor named Turner noted some interesting outcroppings while running a line close to the junction of Turkey Creek and Sycamore Canyon in the 1880s. Being from Lake Valley, a legendary silver camp, he couldn't help but know a bit about ore, as well as the value of keeping quiet. After completing the job he went back into the Mogollons, pausing in Silver City to purchase a saddle. He, like the soldiers, was never heard from again. Some twenty years later a skeleton and saddle were found under a bluff beside Turkey Creek. The saddle had all but disintegrated, but the number of it matched that of the saddle bought by Turner in Silver City. There were eighty-eight spent cartridges near the skeleton, indicating a desperate stand against Indian attack.

After James Cooney had been killed by Victorio's braves, his brother, Michael, resigned his post as a New Orleans customs inspector and headed west to manage the mines on Mineral Creek. James Cooney had found some gold ore on Turkey Creek and Michael became obsessed with finding the lode. He and his brother, Tom, made several vain searches for it, once almost freezing to death when they lost their pack outfit.

A prospector known as the "Dutchman" came out of the Mogollon Mountains with several pack horses loaded with ore yielding high gold and silver content. Mineralogists surmised it might have come from the same ore body discovered by Sidman and James Cooney, but on his next trip into the Gila backcountry the Dutchman disappeared.

Michael Cooney, although still confident he would eventually find the lode, turned his attention to politics. Elected to the territorial legislature, one of his duties was to secure a printer for state documents. He hired a midwestern printer who later commented that he had come to New Mexico expecting to rendezvous with his nephew in Santa Fe. The nephew had written of making a rich gold strike in the Mogollons and wanted his uncle to help him work it. The nephew had never shown up; he was Turner, whose as yet undiscovered remains lay next to the saddle beside Turkey Creek.

In the fall of 1914 Michael Cooney was camped at the junction of Diamond Creek and East Fork of the Gila. At seventy-five he was robust, but he had put on a lot of weight, like a bear getting ready to hibernate. He wore the sort of sweeping goatee popularized by Buffalo Bill Cody. An old Mexican man and an Apache with brick-colored hair happened along with 150 pounds of ore they had broken out from the Turkey Creek area. The Irishman offered to cart the ore to the Socorro smelter in his wagon and

Ruins of old mine buildings in Cooney Canyon.

arrange shipment to the Denver mint in exchange for a cut of the action. An agreement was reached and the party headed out of the mountains for Socorro.

It was high-grade. The sale to the mint brought $4600, which in those days could buy a lot of anything, including lively times. During a binge the Apache killed the Mexican and was promptly lodged in jail. The Indian drew a buckskin map for Cooney, showing the location of the ore body. The idea was that Cooney would bring out a load of ore and obtain the Indian's freedom.

Late October is not a reasonable time to be heading into the high country. When Michael Cooney rode by the 74 Ranch leading a pack horse, the weather was raw and rainy. The owner asked him to linger at the ranch until the storm was over.

"I haven't got the time. I can't stop," Cooney replied and pressed on.

The first eleven pages of his diary recorded terse notations as to campsites. Then, on the sixth of November, he wrote: "Tried to get down Brushy."

November 7—Tried to get out of it.

November 8—Horses left me on last load out of canyon; balked; piled half-load for Tom and got to top of point with provisions. Went back for bedding and while loading Jerry, Tom-horse got off the trail and went crashing over rocks and bushes down the mountain. Cut him loose from pack, and it being now dark, made a rock bed and turned Tom loose and left Jerry loose with bridle on. Slept there all night.

November 9—Piled the bedding and covered with pack covers and led Jerry up to where the————were and so tuckered out slept there. Famished for water.

November 10—Went south making trail to get down to water, came to precipice and had to come back. Got dark and there being good grass, unsaddled and thought Jerry was attempting to take the back trail; got ahead of him and waited awhile for him to eat grass. Then could not find place where I unsaddled. Made a fire and slept within twenty yards of where I left my stuff.

November 11—Woke up tuckered out; tried to eat bread; got some sugar and tried to eat it; got some tablets and sucked them. Will try to saddle Jerry and go back on trail far enough to get down to water, as I hate to have him left here. Been without water since 5th—six days. Will put in tonight, the 11th, on mountain and start for water in the morning. God be with me.

I hunted for game today. I smelt fresh meat cooking; hollered for help but got no reply.

November 12—got down with difficulty and went crash into a pool of water. It started to rain and has kept it up for two days and nights. No place for a bed; wet and cold. Hobbled Jerry and————try to get out. Heard the bell last night but don't hear it any more. Two of the worst days and nights. Matches all wet. Can have no fire.

November 15—Let in a little sun and feels better. [Elizabeth Mc-Farland, *Wilderness of the Gila,* University of New Mexico Press, 1974.]

This was the last entry in the diary. In February a search party found the body of Michael Cooney face down in Sycamore Canyon off Turkey Creek, only about a hundred feet from where Turner's skeleton was found and close to the old prospect of James Cooney that had started Michael Cooney on his long and fatal quest.

The shortest route to Turkey Creek is to drive into the village of Gila, four miles off U.S. Highway 180. An eight-mile paved road follows the eastern bank of the river before abruptly turning primitive at the boundary of Gila National Forest. The last few miles to the mouth of Turkey Creek are recommended for four-wheel drive only.

A trail branches off the Turkey Creek path into Sycamore Canyon and follows it up over a divide of the Diablo Range into the White Creek drainage. There is a ranger cabin at the junction of White Creek and the West Fork of the Gila. At one time the clearing was the site of two settlers' cabins—Ralph Jenks and Thomas McKenzie. Jenks was arrested in the 1890s by a lawman named Keecheye Johnson, after a neighbor accused him of stealing cattle. In a canyon that now bears his name, somebody killed Johnson from ambush—probably an Indian. Or so Jenks told his friends in Mogollon. When a posse came to get him Jenks muttered that "them damn rascals (the posse) are likely to kill me." They did, down near Buckhorn Creek. He went for his gun, they said, although skeptics wondered that the prisoner should have been armed to begin with, and recalled that he left Mogollon wearing thick gloves.

In the spring of 1885 three frontiersmen—Jason Baxter, Wood Poland, and James McKenna—set out for a mysterious, highly mineralized "island mountain" north of the Plains of San Augustin that Baxter had previously visited. He and his companion had been spooked off by Apaches before properly exploring what appeared to be a rich gold deposit. On Elk Mountain the party saw vast herds of antelope and many wild horses, as well as a large flock of untended sheep whose shepherd had apparently been a victim of Indian attack, bear, or disease. On his previous trip to the "island mountain" Baxter had found a deserted sheep camp surrounded by a stone barricade. There were many shell casings in the area, indicating a battle with Indians. Not far away, back in the brush, was a pair of boots, and when he picked one up out tumbled a set of foot bones.

Baxter found the geography of the gold site to have been completely altered since his first trip. Key landmarks appeared to have been obliterated by a cataclysmic earthquake, that ubiquitous villain of most lost treasure.

The prospectors headed back into the mountains. At Snow Creek they observed numerous moccasin prints, which they assumed had been made by Mexicans burning wood into charcoal for mine smelters. The party lingered at the McKenzie cabin on West Fork. Several settlers from the area dropped over to smoke a few bowls of tobacco and jaw for a while. When Baxter mentioned the moccasin prints the men stirred uneasily and one remarked that they might well have been made by Apaches, as a band had recently left the reservation.

After a time, when talk of gold and politics had been exhausted, Baxter began to describe a vision he once had of his own death. It would come while he was camped in a small valley with a stream running through it and a herd of cattle grazing upon a sidehill. After a hush in which the men glanced out at the narrow valley through which the West Fork gleamed in the moonlight, a settler named Prior said, "You'll not be goin' across the border in this valley. For there's never been a cow pastured here yet as far as I know."

Another old-timer, Papineau, remarked that he had no inkling as to the mode of his death, just that it would be sudden.

The campfire was low by the time the gathering broke up. Most of the men had several miles to ride back to their homes. As they started to mount up, a stray dog that had followed the prospectors to McKenzie's cabin began to bark frenziedly. Across the creek, standing out clearly in the light of the full moon, was a herd of cattle cropping at the grass.

The next day McKenzie and his brother went to Alma, and Poland and McKenna fished for trout up the river. Baxter remained in camp. Around sundown McKenna headed back to camp with a string of trout. As he entered the meadow he almost stumbled over the carcass of a horse. The clearing was full of Indians. McKenna was instantly surrounded, grabbed, and shoved back against a tree. He could see Baxter's body next to the campfire and four or five Apaches "dressed like white men" throwing clothes and bedding out of the cabin. Several women passing with brush for a fire spat on McKenna, and one ran a mesquite thorn into his leg. The Indians' horses were being herded up along White Creek when suddenly they broke and stampeded wildly back through camp, probably frightened by a silvertip grizzly. As the Apaches dashed after their horses, the prospector sprinted off in the other direction.

McKenna hid back in the brush until the middle of the night, then cautiously worked his way back to the McKenzie cabin. The Apaches had left. After covering Baxter's body with a wagon sheet and eating some raw potatoes, he started down the trail to Gila Hot Springs. McKenna moved slowly, pausing frequently through the night and during the next day, for bands of Apaches were roaming the area and his moccasins, softened by frequent river crossings, soon were badly ripped by stretches of lava. Pinned to the door of a settler's cabin downcanyon was a notice: "Baxter and McKenna killed at McKenzie cabin. Beware of Apaches. For safety come over to the Wood Place on the East Fork of the Gila River." Exhausted, McKenna lay down and slept fitfully. It rained.

The following morning he started up the divide accompanied by a dog that had been left behind when its owners fled to safety from a cabin near the hot springs. They had not gone far when an immense silvertip grizzly rose out of the bush and charged after the dog, which was never seen again. Delirious with exposure, exhaustion, and lack of food, McKenna back-tracked to his own cabin. A group of Apaches had butchered a steer and were drying the meat. From the opposite side of the river McKenna howled and flailed his arms. The startled Indians, whose culture frowns upon harming the troubled and mysterious spirits of madmen, packed up most of the meat and left hurriedly. McKenna swam the river and ravenously tore into some raw meat. The cold water and food cleared his head and he made his way over to the Tom Wood cabin across the divide. There were a number of settlers gathered there, as well as Poland, who had also escaped the attack at McKenzie's cabin.

The Apaches, who were of Geronimo's band, had killed Prior, Papineau, Tom McKenzie, and other settlers in the Gila before being driven into the Sierra Madre of Mexico.

When not on the lookout for Indians, the settlers in the Gila spent a considerable amount of energy doing violence to each other. In one year alone—1891—men were poisoned, stabbed, bashed to death with axes and crowbars, and shot with virtually every type of pistol or rifle to be found in the territory. After a saloon shootout in Silver City a newspaper reporter who happened to be on the scene later complained that he had not had time to draw out his notebook as he was too busy dodging bullets. The larger part of the mayhem was the result of the classic Hollywood confrontation: man vs. man over pasturage, water rights, mining claims, banditry, or manhood itself. Unlike the adversaries in Western movies, however, most frontier gladiators of the Gila country were usually so deep in their cups that they could scarcely stand, let alone shoot straight, when their moment of truth arrived.

Then, as now, there were arguments over women. The motive for a fatal shooting at Central was described by the press as a "dispute over a frail sister." The dashing young doctor of Kingston, a mining camp, was gunned down by a gentleman who felt his wife was getting more than adequate attention, medical or otherwise. Sometimes a man had cause to be grumpy. A rancher on the Mimbres River discovered his wife had sold the better part of his stock and then hurriedly headed west with the proceeds and his foreman.

Thomas Luke, a Silver City resident, suffered from liver trouble, and for several months he assumed this was why he detected a bitter taste in the water his wife served him each evening in a goblet with cracked ice. He was puzzled, however, as to why he became overwhelmingly sleepy so early in the evening, and was disturbed on certain mornings to find his wife lying fully clothed upon the bed next to him, though his recollection was that she had disrobed to retire the night before. Eventually he suspected that he was being drugged and confided his fears to a doctor. The physician advised him to accept neither food nor drink from his wife. Two nurses were hired.

That evening Mrs. Luke approached one of the nurses with a cheerful smile, expressing wifely concern for her husband's condition. She handed one of them a glass full of liquid, explaining it was a potion the doctor insisted they give to her husband. The nurse set it aside, and the following day the doctor, who had prescribed no such thing, found it to be morphine. Apparently Mrs. Luke had been giving Mr. Luke enough morphine over the months so that he had become not only an unwitting addict, but was in grave danger of death from overdosage. Rather understandably, he divorced the lady.

The *Silver City Enterprise,* which diligently chronicled the violent world of the Gila, was not above journalistic indignation at some of the more dastardly deeds. After an argument at a dance,

> a treacherous brute induced his wife to accompany him to [the] spring, about fifty yards from the house, whence in a few minutes issued the shrieks of the terrified wife and her cries for succor from the murderous assault of her husband. The victim's mother and stepfather . . . ran to the place and found her lying on the ground bleeding freely from many wounds while the cowardly wretch who perpetrated the crime was running towards the woods as fast as he could [*Silver City Enterprise,* April 24, 1891].

Although the woman suffered eight knife wounds, most were minor owing to the dullness of the knife and her thick clothing. She was carried up to the house and makeshift bandages were applied. The next morning someone rode into Silver City to report the "killing" and accordingly the judge summoned a coroner's jury and sent them to the ranch. They found the victim alive. With a bizarre fidelity to instructions, they waited for her to expire so they could begin their inquest. An *Enterprise* reporter arrived that evening to find the woman still alive and the jurymen still waiting. He rode to town for a doctor, who subsequently saved the patient. "In justice to some of the jurymen, it is claimed by them that they wanted to return to town and send a physician to care for the victim but they say the judge insisted upon finding what he came for, a stiff," was the newspaper's final comment upon the affair.

Some of the stories which appeared in the *Enterprise* are intriguing for what was left out. A reported killing in Pinos Altos, "as unwarranted and diabolical murder as ever perpetrated," leaves one dangling without further detail; one Minnie Lee of Deming "so adroitly" concealed two twenty-dollar gold pieces "on her person that it was some time before the officer found it." And what of the two ladies who were found in a corral behind the VV Ranch, each with a bullet through the heart, a pistol in the right hand; one was a governess at the ranch. The newspaper account has little else to add except to state enigmatically that they once occupied a higher station in life.

Two deaths in the Gila country that year might have been subjects of ballads. Calvin Herring, a widower, had a ranch on Meadow Creek, north of Pinos Altos. He worked hard on the property; his two daughters—Sally, sixteen, and Lulu, fourteen—kept the house up. Visitors remarked upon it being a happy, friendly place. Two men working at a nearby sawmill were decidedly impressed by the friendliness of the girls, but confined their calling to times when the rancher was away, correctly predicting he would not welcome the attentions of a man just recently released from the county jail whose companion was a suspected horse-thief. From the young ladies' point of view, not much happened on Meadow Creek. They were charmed with the men, caught up in a new kind of excitement—so much so that they wound up riding into Silver City for a double wedding. Their father was away rounding up cattle at the time.

They registered as married couples at the Tremont House. After which, according to contemporary accounts, the men "proceeded to fill their dirty skins with whiskey." When the girls, very bashful at being in the big town on their wedding night, inquired about the ceremony, the men replied that papers and licenses were being drawn up. When urged to drink, the girls were shocked and would have none of it. Finally, the still-unwedded Sally and Lulu retired to their respective rooms. During the night other hotel guests, passing the rooms, heard the girls protest and beg to be let alone.

The next day a deputy sheriff learned who the girls were and asked them if the ceremony had been carried out. The reply was negative. As any upright man of the era would have done, the deputy then took one of the men—Staples—aside and asked him his intentions. Staples felt it was none of the lawman's business and stated he "would shoot the belly out of any damned son of a bitch who dare say there was anything wrong." The ruckus was overheard by a friend of Herring, who immediately galloped off to tell the father, who was still out on the range.

Staples and his companion made plans to leave on the next cattle train, but deputy sheriffs arrested them as they emerged from the Exchange Saloon, mainly to protect them from the wrath of the father. They had started toward the lock-up when Herring emerged from the Broadway Restaurant. He pulled a pistol from his vest. The deputies moved in front of the terrified prisoners.

"Don't let him shoot me!" Staples cried.

Mr. Herring politely asked the two deputies to each move a few inches to the side so he could shoot Staples and his friend. After a tense moment, during which the lawmen did not budge, Herring allowed himself to be disarmed. He returned to the ranch with his daughters. As they were milking, he questioned them closely as to what had happened during the night. His worst fears were apparently confirmed, for he told the girls to continue with their chore, returned to the house, placed the muzzle of a Winchester rifle against his head and pulled the trigger.

The second tragedy in the Romantic tradition had to do with the death of Jennie Forrest, a victim, some might say, of the footlights. Jennie was an actress, and so consuming was her ambition that she left husband and child for a western tour with the Gem Theatre troupe. Whatever sort of success the members of the Gem Theatre had dreamed of before leaving Chicago—thunderous acclaim, miners throwing gold nuggets at their feet, champagne breakfasts with cattle barons—somehow did not materialize. Jennie wound up in Silver City—alone, friendless, and flat broke.

In desperation, she entered a bawdy house to earn fare back to Chicago. She was alternately garrulous and moody in her new employment. Two days after entering the bagnio she took several stiff drinks, sat at the piano, and began to spiritedly play and sing. Quite abruptly, she broke off, ran upstairs to her room, and died.

The doctor's diagnosis was a diseased heart; the rest of the town felt the cause of death was a broken heart and gave her an appropriate funeral.

The residents of the Gila were generally a hardy breed. They were clawed by bear, thrown from bucking horses, scraped off runaway horses by trees, maimed by blasting powder, had mineshafts cave in upon them— and were generally back about their business within a matter of days or weeks. We are told that a Professor Waring attempted to drive his buggy across a Silver City street in which a river happened to be flowing that day. The buggy was reduced to kindling. The professor and horses, entangled in the traces, were tumbled downstream—or downstreet—for a goodly distance before they could be rescued.

It is reported that a Mr. Shelly, served poisoned bread in a cabin on the Gila River, was so stricken that he could not speak but was able to clamber onto his horse and ride home, where he swallowed quantities of lard. He credited the lard with saving his life, although he was confined to bed for a couple of weeks. In a country where physicans were scarce and usually a long distance away by horseback or wagon, a person needed to be rather handy in the medical arts. A farmer by the name of Bush up on the San Francisco River fell from his mowing machine, breaking an arm in two places. He set the arm himself and it healed splendidly. None of his neighbors were surprised, as he had had some practice in the past, twice breaking a leg and setting it himself.

Although life in the Gila in the 1890s may have had some rough edges, there were a lot of fine times, too. Across the river from where Mr. Bush broke his arm, a hunting party was encamped, and a visitor reports sharing a supper that included quail a la mode, fricasseed chicken, stewed wild pigeon, speckled trout, fresh milk, potatoes, cabbage, and roasted ears of sweet corn. Since the produce came from Mr. Bush's garden, it is presumed he partook of the feast.

Hunting and fishing trips, once merely a simple survival activity, began to be social and festive events. Women often met the returning hunters at the hot springs or other rendezvous, where dancing and croquet were the order of the day. Each sportsman had his own idea of a proper outfit. A Dr. H. P. Huntington set out from Silver City with enough ammunition to start a small war, some soda crackers, a spring overcoat, and a copy of the *Chicago Times* for bedding.

Horse- and foot-racing were popular. An exciting Fourth of July sprint at Kingston was interrupted when a bear cub tumbled off a ledge and tripped the leading runner. Things were a mite testy for a bit, as gamblers had floated a lot of money on the outcome. But things cooled off when the judges called the curious intervention an act of God and nullified all bets.

Some of the more dashing sportsmen of the region came to lamentable ends. A Mr. Clayton, the principal in a sixty-mile horse-vs-bicycle race from Silver City to Deming, was later executed in Mexico on a charge of murder. Charles Howard, a California balloonist, caused the local populace to gasp and shout when he soared above the town. A few months later his balloon burst some five hundred feet above Guaymas, Mexico, and Mr. Howard was no more.

The mining camps of the Gila were becoming substantial places, with churches, schools, banks, and fraternal organizations. Hillsboro built a bottling works that turned out old favorites such as birch beer and sarsaparilla soda (at that time stocked in every bar as a surefire cure for venereal disease that might have been contracted in the upstairs rooms), as well as popular exotics like Pear Champagne, Cherri Ferri Phosphate, and Standard Nerve Food. Silver City boasted a self-regulating steam peanut roaster in front of the post office newsstand.

The women, as women will, were having parties—fan-tan parties, tiddlywinks parties, and gala picnics galore, including a basket lunch on Walnut Creek where a "beautiful veiled prophetess" glided out of the woods and found good fortunes in the palms of all present. Weddings, which only a decade before were generally simple cabin ceremonies, were now often rather elegant. The gift list for one such affair included two baskets of orange blossoms, a cut-glass pickle jar, silver napkin rings, a parasol, a marble clock, a bon-bon box, and a copy of Milton's *Paradise Lost*.

Even though the mining camps of the Gila had lost many of their rough edges by the turn of the century, the mountains remained wild for the most part. Aldo Leopold was a district forester in Albuquerque when he met Clinton Anderson, a newspaper reporter. Leopold felt strongly that the government should preserve wilderness areas for the generations to come. The young conservationist's views found enthusiastic support from men like Gila Forest Supervisor Fred Winn and, later, Theodore Roosevelt. On June 3, 1924, Gila Wilderness Area, the first region to be so designated, was created out of National Forest lands.

Shortly after this historic event Leopold moved back to Wisconsin, where he started the "Wilderness Bulletin." The first mimeographed issue was mailed to less than twenty people. Its first line was a quotation: "The truth is that which prevails in the long run."

The truth which Aldo Leopold perceived—the vast importance of wilderness to an urban and industrialized society—has prevailed. As young men, Leopold and Clinton Anderson often talked of wilderness concepts. Later, when Anderson became one of America's most respected senators, his influence and dedication assured that many of Leopold's dreams would become reality.

It is perhaps fitting that the final stronghold of the Apaches, who loved wild and rugged places, should have become our first wilderness area. The Gila remains a state of mind as much as an actual place.

Guide Notes for the GILA

LOCATION—Southwestern New Mexico. Within the 2.7-million acres of Gila National Forest are the Gila Wilderness (429,506 acres), the Gila Primitive Area (135,978 acres), and the Leopold Wilderness (188,179 acres).

ACCESS—The major access roads are U.S. Highway 180 on the west and State Highway 90 on the south. State Highway 15, which is paved, leads north from Silver City to Gila Cliff Dwellings National Monument. State Highways 61 and 78 (most of which are unpaved) pass through the Gila, and several old mining and logging roads give access to mountainous regions outside of the wilderness areas.

GETTING AROUND—A multitude of trails lace through the Gila, passing through canyons and topping high divides. With a Forest Service map or topographic sheets one can plan day-hikes or plan on being in the backcountry a week or more. The Gila is a beautiful river to canoe during the brief spring run-off, which is usually in late March or early April.

CAMPING—There are a few developed campsites, mostly near the roadheads. Camping is excellent through the Gila backcountry, although one should take note which streams flow all the time and which are intermittent (shown on the Forest Service map).

SUPPLIES—A variety of backcountry gear and supplies can be purchased at Silver City. Small stores at places like Glenwood and Mimbres have a limited stock of provisions.

SPECIAL FEATURES—The mountains, which rise to over ten thousand feet, are bisected by canyons which are better than a thousand feet deep in places. The Gila Cliff Dwellings and other ruins are noteworthy, as are Gila Hot Springs. There are a number of ghost towns in the Gila, as well as abandoned cabins of early-day settlers. Trout—rainbow, brown, and native—are taken from the East, West and Middle Forks of the Gila River, Willow and Negrito Creeks, and portions of Whitewater and Mogollon Creeks. The variety of bird life draws ornithologists from all over the world.

INFORMATION SOURCE—Gila National Forest, 310 W. College Avenue, Silver City, New Mexico 88061.

SEVEN

Desert Trails and Tales
(Southwestern Arizona)

To people who have grown up amid green, leafy trees, brimming creeks, and red barns rising out of clover fields, southwestern Arizona usually seems a desolate place. The immensities of distance may be appalling— vast stony and sandy plains sparsely scattered with thorny plants, where the only sign of life would appear to be the drift of vultures, the tips of their wing-feathers spread as if pressing on a window of blue space. The sun-parched mountains, mostly volcanic, are abrupt and gaunt rising from the desert floor like improbable mirages. On an average blistering summer day—say, 103 degrees in the shade—the baselines of such ranges do indeed wobble and often the entire mass will appear to lift completely from the ground. The heat of this country, although dry, is intense. So, too, is the bitter cold of the desert ranges when the sun has dropped.

Most people who have experienced this part of the country have done so briefly—deliberately—leadfooting their way across it upon Interstate Highway 8 or 10, pausing only when necessary to gas up, throw down a soft drink or beer, and then press on to destinations where the land is not so raw and somehow . . . unfinished.

A number of people, including myself, find this fascinating country. Appearances can be deceptive. Although it is scarce, there is water here, springs both cold and warm as well as *tinajas,* natural scoops in the rock which may hold water for weeks after a rainfall. In places, springs or underground water sources provide enough constant moisture for an oasis such as the canyon of wild fan palms which lies high amid the burned, barren cliffs of the Kofa Mountains. A variety of mammals, including badgers, mule deer, bobcats, foxes, and bighorn sheep, rely upon the *tinajas* and springs for their water supply. Other desert dwellers, such as the kangaroo rat, are so adapted to their environment that they can obtain virtually all the moisture they need from the plant life they feed upon.

Much of southwestern Arizona, including some starkly beautiful desert ranges, has been given to the military so they can practice making war. Luke Air Force Gunnery Range stretches from the Papago Indian Reservation almost all the way to Yuma, a distance of about 130 miles. The Yuma Proving Ground of the U.S. Army lies to the north and east of Yuma. Travel in these areas is restricted; reasonably so, as it is discouraging to see a camp or companions reduced to a missile crater. If no tests are immediately scheduled, however, it is sometimes possible to obtain permission to enter these areas.

There are three wildlife refuges in this region: the remote and roadless Cabeza Prieta Game Refuge, whose southeastern corner adjoins Organ Pipe Cactus National Monument; the Kofa Game Refuge, which embraces the rugged Kofa and Castle Dome mountains; and the Imperial National Wildlife Refuge which borders a goodly stretch of the Colorado River.

The Kofa Mountains lift steeply from the desert floor into a jagged skyline of pinnacles, towers, and ramparts. Few plants find purchase upon the steep, granite cliffs of the range, and vegetation is sparse in the draws—cactus, creosote, palo verde, catclaw, and ironwood, as well as scrub oak on the higher elevations. There are only a few dependable *tinajas* here. Until recently this remote and forbidding range was visited rarely—first by Indians hunting deer and desert bighorn sheep, later by prospectors.

It was a prospector, John Ramsey, who in 1910 looked down from a pinnacle into a cleft filled with tall palm trees—a hidden strand of green in a dry and almost vertical canyon. The palms were by and large regarded as a burro thumper's tall tale until the 1930s, when the existence of the grove was verified by botanists. Several thousands of years ago, species *Washingtonia filifera* was common throughout southwestern Arizona, southern California, northern Mexico and Baja California. A gradual climate change eventually destroyed the palms except for isolated groves in southern California and northern Baja California, and canyons high in the Kofas.

To reach Palm Canyon one takes Arizona Highway 95 eighteen miles south from Quartzsite or sixty-four miles north from Yuma. A sign marks the turn onto a seven-mile graded dirt road leading to the trailhead. Highway 95 is one of the loneliest stretches of blacktop in the Southwest. Only at Stone Cabin, a gas station and store nine miles south of the Palm Canyon turnoff, is there habitation on the entire stretch of road. Driving toward the almost vertical western wall of the Kofas, one may see that curious, swift, and seemingly tireless bird, the roadrunner, which can fly but prefers to jog upon X-shaped clawed feet, using its long tailfeathers

A *tinaja* after a rain.

The Kofa Mountains. Saguaro and "teddy bear" cholla cacti in the foreground.

both as steering rudder and braking device. Desert country legend has it that the roadrunner will surround a slumbering rattlesnake with a corral of cholla cactus. Upon awakening, the snake, hopelessly trapped, will bite itself to death in frustration. The roadrunner, in fact, does regard rattlesnake as commendable dinner fare, but relies upon agility rather than cactus to obtain it. The nimble bird will hop around the snake, dodging strikes until the serpent is exhausted. The bird then kills it with powerful thrusts of its long bill.

One may also see the antelope jackrabbit, a stringy hare with huge flaps for ears. The rabbit, whose meat is prized by a number of predators such as the coyote, is a difficult beast to catch. In addition to possessing running speeds of up to thirty-five miles an hour, a frightened jack will zigzag while the color of its flanks rapidly changes back and forth from tan to white. This curious device, apparently a baffle to pursuers, is accomplished by muscles which can instantly raise the tan fur of either flank, revealing the white underneath.

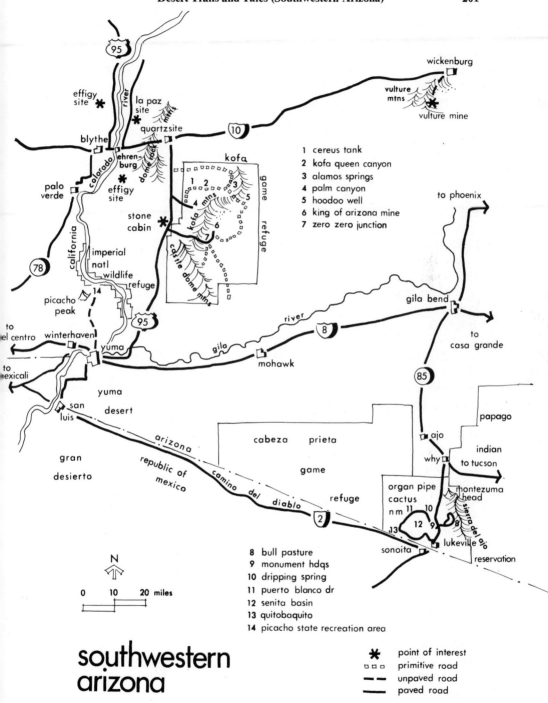

1 cereus tank
2 kofa queen canyon
3 alamos springs
4 palm canyon
5 hoodoo well
6 king of arizona mine
7 zero zero junction

8 bull pasture
9 monument hdqs
10 dripping spring
11 puerto blanco dr
12 senita basin
13 quitobaquito
14 picacho state recreation area

southwestern arizona

✻ point of interest
▫▫▫ primitive road
--- unpaved road
— paved road

The dirt road ends in a scraped-out turnaround where one can leave vehicles. A well-delineated trail leads up a boulder-strewn canyon for perhaps half a mile before the palms can be seen, growing in a narrow side cleft some three hundred feet above the main canyon. It is a steep, tough scramble up to the narrow portal of this side canyon. Barren, vertical rock soars up on all sides. To reach the largest stand of palms it is necessary to squeeze through a two-foot slot. The palms themselves range up to thirty feet high and climb the precipitous cleft almost to its head—truly a green and magic place.

Most people who go to the Kofas these days merely hike the half-mile into Palm Canyon, gaze at the green slot high above them, and head back to their cars and other destinations. There are, however, a number of primitive roads and trails all through the craggy range. For some a pickup is adequate; others require four-wheel drive or a pair of hiking boots. I highly recommend that anyone planning to prowl the Kofas or nearby Castle Domes stop by the refuge headquarters in Yuma. There one can pick up detailed maps and obtain current information on road conditions.

About midway between the turnoff on Highway 95 and the entrance to Palm Canyon, a jeep-trail hooks to the north briefly and then heads east into Kofa Queen Canyon, a deep and spectacular defile. One passes Cereus Tank—one of several tanks, small springs, and seeps scattered throughout the refuge where deer, bighorn sheep, and other animals water. One can continue through the heart of the range to Alamo Springs off to the north or Hoodoo Well on the eastern flank of the mountains. These tracks join with yet others, and trails branch off in many places. One can spend a lot of time prowling the Kofas, a region of some twenty by forty miles in extent.

An estimated 250 desert bighorn sheep range the Kofa and Castle Dome mountains. Most people who come to the Kofas do so to see the palms or the sheep. The palms, being stationary, rarely disappoint them, but the sheep, who are wary and constantly on the move, often do. Nevertheless, those fortunate enough to come upon some sheep will be treated to a rare vision of beauty and cliff-ledge dexterity.

From Stone Cabin on Highway 95 a twenty-two-mile graded road leads around the south flank of the Kofas to a cluster of mining properties —the King of Arizona, North Star, and Rob Roy. After crossing a low spur of the Castle Dome Mountains, where saguaro cactus stand against the horizon, the road descends into the empty vastness of King Valley. The Kofas loom to the north, while the Castle Domes, another gaunt desert range, rise sharply to the south. Far out in the valley at a dusty crossing named Zero Zero Junction, the route heads north toward the Kofas.

A prospector named Charles Eichelberger discovered gold on this side of the mountains in 1896. He named his mine the King of Arizona, which

Palm Canyon, a hidden oasis in a rocky desert.

mapmakers later abbreviated to give the official name of Kofa to the mountain range. Previously prospectors had referred to the range as the SH Mountains, apparently inspired by a prominent rock formation which had the slant-roof appearance of a familiar outbuilding of the era. For three years the ore was shipped out by ponderous wagons to Mohawk on the other side of the Gila River, and then deep wells were dug to provide water for a cyanide mill. The King of Arizona produced three and a half million dollars worth of gold and silver before the rich surface ores played out and operations ceased in 1911. The nearby North Star Mine produced over a million dollars worth of gold before it, too, became unprofitable to operate at about the same time. A few weathered shacks, shaft openings, tailings, and scattered ruins and rusted machinery mark the sites of these once-booming mines. There is still gold in the area, and caretakers live at some of the mining properties, waiting for the price of minerals to go up.

The russet, worn cliffs of the Kofas rise starkly behind the mines. In early morning or late afternoon light they rather resemble the walls of an ancient fortified city, a place deserted in the early days of time when gods yet walked the earth and buildings were plated with gold. The first Europeans to come into this country were seeking such places of legend—the Cities of Cibola and the Land of Quivira. In 1540 Francisco Vasquez de Coronado led an expedition across the foothills of the Sierra Madre and into southern Arizona, while Hernando de Alarcon, in command of three ships, sailed up the Gulf of California. After nearly floundering upon sand bars at the mouth of the Colorado River, the ships twisted their way through a labyrinth of channels to where, as Alarcon reported, "We found a very mighty river, which ran with so great fury of a storm, that we could hardly sail against it." With the aid of Cocopah Indians, who towed the vessels through shallower stretches, the Spaniards reached the mouth of the Gila and pushed on to a point some one hundred miles above it. Finding no gold, nor being able to make contact with the land expedition, the ships sailed back out into the Gulf at the end of the summer.

More than three centuries later, in the 1850s, gold placer was discovered on riverbanks which the Spaniards had sailed past and walked over. The first strike was close to the mouth of the Gila, and soon there were mining camps upriver—La Paz and Ehrenberg. The strike at La Paz was made by Pauline Weaver, whose tombstone in the old capitol grounds at Prescott identifies him as a "Pioneer, Prospector, Scout, Guide, Free Trapper, Fur Trader, Empire Builder, Patriot." Weaver, whose mother was Cherokee, gained a reputation as being one of the most resourceful of mountain men before coming to Arizona as an agent of the Hudson's Bay Company. During the Mexican War he guided the Mormon Battalion from the headwaters of the Gila River to California.

A freighter who brought a wagonload of flour from San Bernardino,

California, to the gold strike at La Paz arrived one suppertime. Men were cooking fish and beans over campfires, and virtually everyone not rustling up food was playing Mexican Monte.

"They had little piles of nuggets laid out all along the edge of the blankets and, when a man wanted to bet, he just shoved out a handful. I saw more gold as I walked down that street and watched the gambling than I'd seen since I was born. I got my share of it, too, for the people of La Paz hadn't seen a sack of flour for a month. . . ."

River water to work the dry diggings was carried in rawhide bags by strings of pack animals. For drinking water a miner could either settle out a pan of the muddy Colorado overnight or else pay two dollars a gallon for spring water hauled in from distant sources. There were soon numerous adobe huts and at least one store. La Paz became a stop on the overland stage route between northern Arizona points and San Bernardino, a respite of willow trees and flowing water in the heart of a wide, dry desert. Wood was scarce, and the shipping cartons which came in filled with merchandise were sold for furniture or coffins as soon as they were emptied out.

For a giddy, brief period, La Paz was the largest town in Arizona and was making a strong bid to become the territorial capitol. It was a river port of considerable importance and a supply center for distant desert mines like the fabulous Vulture near Wickenburg. Within a decade after La

Looking toward the Castle Dome Mountains.

Paz's raw beginnings, the price of gold plummeted. The placers, already well chewed over, were now no longer profitable. In 1870 the unpredictable Colorado River cut a new main channel that left La Paz, once a river port, two miles away from navigable water.

Most of the inhabitants moved downriver to the mining community of Ehrenberg, which boasted a steamboat and ferry landing, as well as a bank, stage office, and the River View Hotel. Ehrenberg had some rough edges in the early days. A wooden headboard in the old cemetery simply read: "J. C. 1867." The date signified the year a stranger was gunned off a horse whose brand was J.C. Martha Summerhayes, the wife of an Army officer, was not impressed by Ehrenberg when she first paused there on a river steamer: "I did not go ashore. Of all the dreary, miserable settlements that one could imagine, that was the worst." Later she was forced to live there for a time, and the intimate contact did little to alter her first judgment. She would later recall as particularly unpleasant the experience of walking past the cemetery just as coyotes were digging out a body.

Be that as it may, several million dollars worth of gold were washed from the placers at La Paz and Ehrenberg.

Upon hearing of the gold strikes on the Colorado, a citizen of Los Angeles named Joshua Talbott mounted a twenty-foot sailing craft upon wheels. The contrivance was drawn by a team of horses over the stage road which crossed the desert. It was his plan to use it as a ferryboat on the river. Somewhere deep in the land of mirage, probably on the fringe of the Chocolate Mountains, the outfit became hopelessly thwarted by steep grade and deep sand and had to be abandoned.

Talbott's was not a solitary vision. In November of 1852 the *Uncle Sam,* a sidewheeler which had been brought to the mouth of the river in sections, started up the river with a load of military provisions destined for Fort Yuma. Her engines were not powerful enough for the current, and the cargo had to be unloaded some fifty miles below the fort and transported the rest of the way by wagon. Nevertheless, the *Uncle Sam* started an era of steam navigation upon the shifty and shallow Colorado that would flourish for better than half a century until competition from the railroads effectively put the steamers out of business.

The steamers carried all manner of goods from the mouth of the Colorado all the way up to what is now Lake Mead. Supplies for military forts, mining camps, and farming settlements were hauled upriver while farm products from the Virgin and Muddy river valleys were shipped south to mining districts from which, in turn, ore was carried down to the Gulf of California and transferred to ocean-going vessels. An average vessel would be roughly 175 feet in length, 30-some feet in beam, and could work in as little as three feet of current when fully loaded. Heading downstream without a load, it was said, they could maneuver upon a heavy dew.

Piute Indians were helpful to the river traffic in two quite distinctly different ways.The first steamboats burned sage, greasewood, and whatever driftwood they haphazardly came upon. An estimated quarter-million cords of pine, cottonwood, and fir were, before we blocked the flow with dams, carried down the Colorado during the annual spring runoffs. Soon Piutes manned a number of scows and flatboats all along the river, using them principally to gather driftwood. They dragged the wood ashore, cut and dried it, and then sold it to steamship companies from specified locations.

The Piutes assisted navigation in another curious way. The lower Colorado is notorious for the sudden shifting of its channels. Learning of such a convulsion, Indians would gather upon the banks, hoping that the boat might flounder upon a sandbar and could then be looted. Steamboat captains learned that such a gathering generally meant low water. Often they would cautiously approach a sandbar stern first so that the paddles could wash away the obstruction.

The Colorado River near La Paz and Blythe.

Although few steamboats were ever completely lost on the river, a number of them rammed rocks, snags, or submerged logs and sank. They were usually raised to churn muddy currents once more, or were sold for salvage. The *Explorer* was a steel paddlewheeler originally engaged by Lieutenant Joseph Ives to probe the lower Colorado to the head of navigation at Black Canyon. Later it was used for freighting. On a run in 1864, heavily loaded with wood, it spun out of control where the Gila enters the Colorado. After a wild ride the crew managed to get the boat to a cutbank and tied it to a huge cottonwood tree. Almost immediately the bank caved in and the *Explorer,* still lashed to the cottonwood, was swept some eight miles downriver and finally drifted into a slough. Somewhat later the river changed course, leaving the rusting hulk twenty miles from the main channel.

By the first decade of the present century, the Colorado River steamboat trade, as well as the ports it served, had been bypassed as surely as the stranded *Explorer*. The completion of competing railroads and a decline in mining activity both contributed to the close of a short, colorful era.

Today, little remains of Ehrenberg. Interstate 10 passes close to a few adobe ruins, and the cemetery, just to the north, is interesting and not hard to find. It is the most tangible residue of what was once a booming mining camp and river port. Of La Paz, once reckoned to be the largest town in Arizona Territory, there is even less. About thirteen miles from Ehrenberg on the oiled road which leads up to Parker are the ruins of the Golden Belt Mill in La Paz Wash. The mill, which operated until the late 1930s, is close to the road on a low hillside to the east. To the west, a half-mile to a mile away, is the site of La Paz itself—a few mounds of adobe—lost in an all but impenetrable thicket of mesquite and bordered by stagnant sloughs.

The town of Picacho, on the California side of the Colorado River, was also once a mining center and river port. Gold production began to boom in the 1880s, and by 1904 there were over 2500 people living in the town. An estimated fourteen million dollars worth of gold was stripped from the rock and shipped down the Colorado in steamboats. Today most of the old town of Picacho is underwater. The site is now the headquarters of the Picacho State Recreation Area, which in turn adjoins the Imperial National Wildlife Refuge. One gets there by driving north on an eighteen-mile gravel road that heads out from Yuma almost immediately after the Colorado River is crossed. Ahead, 1947-foot Picacho Peak pokes a dark, volcanic fang against the sky. It is one of the most prominent landmarks along the lower Colorado.

There are developed campsites at the recreation area headquarters, tables and fire rings shaded by large trees and rocks. There are rest rooms, showers, drinking water, a marina where sailboats can be rented, as well as a store selling groceries, gas, and fishing supplies. The best fishing is for black bass, channel catfish, crappie, and bluegill. Predictably, this core location can get crowded, especially during vacations that fall during the winter months. There are, however, some fine primitive campsites and all manner of interesting backcountry in the several thousand acres of the recreation area.

When Spanish explorers such as Hernando de Alarcon sailed up the Colorado, this region was inhabited by tribes of Indians who spoke Yuman dialects. The Indians poled back and forth across the river on log rafts and chiefly subsisted on fish, corn, beans, and squash. A number of ancient trails wind along the river and up side canyons, and pottery shards are scattered throughout the area. There are some remains of the gold boom, most notably the twenty-ton mill at the Diablo Shaft. The refuge itself hosts numerous waterfowl such as geese, blue heron, ducks, ibis, snowy egrets, and cormorants, as well as hawks, quail, owls, wrens, white-winged doves, and other desert dwellers. Perhaps the best way to enjoy the Imperial Wildlife Refuge is to drift down the river to Picacho from either Ehrenberg or Palo Verde. There is no fast water to speak of, yet shifting sand and mud bars can make navigation interesting. Mosquitoes are usually bad only in late spring and early summer.

In the backcountry of southwestern Arizona it is not surprising to come upon wild burros—inquisitive animals which readily adapted to the natural environment once they had escaped from or been turned loose by prospectors. For a good many years wild camels were also seen in lonely desert ranges. Camels were originally shipped to this country from Egypt and Arabia in the 1850s to serve as pack animals on the deserts of the Southwest. Largely through the persuasion of Secretary of War Jefferson Davis, Congress appropriated thirty thousand dollars to procure the camels. In all, seventy-eight camels were brought to Val Verde, an army camp sixty miles northwest of San Antonio, Texas. As the camels approached the camp, bells jingling at their necks, an observer noted that "The horses and mules were wild with fright at first sight of these ungainly beasts. They dashed around the corral with heads erect and snorting in wild alarm." The camels and mules soon got used to each other, however, and in June of 1857 an expedition under Lieutenant Edward Fitzgerald Beale headed west to survey a wagon-road to California. The caravan consisted of 25 camels, 8 mule-drawn wagons, 56 men, and some 350 sheep. From Zuni, New Mexico, the party trekked through wilderness to Fort Tejon, close to present-day Bakersfield. The route blazed is very close to that followed by Interstate 40 today.

The camels were under the charge of a small, energetic Syrian named Hadji Ali, which his new companions soon contracted to Hi Jolly. Beale was impressed with the camels, noting they could carry more weight than a mule, seemed to thrive on creosote and other desert shrubs, and did not become lame as easily as mules. Nevertheless, the Camel Corps was short-lived. Soldiers complained of seasickness when riding camels. Men accustomed to horses and mules resented the peculiarities of the camels, and the camels, in turn, apparently resented the men at times. As one corporal noted in his journal: "The beast was most willing to sink its teeth into any part of the soldierly anatomy coming within reach of its long neck."

Eventually the army sold a number of the camels to zoos or companies which transported supplies to mines. Many were simply turned loose on the desert, soon turning wild. Hi Jolly worked as a mule driver, a scout, and even, at one point, purchased some camels for a transport business of his own.

Most early-day prospectors had at least one camel story; some were rather eerie. Back in desert ranges like the Kofas or on Mexican *ranchitos* over the border, people still speak of a red camel, the *fantasia colorada* ("red ghost"), which is seen in remote places with a skeleton lashed to its hump.

There is something about the desert that seems to invite mystery and legend. Lost mines and treasure, of course, are ubiquitous in the Southwest. George Rohwer, a prospector, claimed to have discovered a ledge of gold ore while trekking from Stone Cabin to Ehrenberg in 1870. When he reached town half the population was heading out for some new strikes on the Colorado River to the south. Rohwer and his brother followed, and developed the Red Cloud Mine, from which they shipped out thousands of dollars worth of rich silver ore by river steamer. Rohwer eventually sold the Red Cloud, went to Missouri, married, and settled on a farm. A number of years later he returned to prospect for the lost ledge. The ledge was apparently close to an antimony deposit, of which there are known ore bodies in the Dome Rock Mountains. Rohwer probably would have passed through the Dome Rock Mountains on that long-ago journey to Ehrenberg, but although he and others have searched diligently for it, the ledge remains lost to this day.

One of the stores in La Paz used to exchange merchandise for gold. The dust and nuggets were kept in either a metal box or a wooden cask which was stored in a hollow beneath the building. After a flood swept away the structure, drowning one of the owners, his partner returned to the site and dug about in vain for the treasure after the water subsided. It may be there yet for anyone willing to bushwhack a way through the mesquite and quicksand to La Paz and then figure out which foundation was that of the store.

One of the most persistent legends of the desert country to the north of the Gulf of California concerns treasure-ships left high and dry. In 1933 Louis and Myrtle Botts of Julian, California, were out camping and gathering wildflowers on the western side of the Salton Sink, a vast basin which lies below sea level. A grizzled prospector who dropped by their camp told them he had seen an old ship sticking out of the clay wall of a nearby canyon. The Bottses put little stock in the story, but the following morning did enter the canyon to look for flower specimens. Pausing to rest, they looked up to see the forward portion of a large, ancient vessel jutting overhead. A curved stem head was attached to the prow. As there was no way to reach the ship from the canyon floor, they returned to the canyon mouth to speculate on what it might have been and how it could have been deposited there. At that point the couple were knocked to their knees by an earthquake, the same tremor which leveled much of the city of Long Beach. The following weekend the Bottses returned to the canyon—only to find that millions of tons of earth and rock had been shaken into it, thoroughly burying the mysterious ship.

In 1615 Captain Juan de Iturbe was returning to San Blas on the west coast of Mexico with a load of pearls from the beds of Baja California, when his vessel was pursued by a Dutch corsair. Iturbe fled up the Sea of Cortez with the corsair pressing closely after him, hoping to trap the Spanish vessel at the head of the Gulf. There Iturbe noted a wide channel and passed into it with the tide. Since his charts showed Baja California to be a peninsula rather than an island, he was astonished to find himself in what appeared to be another large sea. He sailed north, hoping to find passage around the mountains to the Pacific, but found his way eventually blocked by a rim of sand dunes. Sailing south once again he was dismayed to find that the wide channel back to the Sea of Cortez was now scarcely more than a shallow creek. The ship grounded, and Iturbe and his crew made a harrowing overland journey back to a Spanish outpost.

Is Iturbe's story plausible? When explorer Melchior Diaz journeyed to the mouth of the Colorado in 1540 he reported no inland sea, nor did De Anza when he passed through the region two centuries later. Yet the Salton Sink, once a part of the Sea of Cortez and lying below sea level, has in the past been inundated by a shift of the river-flow to the inland depression. The present Salton Sea, which is evaporating at a rate of six feet a year, was created in a mere year and a half when the Colorado rampaged into the valley through irrigation canals cut after the turn of the century. If Iturbe's vessel was carried up the Colorado upon a tidal bore and then entered a lake filling up in the sink, there may indeed be a ship loaded with pearls somewhere under shifting sands.

Perhaps an even more intriguing mystery of this desert concerns things found rather than lost. On mesa tops near the Colorado River there are some giant effigies which have been created by scraping tan gravels back to expose lighter soil beneath. There are human figures, four-legged animals, circles, a design which may represent a serpent, and another which resembles a Maltese cross. One of the figures, thought to be a female effigy, is 170 feet long, with arms outflung for a distance of 158 feet. It has exaggerated fingers and toes, an elongated neck, and quartzite stones marking eyes, nose, mouth, and breast. The figure has six strands of hair on one side of its head, seven on the other. The figures stand out boldly when viewed from the air, but are all but impossible to see from ground level; there are no elevated viewpoints from which they can be seen. The unknown creators had no way to see their finished product.

Present-day native Americans of the region claim to know nothing of the effigies; nor did early-day explorers record hearing of them. When were they made? The two animal figures have the hammer heads and long, dropping tails characteristic of the horse. The Pleistocene horse which once roamed America is believed to have become extinct ten thousand years ago. The figures could date from that period, but the amount of patina or desert varnish on the scraped areas would tend to argue against it. The patina is formed when certain lichens act as catalysts for deposits of iron and manganese, which under intense desert heat turn rock or gravel to darker hues. Experts believe more patina would have formed within ten thousand years. This leaves the possibility that the effigies were created after the Spaniards arrived with horses in 1540.

The Pima Indians, who live halfway across the state from the Colorado River, have a legend about a strange child who was born to a woman of their tribe. The infant had long, sharp teeth, and claws instead of fingers and toes. She was called Ha-ak, which means "ferocious." Ha-ak ate only meat—any sort of meat, raw or cooked—and in four years reached maturity. When she began to kill and eat children, the people, horrified, drove her away to a cave. They beseeched their powerful deity, Elder Brother, to destroy her. He did so, and the Pima commemorated the event by making a giant effigy of him.

There is no evidence the Pima were ever in the region of the Colorado, but a tribe of their allies, the Maricopa, did live there until 1775, when they moved eastward after feuding with the Yuma Indians. Possibly the Ha-ak legend and the commemorative effigy were passed to the Pimas from the Maricopas, even after it had been forgotten by that tribe and their former neighbors, the Yumas. We may never know for sure.

The mysterious effigies lie north of Blythe, off U.S. Highway 95, as well as across the river from Ripley.

Below Yuma irrigated fields soon give way to a vast desert where little of anything grows, and there are endless waves of large sand dunes. This is the northern extension of the Gran Desierto of Mexico, called the Yuma Desert on our side of the border. To the east of this barren land the border country has a different aspect—a series of low volcanic ranges separating wide valleys. A dry country and a hot one in the summer, yet at the same time it is a wilderness containing a wide variety of plant and animal life.

California gold-stampeders passing across this region on any of several trails called them collectively the Camino del Diablo (Road of the Devil). The argonauts were usually burdened with cumbersome wagons, had no reliable maps, and were often misinformed about what few springs and *tinajas* existed. Indians skewered their stock with arrows. Those who survived the trek rarely remembered it with fondness.

Today this lonely country offers some of the more interesting desert rambling to be found in America. From November to May the weather is generally pleasant—warm days and brisk nights. The best approach to this country is made by heading into Organ Pipe Cactus National Monument, which lies against the Papago Indian Reservation and directly above the Mexican border. Coming in on Highway 85 from the American side, one

The desert in Organ Pipe Cactus National Monument.

passes a majestic citadel of volcanic rock, 3634-foot-high Montezuma Head. As with other peaks and ranges in this part of the country, there is no preamble of foothills and gradual buildup of shoulders, connecting ridges, and saddles. The rock simply juts up from the plains—massive, eroded, and mostly vertical—a challenge to climbers and a haven for eagles. Not far beyond lies a rugged crest topped by 4843-foot-high Sierra del Ajo. This is the best area in the monument for observing desert bighorn sheep. Trails lead back up into this rough country. One of the most interesting winds up through the Bull Pasture, a large, hanging shelf. In years past cattle grazed here after climbing up for more than a mile from the valley floor.

Before heading into the backcountry of Organ Pipe Cactus National Monument or Cabeza Prieta Game Refuge to the west, one should stock up on water at the monument headquarters and obtain trail information from the rangers. For any sort of extended trip current data on waterholes is essential, as few are dependable year-round. As with the Kofas, the region has four-wheel-drive routes as well as foot-trails. Cross-country walks are also enjoyable.

As well as the myriad varieties of cactus found in southwestern Arizona, the national monument contains numerous organ pipe cactus— the only place where they grow on this side of the border. The organ pipe is an impressive cactus. Numerous graceful, spiky arms grow out and up from a single stem. The tallest stems may reach a height of fifteen to twenty feet, drawing energy from almost constant sunlight and storing moisture within the thick stems. They grow only on south-facing hillsides.

One of the best introductions to the region is Puerto Blanco Drive, a fifty-one-mile loop through the western portion of the national monument. The dirt road crosses valleys where cactus grows thickly and more open country where antelope may regard your approach with curiosity before bounding away. Stark and colorful ranges lift close at hand as well as blue in the distance. One passes an abandoned miner's shack, and, farther on, an old well, windmill, corral, and line shack. Dripping Spring, close to the road, is a cool grotto set back under an overhang from which water drops softly and steadily. There is a deep pond, from which a small stream winds between watercress before disappearing underground. A trail behind the spring leads to the Puerto Blanco, a notch in the white ridge from which one can see out across the Senita Basin to the mountains of Mexico.

After passing through a broad sweep of wild desert country—through ravines, around mountain shoulders and across sandy plains—the road comes finally to Quitobaquito, a pool shaded by large cottonwood trees, an oasis visible from miles away. Here desert pupfish live in the spring-fed stream which enters the pond.

From this remote, lovely spot, where quail call in the glow of the rising sun, the loop road leads back to monument headquarters. In the other direction trails lead off toward secret springs, old mines—the immensities of an exquisite and little-known region.

Guide Notes for DESERT TRAILS AND TALES

LOCATION—Southwestern Arizona.

ACCESS—From Interstate Highways 8 and 10, U.S. Highway 95 between Quartzsite and Yuma, Arizona Highway 85 between Gila Bend and Lukeville.

GETTING AROUND—Although there are a few secondary roads in the region, most routes are suitable only for four-wheel-drive vehicles. In Organ Pipe Cactus National Monument and the Kofa Game Refuge it is prohibited to drive vehicles off designated routes. There are numerous foot-trails in the area, but most are primitive and not maintained. Some are old Indian trails, others were wagon routes or were used by prospectors. Float trips can be made down the Colorado River from Ehrenberg or Palo Verde to Picacho State Recreation Area. Water is a prime consideration away from the river, as there are few dependable springs or *tinajas* in the region. Always inquire locally before setting out on an extended trip. November to May is the most comfortable time in the desert—the summer months are scorching. Although the threat of rattlesnakes is generally exaggerated, one should always carry a snakebite kit. On the other hand, the solitude of the region can pose a real danger should one turn an ankle, become lost, or miscalculate water or provision rations. Always let someone know where you are headed and how long you figure to be gone.

CAMPING—Except at Organ Pipe Cactus National Monument, Picacho State Recreation Area, and a couple of other places along the river, there are no developed campsites in this area. In selecting a campsite one should avoid arroyo bottoms, inviting as they might seem. One might bed down under a clear sky and still be hit with a flash flood from a distant storm before morning. Shade is desirable for a campsite, as is proximity of dead wood for good burning from desert growth such as ironwood, palo verde, or mesquite. Some sort of small trail-stove may come in handy. One should always carefully check out the ant situation before laying out a sleeping bag. Although I have never used nor missed a tent while camping in the desert, some folks like to take along a light, self-standing model for wind protection and to keep critters away. Although the chances are probably a million to one, snakes have crawled into sleeping bags when seeking warmth. A warm sleeping bag is essential for winter camping.

SUPPLIES—If traveling in a four-wheel-drive vehicle, stash extra gas, water, and groceries for emergencies. Carry a shovel. In desert country freeze-dried foods are not weight-savers, as one has to pack in extra water to reconstitute them. The freeze-dried dinners which are prepared merely by pouring hot water into their cardboard and plastic packages do simplify pot cleanup where water is scarce. Likewise, if you carry in canned goods, you can avoid unnecessary washing up by eating out of the can hobo-style. Be sure to pack all containers out—things deteriorate slowly on the desert. Fresh fruit, such as oranges and apples, is mighty good in dry country, and bacon goes a long way.

Water is crucial. The amount of water one needs to be comfortable, or even to survive, increases dramatically with each ten degrees of temperature. In other words, any rule-of-thumb as to an amount to carry in this desert might be misleading. Once again, talk to rangers at either Organ Pipe Cactus National Monument or the Kofa Game Refuge office in Yuma before setting off into the backcountry. One should bring an ample supply of salt tablets and take them as directed.

If you are planning to use trail foods you should pick them up before heading into this region. Everyday groceries, of course, are available at the larger towns such as Blythe, Yuma, and Ajo.

SPECIAL FEATURES—A wide variety of plant and animal life, some of which are all but unique to this region. Steep and eroded mountain ranges. Relics of ranching and mining. Thousands of acres of wild and seldom-visited country.

SOURCES OF INFORMATION—Superintendent, Kofa Game Refuge, 356 First Street, Yuma, Arizona (P. O. Box 1032, Yuma, 85364); Superintendent, Organ Pipe Cactus National Monument, Box 38, Ajo, Arizona 85321.

EIGHT

The Sierra Madre (Mexico)

The Sierra Madre Occidental stretches for some eight hundred miles through northwestern Mexico, a tangle of thorny and forested slopes and deeply slashed canyons that averages 130 miles wide and 6,000 to 10,000 feet in elevation. The central basin of northern Mexico slopes gradually up to the Continental Divide much like the back of a slowly building wave, then breaks sharply to the west, where the escarpment drops quickly to the Pacific coastal plain. The mountain summits are, for the most part, blocky, easy knobs of weathered rock, yet the rivers that drain their western slopes have carved chasms of great depth and almost vertical walls. The region is like a leaf pattern of knife-edge ridges that has been cataclysmically turned upside down. Four canyons in the Barranca del Cobre area are thought to be as deep or deeper than the Grand Canyon. No one knows for sure; no one has ever accurately mapped this country.

The first time I came into the Sierra Madre was back in the late 1950s, with three friends in a jeep. We were students at the University of New Mexico in Albuquerque. Maps showed that the Sierra Madre was crossed only by the highway connecting Durango with Mazatlán. Another student, however, had driven a road that roughly followed the Chihuahua al Pacífico Railroad from Chihuahua to Creel, far back in the mountains. Not far from Creel the rails reached the crest of the Sierra, at Sanchez, and construction was in full swing upon the 122 miles of roadbed that tortuously dropped seven thousand feet to the seaplain. One might, he surmised, be able to cross the mountains by using a combination of old wagon tracks, logging roads, and the bed of the railroad itself, since ties and rails had yet to be placed along most stretches.

We decided to try it. Instead of entering Mexico on the main highway at El Paso and Ciudad Juarez, or even the secondary road south of Columbus, New Mexico, a dusty border village once raided by Pancho Villa, we decided to approach Mexico from the extreme southwestern corner of New Mexico. Here, long valleys with dry lakes, isolated ranches, and lots of dust devils are bordered by gaunt mountains pocked with prospect holes and occasional mines that once were worked for a decade or two. There is a feeling of good raw country here, of remoteness; little has changed from when the last defiant Apache bands rode through, eluding the U.S. Army Cavalry. As I recall it, Antelope Wells, the border crossing, was a house trailer upon the American side and two whitewashed adobe structures on the Mexican. The trailer was the home and office of the American border official; the largest of the adobes served the same function for his Mexican counterparts. The second adobe, we were told later on, was a small and certainly isolated bagnio. The three- to five-girl staff apparently catered to lonely ranchers on either side of the border.

Below the border the dusty road wound through hill country spiky with cactus and creosote and across bunch grass prairie into Janos, a quiet town that was once an important outpost of the Spanish empire.

The country became greener as we entered the Casas Grandes Valley south of Janos. There were irrigated fields and a number of orchards. The town of Colonia Dublan, in contrast to the adobe villages we had passed through, had Victorian brick houses with climbing roses and white window trims. Colonia Dublin, like nearby Colonia Juarez, was settled in the 1880s by Mormons fleeing federal authorities in Utah who took a dim view of polygamy. It is estimated there were ten thousand Mormons living in the region until Pancho Villa drove them out. Some eight hundred of their descendants have now moved back into the area and are industrious and successful farmers.

We drove on through Nueva Casas Grandes to the Casas Grandes ruins—an adobe-brick pueblo similar to those found in the southwestern United States. The ruins were situated on a ridge with sweeping views of the surrounding area. That evening we rolled out sleeping bags on a level spot not far from the ruins. It was a busy place. All evening people passed by on foot or on horses and mules. Once a burro train carrying firewood almost walked over us. The next morning we awakened to find a *soldado* standing next to our jeep as if guarding it. We exchanged greetings, rather stiff on his part, and then we rolled up our bags preparatory to leaving.

"Alto!" He clamped a hand upon the tailgate of the vehicle as if to hold it there by force if necessary. It seems we had inadvertently camped on a wide spot in a principal trail between villages—a serious offense, apparently. The soldier, face stern as a spade, muttered something about jail that we could not quite make out, and then made it very clear he would

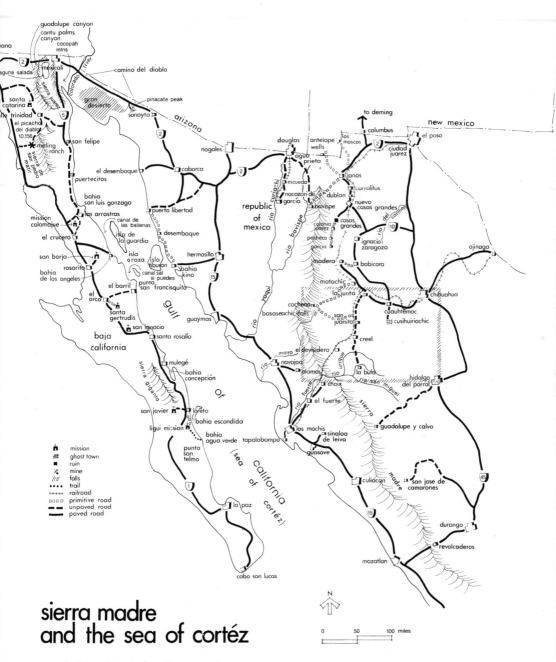

guadalupe canyon
cantu palms
canyon
cocopah
mtns
juana
camino del diablo
laguna salada
mexicali
sierra juarez
colorado river
santa
catarina
gran
desierto
pinacate peak
alte trinidad
el picacho
del diablo
10,156
5
sonoyta
arizona
to deming
new mexico
columbus
el paso
meling
ranch
san felipe
nogales
douglas
antelope
wells
los
moscos
2
ciudad
juarez
sierra de
san pedro
mártir
el desemboque
caborca
agua
prieta
janos
puertecitos
2
rio curiachi
escueda
corralitos
bahia
san luis gonzaga
nacozari de
garcia
dublan
nuevo
casas grandes
rio del carmen
mission
calamajue
puerto libertad
republic
rio bavispe
bavispe
colonia
juarez
casas
grandes
10
el crucero
canal de
las ballenas
desemboque
pacheco
garcia
ignacio
zaragoza
ojinaga
san borja
isla de
la guardia
babicora
bahia
de los angeles
isla
o raza
isla
tiburon
hermosillo
madera
rosarita
bahia
kino
matachic
el barril
canal sal
si puedes
15
cochena
la junta
chihuahua
el
arco
punta
san franciscuito
guaymas
basaseachic falls
san
juanito
cuauhtemoc
cusihuiriachic
santa
gertrudis
san ignacio
rio yaqui
creel
baja
california
santa rosalia
rio fuerte
mayo el devisidero
navajoa
la bufa
rio urique
mulegé
bahia
concepción
alamos
choix
rio san miguel
hidalgo
del parral
san javier
loreto
el fuerte
sierra
ligui mission
bahia escondida
bahia
agua verde
topolobampo
los mochis
sinaloa
de leiva
guadalupe y calvo
punta
san
telmo
guasave
45
1
culiacan
san jose de
camarones
madre
la paz
15
durango
revolcaderos
cabo san lucas
mazatlan

gulf

of

california

(sea of
cortéz)

**sierra madre
and the sea of cortéz**

a more detailed map of the region shown within
shaded borders will be found on a later page

N

0   50   100 miles

mission
ghost town
ruin
mine
falls
trail
railroad
primitive road
unpaved road
paved road

accompany us back to Nueva Casas Grandes. He perched on the tailgate of the jeep, rifle between his knees.

At best, it appeared we would cool our heels in the police department for a while—or shell out an exorbitant fine we could ill afford. At worst, we might spend our second night in Mexico in the lockup. It occurred to one of us that we knew a man who had been in charge of a dig at the ruins. Possibly he was still there. The *soldado,* although skeptical, allowed me to hike back to the ruins to check, and as luck would have it, our anthropologist friend was indeed there. He and our captor spoke in rapid Spanish for a few minutes.

"Legally, it appears to be a very complicated matter," observed our friend. "Our man here realizes you would be inconvenienced by a delay. He has offered to take care of the matter. I'd say a consideration might be in order—um, say forty pesos."

And so we forked over our first *mordita* ("bite"), although certainly not the last. Official pronouncements to the contrary, small bribes are still an acceptable way of expediting things when dealing with minor officials in Mexico. The average Mexican, official or otherwise, barely makes a living wage. The *mordita* has none of the aura of corruption that surrounds a bribe on our side of the border, where the transaction usually involves lots of money and high officials. The *mordita,* when red tape occasions it, might be likened to slipping a couple of dollars to a head waiter in order to insure a good table.

For the record, I should hasten to add that in all the innumerable camps I have since made in the Sierra Madre, I have never been bothered by police, bandits, or other annoying folk. There are certain considerations one should keep in mind when camping in Mexico, but more of this later.

From Casas Grandes we drove south through foothill country, where there were grassy valleys rimmed by piney ridges. Below the town of Ignacio Zaragoza we entered the old Babícora Ranch, once a cattle empire of better than a million acres. George Hearst originally purchased the ranch through his friendship with President Porfirio Diaz. Later, when ownership had passed to his son William, and revolution raged across Chihuahua, Pancho Villa attacked the ranch and ran off several thousand head of cattle.

William Randolph Hearst was outraged. Hearst newspapers carried inflammatory headlines, such as "BANDITS JOIN CARRANZA TO FIGHT U.S." and "MEXICANS PREPARE FOR WAR WITH U.S." A story in the New York *Journal* of June 19, 1916, stated that ". . . We are no longer planning to catch this bandit or that. We are GOING INTO MEXICO. And as far as we GO, *we'll stay."* Fortunately for our relations with Mexico, American leaders were a good deal more concerned about war clouds gathering in Europe than Hearst's problems as an absentee landlord.

In 1953 the Babícora ranch was sold to the Mexican government for 2.5 million dollars.

A gray-haired woman named María who lives in the village of Babícora showed us the old Hearst ranch house, now dilapidated and partitioned off into offices. Only three are still in use; they are sparsely furnished cubicles with old tables, chairs, and filing cabinets. María told us she had once worked as a maid in the ranch house. She led us into the patio, which was surrounded by a high adobe wall in which shards of broken glass had been imbedded to keep out prowlers during more prosperous times. Now they guarded only a dusty yard where weeds pushed up at the edges. There had been a lovely garden here once, we were told. Passing one of the unused rooms, I peered in through a dingy window and saw a long, elaborately carved table standing alone in the center of what was once a dining room.

The Casas Grandes ruins, an archaeological mystery at the fringe of Mexico's Sierra Madre.

Although some of the villagers recall with a certain nostalgia how resplendent the old place once was, all celebrate the twelfth of August with gusto—the date the ranch was reclaimed by the government and divided into *colonias* for the people. The departure of the foreign landlords is celebrated with dances, fireworks, and a rodeo.

From Babícora we followed a rough, rutted track that twisted its way over a volcanic ridge where there were thick stands of pine. Ravens flapped lazily out of oak thickets. There are over a hundred varieties of oak in the Sierra Madre—great campfire wood, hot and slow-burning. We descended to the smoky logging town of Madera and followed a graded road south through high plateau grasslands.

At La Junta the road began to climb a series of wooded arroyos. La Junta itself was, and still is, an important railroad town. The main trunk of the Chihuahua al Pacífico, first visualized by a man who wished to link his Utopian colony at Topolobampo with the markets of Kansas City, passes through La Junta. A branch line runs in an arc to the northeast, passing through Madera and Nueva Casas Grandes *en route* to Ciudad Juarez. At La Junta we paused at the station as the train to Creel briefly halted there. Knowledgeable Mexican passengers flocked to the open vestibules at the end of each car, buying *tamales* and *quesadillas* from old women with baskets and oranges from youths who clamored of the delights of their fruit. People leaning out of the vestibules exchanged gossip, quips, and ribald stories with people on the platform. Lively. Noisy. Fun. The entire stop was probably for no more than five minutes, and yet all manner of exchanges had taken place.

Our dirt road more or less paralleled the railroad until we reached the logging center of San Juanito. From there it took a wide detour through stands of pine, fir, and madrone—the beautiful, contorted tree whose bark is the color of burgundy wine. In most of the mountain villages we passed through there were no restaurants as such, but we soon learned that there would always be at least one private home which would serve beer, soft drinks, and a simple, hearty meal to travelers. It was a rocky road, traveled almost exclusively by logging trucks. At one point we blew a tire. Our spare was already flat and we had not seen anyone for hours. We set up camp, figuring it might be a long wait before a logging truck could be flagged down for a lift. The first vehicle to appear was a truck hauling supplies and about twenty-five people—men, women, and children. The driver, a jaunty youth with a hairline mustache, insisted upon fixing the tire upon the spot. He had the proper tools and did it. Meanwhile the rest of the people had swarmed out of the back of the truck. The men gathered firewood; the women got tortillas and beans together. We happened to have a bottle of tequila, which we passed around to the men, and also some jelly beans, which were enjoyed by the women and children. The tire was fixed, a meal was enjoyed. The truck driver would accept no money for his work on the tire, not to speak of the three hours he had lost. One of us had an old jackknife and offered it to him. He accepted it with pleasure.

This incident is typical of most of my experiences with the Mexican people. They are among the most friendly and generous souls to be found anywhere. As with all cultures, the Mexicans have their share of sharks, deadbeats, wheedlers, thugs, and panderers of every persuasion. Fortunately, however, these buzzards concentrate their particular hustles upon places where well-heeled *gringos* flock, such as Acapulco, Mexico City, Cozumel, Cuernavaca, Puerto Vallarta and the like. But once away from the tourist traps, most travelers will find the Mexican people to be *muy simpático*. They are, indeed, the ultimate treasure of the Sierra Madre.

The logging road came back to the railroad at Bocoyna. From here we drove fifteen miles eastward to Sisoguichic, where Jesuits founded a mission in the late seventeenth century. By and large, the Tarahumara Indians who lived in that region took to the Catholic faith, but in much the

A Tarahumara Indian family home at Sisoguichic.

same spirit as all Indian people throughout the Land of Clear Light have been converted. Christ and the Virgin Mary were placed beside and mingled with ancient tribal deities; the Holy Ghost was simply another god with the wind.

The Tarahumaras carve violins out of native woods, and their large, two-headed hand drums have beaded wildcat gut across their back, creating a snare drum effect. With an old, toothless Tarahumara man as guide and companion, we prowled the region, ostensibly seeking violins or drums, but really just walking around, looking and enjoying. At one point a youth loped past us, his sandals made from cutoff automobile tires, leaving a tread upon the trail. The Tarahumaras are perhaps the finest natural distance-runners in the world. They are capable of jogging a deer to death; in tribal contests they have been known to run for more than forty-eight hours without stopping. Our old man, although never breaking into a canter, moved right along. Before approaching a divide in the piney hills he would pick up a rock, carry it to the crest, and deposit it on the cairn of rocks which would be there. Each rock thus deposited is a prayer of thanksgiving, an expression of joy at being yet alive and not a spirit, which the Tarahumaras believe take the form of butterflies by day and bats by night.

Back at the mission school in Sisoguichic, a novitiate priest showed us the boys' dormitory, where well-made beds and neat lockers stood with military precision. "Most of the children who stay with us for any length of time," the priest commented, "are Mexican. The Tarahumara children come, often half-starved. They are very watchful. Some, I think, are very bright—could be good students. But after a short while, they get restless. They leave. They are like wild birds."

Not far beyond Creel, which is a trading center for the Tarahumaras, the rails ended and we started down the serpentine road which more or less followed the route of the difficult section of the railroad—the abysmal drop from the crest of the sierra to coastal plain. When completed, there would be eighty-nine tunnels and forty-eight bridges.

Most of the tunnels, we discovered, had already been blasted, although no ties had been laid down as yet. It is a curious experience to drive through a long tunnel, cut high and narrow for trains, guided by your headlights. We always half-expected to suddenly hear the shriek of a whistle and see the rolling Cyclops eye of an express hurtling toward us. Of course, there was never that—just the darkness, the feeling of the millions of tons of mountain over our heads. Occasionally a large rock would drop from the roof. The tunnels were very new and little shoring had been done as yet. The mouth of blue marking the end of the tunnel was always welcome.

None of the bridges had been completed. Consequently, our road made frequent, lengthy traverses around arroyo heads. Sometimes we took a wrong fork and wound up in hamlets where everyone would turn out to gaze and touch the jeep with wonderment, as if they had never seen such a contraption. Perhaps they hadn't. Villagers such as these were usually rather shy around the two big, bumbling, Nordic-type males in our party, but related immediately to the petite, dark-haired woman with us. She was, in fact, part Chippewa Indian and did not know a word of Spanish. She would smile; the children would run off to return with beautiful pebbles, wildflowers, or, in one case, the skull of a fox. And she, in turn, doled out the last of the jelly beans.

In one place the jeep trail wound high above a steep-sided gorge. Far below there was a large, ruined hacienda. As we watched, a flock of green parrots swept out of a neglected citrus orchard and wheeled around the broken adobe walls. Not far beyond, we showered in a waterfall the color of pale turquoise. At the Rio Fuerte, now spanned by an impressive railroad bridge, a narrow bed of concrete had been laid across the river during some dry season to facilitate a ford. The water was up when we started across, however, and the current pushed strongly at the base of the jeep. Had the engine died, there was a good possibility we would have been swept off the concrete apron into the fast water below. The jeep, cantankerous and prone to stalling under the best of conditions, bored through the fast, deep water (slopping over our boots at one point) as if it had been created solely for this supreme effort. On the other side, dripping muddy water, it sputtered and died.

Eventually we reached Los Mochis, the agricultural center which was to be the Pacific terminus of the railroad, and hopped a crowded local bus to Topolobampo on the Sea of Cortéz. Topolobampo is a small fishing port, perched upon a cactus-studded hillside that drops sharply to the waters of a sheltered bay. A fine village to prowl. The good beaches, however, must be reached by boat. We ambled down to the wharf and hired a fisherman to take us out to an island beach in his skiff.

There, on smooth, white sand across from Topolobampo, we sipped Bohemia beer and watched a brace of sleek porpoises finning in the bay. We talked about the Sierra Madre—"Got to go back there," we said. And have, many times since.

One of the most important keys to enjoying the backcountry of the Sierra Madre is to be able to communicate with the people. Some knowledge of Spanish, even if unpolished, is important. Carry a pocket dictionary and don't hesitate to haul it out frequently if needed. Even if you know little Spanish and sometimes get your tenses hopelessly snarled, people are usually responsive and helpful if you make an effort. Most of them will know a little English, and with the help of gestures one can usually communicate to a degree. An occasional blunder is to be expected, although it can be embarrassing.

One Thanksgiving, hankering after a suckling pig for our campfire spit, I startled my companions and some men who were pitching hay at an isolated *ranchito* in the Barranca del Cobre country by jovially stating that *"Mi compañeros y yo queremos una lucha"* ("My friends and I would like a fight"). The men stiffened and a couple of pitchforks tilted defensively in our direction before one of my companions straightened things out by explaining we were in the market for *luchón* ("suckling pig") rather than a *lucha* ("fight"). The pig, I might add, roasted slowly over madrone wood, was superb.

Unless they are hunting or fishing, most people who head into the outback on our side of the border would never dream of hiring a guide. There is much to recommend using guides for the Sierra Madre. They are inexpensive, for one thing: local farmers or their sons will generally hire out for between thirty and fifty pesos a day. It is customary for you to provide a guide's food for the journey, as well as to advance some money he can leave with his wife or family. A pack burro will run five or ten pesos extra a day. (There are about twelve pesos to the dollar at the current rate of exchange.)

One will find a guide the same way as anything else in Mexico—ask around and wait to see what happens.

The Sierra Madre, while wild country, is not a wilderness in the sense that we are accustomed to. Seventy-five percent of Mexico's people live in isolated family units or in hamlets of less than two hundred population. Even in the most rugged and remote corners, there are Mexican and Indian *ranchitos*. Consequently, the backcountry is a maze of paths. Maps are highly inaccurate. It is easy to get lost, and in many places one has to know where to look for sweetwater springs or running creeks. One of the best reasons for hiring a guide is that while most people of the sierra backcountry are friendly, they tend to be wary of strangers. In some areas the Indians have seen few, if any, Americans except on occasional journeys to distant villages where they trade. When they see some very large, odd people with bright orange and blue humps thrusting up from their backs to a height as tall as, or taller than, their heads, as like as not jabbering in a loud, strange language, the Indians do what any sensible folk would do under similar circumstances: get everyone inside and firmly secure the door until the interlopers have gone.

Your guide will be a reassurance to them. You may be invited to draw up a stump and have coffee (the Tarahumara Indians use sections of wood for seats. Balancing upon these slender pedestals of hospitality can be tricky). It is often possible to purchase simple, satisfying meals—beans, rice, and eggs—at these *ranchitos*. If you are traveling with several friends, you may want to negotiate for a *cabrito* ("young goat").

Your guide will probably make up a batch of tortillas for himself each evening. One should definitely consider buying him some extra *harina de maíz* ("corn flour") at the outset, and paying him a little more to make some for you and your party. Tortillas are superb with beans and *carne seca* ("dried meat"), and complement everything from marmalade to chicken stew.

Finally, a guide affords a certain amount of protection. There are few bandits of the crossed *bandolero* variety in the sierras today, and those that are around seem interested in rural banks and mining-company payrolls rather than hikers. However, should you spot someone with a businesslike rifle in the backcountry, as a friend of mine once did, it is advisable to merge quickly with the landscape. Any rifle larger than twenty-two caliber is prohibited in Mexico. Although bandits as such are an almost nonexistent danger these days, a good many people in the hills of Mexico distill tequila without paying the government tax. Like our own moonshiners, they are touchy folks, and it is advisable to give their illicit operations a wide berth. The same holds true for the numerous farmers whose basic cash crop is marijuana. For all they know, you may be an American plain-clothes narcotics agent. A local guide will be able to route you away from potentially sticky encounters.

July and August constitute the rainy season in the Sierra Madre. It can be a muddy, miserable time to prowl the backcountry, although waterfalls and river rapids are spectacular. Mid-fall or mid-spring is, in my opinion, the best time to visit the Sierra Madre. At those times it is neither too cold upon the canyon rims (which are from six thousand to eight thousand feet in elevation) nor too hot in the depths of the canyons, which are several thousand feet lower and in a tropical vegetation zone. Most of the year precipitation is slight. Insects, except during the summer months, are mostly quiescent. Consequently, a tent of any sort is about the most worthless item one can lug into the Sierra Madre, unless desired for privacy. A good water-repellent poncho will suffice for what few brief showers one will encounter. A warm sleeping bag is important, as it is cold in the high country during the winter months, and sometimes there are snow flurries.

Freeze-dried and dehydrated foods are not the most practical thing for trips into the Sierra Madre. For the exorbitant amount of money one would lay out for such specialty items, one would be better off renting a pack burro and loading it with fresh meat, eggs, fruit, vegetables, and the like. If you opt against a burro, be sure to pick up a package of *refritos rápidos* ("instant refried beans") at a supermarket in Ciudad Juarez, Nogales, or Chihuahua—great stuff. It is handy to bring at least one plastic egg carton (available at all backpacking stores) to Mexico. Every *ranchito* in the Sierra Madre has a few chickens scratching around the yard, and one can usually purchase fresh eggs hither and yon. Your Spanish dictionary will identify eggs as *huevos*. If you ask for *huevos* in the Sierra Madre, you will probably receive calf testicles, if they have them, and should you be a woman or a man with a woman, the query will stimulate much ribald amusement on the part of any Mexican men within earshot. In this part of the country eggs are referred to as *blanquillos* ("little white ones").

Getting to good walking country is fairly easy. One can, of course, drive, and I would recommend a sturdy vehicle with high clearance. When you leave your car to head into the outback, it is sensible to ask someone to look after it. In Mexico, where a person will protect someone else's property out of hospitality or for a very insignificant sum, it is assumed that an American who simply abandons a car for a period of time must be so wealthy that the loss of some hubcaps, a battery, or even a transmission would be too trivial to even concern him.

By and large, Mexico is a very poor country. Few people have cars, and consequently the public transportation system is excellent. Sleek, large buses modeled after our Greyhounds hurtle between major cities. Shabbier (but often more interesting) buses serve the out-of-the-way places. In Mexico, almost without fail, where there is a road, however marginal, there is a bus that goes there. To find out what goes where when, one must go to a Mexican bus terminal and ask. Your home town travel agent probably knows as much about backcountry Mexico as about the dark side of the moon.

Some of the most interesting and remote villages in the Sierra Madre can be reached by small planes that bring mail and freight from the Chihuahua airport. Schedules are as flexible as salt-water taffy, and one should go to the airport to check them out. Letters and phone calls are a waste of hand and voice; nothing is ever really scheduled or organized in Mexico, although lots of people bustle about in various uniforms to give the appearance of it, Gilbert-and-Sullivan style—a major reason I am so fond of that country. Very little is fed into computers.

Trains are possibly the best way to get back into the Sierra Madre. The Chihuahua al Pacífico Railroad, over whose uncompleted roadbed I first crossed the Sierra Madre, now links Ojinaga on the Texas border with Los Mochis by way of Chihuahua. A branch of the line loops up from La Junta through Madera and Nueva Casas Grandes to Ciudad Juarez. On the western slope a mixed passenger and freight train makes biweekly runs to the mountain town of Nacozari de Garcia from Agua Prieta, immediately south of Douglas, Arizona. On the main line of the Chihuahua al Pacífico, the best places to get out and start walking are Bocoyna, Creel, Divisidero, Cuiteco, Temoris, and El Fuerte. On the northeastern branch, the best places to hop out of the train with your gear are Nueva Casas Grandes, Madera, or Juan Mata Ortiz (also known as Pearson).

A word of caution—the Chihuahua al Pacífico run from Chihuahua to Los Mochis is one of the most beautiful train rides upon our planet. Yet the food is poor and overpriced. I generally take a basket lunch with barbecued chicken, fresh bread, and the like. I always buy fruit and the *burritos* ("beans and chili wrapped in a tortilla") sold by venders at La Junta, which are excellent.

In the mountain villages of the Sierra Madre, the ghost of Pancho Villa is very much alive. To hear the stories that old-timers tell on the *ranchitos,* the mustachioed revolutionary must have had some sort of contact with every man, woman, and child in the backcountry.

The silver-haired woman in a black dress had the sort of matronly warmth one associates with Midwestern farm grandmothers, porch swings, embroidery samplers, lemonade, and freshly baked sugar cookies. In her home, however, there was a curious melange of mementos: an antique clock sprouting a bronze lion's head, pith helmets, a sword inscribed "When this sword bites you there is no remedy for you in any drug-store," an exquisite silver tea service, a human tooth in a velveteen jeweler's box. Back in the patio, the bullet-riddled shell of a black 1919 Dodge rested upon frayed tires. From the wall of the elegant sitting room, a mustachioed face stares jauntily from a photograph, *bandoleros* crisscrossing his chest— Pancho Villa, who was once the master of this house and most of northern Mexico.

There are those who say Pancho Villa was one of Mexico's greatest revolutionaries, others who assert he was a Mexican Robin Hood, and still others who regard his career as that of an opportunistic bandit. There is probably some truth in all of these views.

Señora Luz Corral de Villa, who still occupies the bullet-pocked mansion in Chihuahua she shared with her husband fifty years ago, possesses an oil-on-velvet painting of the late President Kennedy, as do many people of Mexican descent in the United States. She often likens the assassination of her husband to that of President Kennedy. "Both of them were crucified for the same reasons. They were too powerful with the people. Too popular. They were very similar in their beliefs. . . ."

Señora Villa was only a girl of seventeen when Pancho Villa and some of his band reined up at her mother's store, demanding free supplies. At his first sight of the girl, he was captivated. As Señora Villa recalls: "My mother told him to get his revolution over, come back and get acquainted, and if we wanted to get married then, we could."

Perhaps not even Villa himself could have predicted how quickly his revolution would spread. Peasants by the thousands flocked to join his forces, as well as middle- and upper-class people who felt oppressed by the existing regime, or at least saw which way the wind was blowing. Federal garrisons fell like dominoes.

Villa was beginning to gain financial support and even recruits from the American side of the border. In one of the more bizarre footnotes of history, Villa contracted with an American company, Mutual Films, to let them make a documentary of his revolution. For twenty-five thousand dollars and a cut of the profits, he agreed to battle only during the daylight hours. Frequently during the filming, attacks were delayed until cameras were in position, or the lighting and angles right. It was probably the only serious war ever waged on a film shooting-schedule.

In due course Villa was to sit proudly in the president's chair in Mexico City, side by side with Emiliano Zapata, the revolutionary from the south of Mexico. And he would return to woo and wed the girl he had once met in her mother's store.

His fall was almost as meteoric as his rise. A counterrevolution, led by his former allies, Generals Obregón and Carranza, soon had his dwindling army on the run. Forced back into the Sierra Madre, Villa crossed the mountains to make a daring attack on the Carranza garrison at Agua Prieta. But the opposition had learned of the proposed night attack, and in the blinding glare of giant searchlights most of Villa's troops were cut down. From across the border, Americans with field glasses watched the bloody spectacle much as they might have taken in a bullfight.

His battles over, Villa lived peaceably on a hacienda until he was riddled with bullets while riding through the streets of Hidalgo del Parral in 1923.

One might imagine the widow of such a man to be a recluse, yet quite the opposite is true. Señora Villa herself sometimes guides tourists through the two rooms of the mansion which are open to the public much of the time. The entire building has over fifty rooms and several secret passageways. When talking about the past to these travelers, Señora Villa's patter in English reminds one of a singer who has perfectly mastered a song in a foreign language, yet understands none of the words.

". . . and this picture is of Pancho Villa with two of his generals; here, a telephone used many times during the revolution . . . we have many people come here from the United States, France, Africa, Venezuela. . . ." The señora leaned upon her cane with one hand and gestured toward various mementos with the other.

One would be greatly mistaken to assume, with sadness, that she is merely a nostalgic record to be wound up and played out for her visitors (who are asked to leave a contribution for the Pancho Villa Museum). In her own room, when the pilgrims from Vera Cruz, London, or Omaha have departed, she is still constantly talking—to whomever is there, or over the telephone. The canned patter is gone, her English more broken. She speaks with a clarity and animation that belies her seventy-eight years. We talked of New Mexico, which she has visited; or some recent additions to her stamp collection; of politics (she dismissed former President Nixon with an elegant gesture of exasperation). Señora Luz de Corral Villa, a figure out of history, is very much a woman of the present.

Back in the patio, the black, bullet-punctured shell of the Dodge sat in shadows. Nearby, two small children laughed and tumbled in sunlight, while brightly colored laundry flapped upon a clothesline.

Nueva Casas Grandes is the gateway to the wild mountain country of the northern Sierra Madre. It can be reached by the northeastern loop of the Chihuahua al Pacífico Railroad, as well as by Highway 2, a paved road connecting Ciudad Juarez with Janos. One can also strike this road by crossing the border between New Mexico and Mexico at Columbus, Los Moscos, or Antelope Wells. Another approach is to take the main highway from Ciudad Juarez toward Chihuahua, and then turn west close to El Sueco. This route cuts across dry, flat rangelands until, abruptly, the road drops into the valley of the Rio del Carmen. The lovely village there, Flores Magon, is set in lush, green fields that border the river.

The Casas Grandes ruins were long thought to be of typical Anasazi and Pueblo cultures whose ruins are scattered throughout the southwestern United States. Comparatively recent excavations, however, have turned up some curious things—stone buildings; metal objects; an elaborate ceremonial life associated with ball courts, pyramids, and suggestions of human sacrifice. All of these things were a part of the Aztec and other cultures of central and southern Mexico. Here, in the foothills of the Sierra Madre, apparently two highly divergent cultures mingled and flourished until they ceased to exist around 1565. There are many riddles posed by this large and curious site.

A few miles by paved road beyond the ruins, one comes to Colonia Juarez, a Mormon settlement with brick buildings and lots of shade trees, things one does not see too much of in this part of the country. The Mormons, although generally first-generation Mexican citizens, still have close ties with Utah. Many of their children are sent to Brigham Young University for their higher education. Their economy focuses upon irrigated farming, and they are known for the quality and quantity of apples, peaches, and poultry produced for the Mexican market.

Prior to the revolution some English entrepreneurs constructed a bed for a railroad to be used for a logging venture. Today a rough road follows the route of this abandoned project south from Colonia Juarez through the village of Pacheco, a good place for setting off on pack trips into the high country. García, thirty-five miles beyond Pacheco, is also deep in the mountains. This is a forested region where there are deer and bear, as well as numerous fast trout streams. Brook trout lurk in the four high-country tributaries of the Bavispe River, and rainbows ranging up to twenty inches can be taken from many streams that tumble down from the divide on either side. There are some beautiful canyons.

One can also approach the northern highlands from the western slope, the state of Sonora. Nacozari de García, seventy-eight miles south of Agua Prieta, can be reached by either train or car. Between Esqueda and Nacozari the route follows the Curiachi River, which snakes its way up San Nicolas Canyon through the old mining town of Hidalgo before reaching Nacozari de García in the highlands. This was once a booming copper-mining center of twenty thousand population. The richer ores have played out and the town today is a sleepy, bypassed place. A two-mile hike brings one to the Montezuma Copper Company's Lake, from which there is a fine view of the valley below. November 7 is fiesta in Nacozari. This date commemorates the death of Jesus García, an engineer who in 1908 backed his locomotive to couple with two flaming boxcars filled with explosives. He pulled them to the edge of town, where they exploded, killing himself and twelve others. The town itself and countless lives were spared by his heroism. From Nacozari there are a number of trails that head into the backcountry.

Like Nacozari, Bavispe is a pleasant place to linger for a couple of days before heading into the Sierra Madre. A dirt road heads southwest from Agua Prieta to San Miguelito, a ranching center, and nearby Bavispe, which is older and more colorful. Both towns are close to the continental divide and good jumpoff places for pack trips. Although few maps show it, a road passable for pickups or other high-clearance, sturdy vehicles con-nects Bavispe with Janos, thus providing continuous linkage from Ciudad Juarez all the way to Tijuana in Baja California.

The Sierra Madre has been, and still is, a storehouse of minerals. During the eighteenth and nineteenth centuries a number of important silver strikes were made in remote and all-but-inaccessible sections of the mountains. The ore, after being crudely refined on the spot, was shipped to Chihuahua by mule-train over a trail that connected Culiacan, Alamos, Batopilas, and other mining centers. Portions of this trail still exist. Near Sisoguichic soft volcanic tufa has been worn several feet into the rock by the hooves of pack animals.

The minerals were brought to Chihuahua for smelting, and now, as then, Chihuahua is the principal gateway to the central section of the Sierra Madre. Chihuahua was founded in 1709. It is a pleasant university city, with clean, wide streets and a number of imposing churches and other colonial buildings. A historical mural that covers the inside walls of the federal building is impressive, as are the mineral exhibits housed in the ornate mansion that once belonged to a silver magnate. The mansion is but a short walk from the home of Señora Luz de Villa. A bit of prowling will uncarth several unpretentious, inexpensive, and excellent eateries, such as Tio Pepe's, which features *cabrito,* "barbecued kid," and Casa Carlos, whose specialty is *comida corrida,* a number of dishes served family style. For a couple of dollars one can gorge on the likes of chicken soup with lime juice, seafood *paella,* baked pork chops, chicken mole, fresh fruit, and, of course, the inevitable stack of fresh, hot tortillas. The bar of the Hotel Victoria is a good place to strike up conversation with old miners and ranchers, most of whom have great anecdotes about the Sierra Madre once you get them going. Chihuahua is a pleasant place to spend some time before heading into the interior. One can stock up on provisions at the inexpensive, extensive public market.

The landscape west of Chihuahua is of arid, rolling hills—grazing country—until one reaches the vicinity of Cuauhtémoc, which is surrounded by a steppe extensively farmed by the thousands of Mennonites who have emigrated to the region from Canada. Most of the Mennonites live in small communities, *colonias,* where the only concessions to the twentieth century seem to be tin roofs, windmills, tractors, and spotless cheese-making apparatus. Their cheese, *queso Mennonito,* is excellent and

The Sierra Madre: a view from the west.

of no risk to the health, which cannot be said of many Mexican dairy products. The cheese can be purchased in most of the larger villages in the Sierra Madre. One often passes a Mennonite family heading to or from town in buckboards or springwagons, the men ruddy and fair-complex- ioned, wearing bib overalls and straw hats, the women usually in long, dark dresses and black veils.

If you are driving, a side trip to Cusihuiriachic is interesting. The town, which strings along a narrow canyon several miles south of Cuauhté- moc, is over 250 years old. When I first visited "Cusi," as local people call it, dusk was becoming night. Although there were a couple of burros and a few pigs in the long, single street, the houses and stores were all lightless. The place seemed completely deserted until, after passing an ancient, imposing church, we came to an adobe house whose windows glowed with the soft light of kerosene lamps. We stopped and talked to the occupants, a family whose chief income came from grazing flocks of goats. When we asked about the age of the town, the gnarled grandfather leaned forward and remarked that the town was there before he was born, and that he was one hundred years old. We were told there were only about fifty people still living in Cusi. Historians, we later learned, estimate that the population was better than ten thousand at several times during silver booms over the past two centuries. Pancho Villa used Cusi silver for his revolutionary pesos. Our host remarked that many people had been driven out by flash floods from time to time. "The last big one was in September of 1964," he told us in soft Spanish, "but there was almost no one left then. The water just filled empty rooms. And washed away some walls."

Both road and railroad fork at La Junta. Some sixty miles west of La Junta a tributary of the Rio Mayo cuts a straight, deep channel to the lip of an immense cliff and plunges off into space. The sheer drop is 1010 feet, making Basaseachic Falls the highest single jump waterfall in North America. From Matachic or San Juanito, both reached by fairly good roads, one can take a jeep or truck through the high country to the hamlet of Concheno, from which it is about a five-hour hike in to the falls. There are a series of jade pools below the falls, which can be reached by a torturous trail from the rim.

This is a region of thick forests and deep canyons, a magnificent solitude of wilderness.

The Barrancas del Tarahumara form the most dramatic backcountry of the Sierra Madre. Here, four tributaries of the Rio Fuerte—the Rio Urique, Chinipas, Batopilas, and San Miguel—may rival the Grand Can- yon of Arizona in depth, although precise mapping has yet to be done. Each of these larger *barrancas* (or "gorges") is, in turn, fed by still other canyon systems, so that an area roughly the size of Connecticut has been carved into profound and exquisite gorges. The uplands between the *bar-*

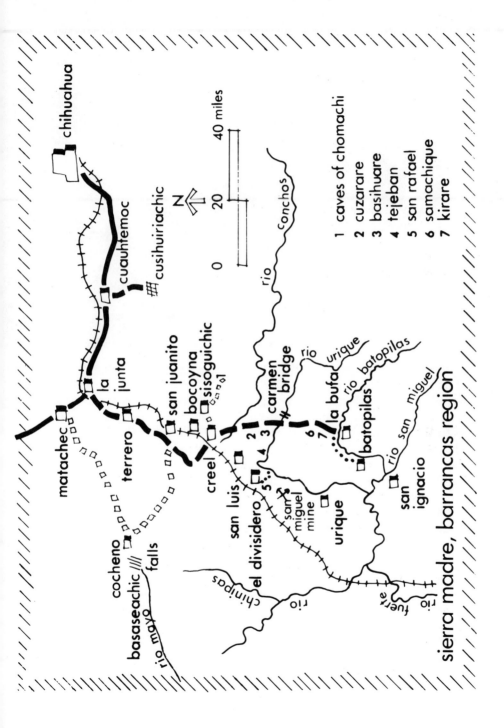

sierra madre, barrancas region

Tarahumara Indians celebrating Holy Week at San Luis, close to the rim of the Barranca Urique in the state of Chihuahua, Mexico.

rancas are from seven to nine thousand feet high, ridges and plateaus of broken volcanic rock serrated into pinnacles and massive, dark stubs worn as the molars of an old bear. There are wide meadows here, too, as well as forests of juniper, ponderosa, and fir, much of them upon isolated islands of land that would take a helicopter fleet or the archangel Gabriel for a successful logging operation.

There are other things: caves of calcite crystals, where a single candle can turn the walls and ceiling into a glittering, strange universe for as long as you would meditate there; remote villages, where during the days leading up to Easter Tarahumara Indians apply ocher and ash streaks to their faces and, stimulated by flutes, drums and homemade violins, ritually dance the struggle between Moors and Christians and then elaborately satirize and in due course condemn to death a *mono* ("monkey"), a life-sized mannequin stuffed with straw, which represents Judas. In the end a *Santo Niño,* an elaborately carved Christ-child of the Spanish colonial period, is carried into a church where no priest has entered for a hundred years or more.

Perhaps the most fascinating aspect of the *barrancas* is the contrast between the conifer forests of the rim and the tropical depths of the canyons, where flocks of parrots sweep over orange, kapok, laurel, and tamarind trees while brilliant butterflies fan around ponds where hot springs issue from joints in the rock. Bamboo thickets and orchids grow beside the streams; orchids and a variety of cactus and thorny shrubs grow upon the slopes. A warm sleeping bag is essential for the rim country from autumn through spring; a day's hike away, at the bottom, you will probably sleep on top of it.

Although there is a variety of wildlife throughout the *barranca* country—deer, some mountain lions, wild turkey, hawks, buzzards, the rare and graceful solitary eagle, and some unique subspecies of fish—there is not a lot of game in the area, nor edible plants. This is because this rugged and seemingly unoccupied country actually has Tarahumara Indians scattered throughout. They are a hungry people, expert hunters and knowledgeable of all plants that give even marginal nourishment or have medicinal properties.

A couple of decades ago their infant mortality rate was staggering; only one out of five Tarahumara babies lived to age five. Expectant mothers would, far from husband or family, grip a tree trunk and squat to deliver the child, and be back at their chores within twenty-four hours. Tarahumara infant mortality is down now, due to the combined efforts of a volunteer corps of concerned American doctors, who fly in by bush plane, and increasing interest on the part of the Mexican government. Yet as infant mortality declines the Tarahumara procreate upon a land that increasingly cannot support them.

One has to feel at least momentary sadness in considering the future of the Tarahumaras, as well as the Navajos upon our side of the border; a healthy, growing tribe will soon reproduce more people than an already sere and taxed environment can support. It becomes a scary sort of altruism when a baby saved will become a beggar in distant places, and a dubious proposition that the glory of Tarahumara Indians would lie in a Ciudad Juarez factory, the quiet grace of a Navajo be satisfied by taking out transmissions in Los Angeles.

I digress.

By and large, the Tarahumara people live in the highlands and drive goats down into the depths of the *barrancas* for grazing. A man's wealth is measured in goats, cattle, and horses, and they are important for a number of reasons, not the least of which is arranging marriages. Tarahumara young men and women are very shy, rarely looking into each other's eyes unless they are ready to couple for life, as do the eagles that wheel upon the convective currents that rise from the canyons.

Anthropologists talk about the Tarahumaras as a shy people, and journalists who have wandered into the area sometimes talk about them as a stiff, stern people that express almost nothing at all.

Bring a frisbee into Tarahumara country, and after a day or two you will find how shy, stiff, and stern the Tarahumaras are. Once they relax around you they will play bamboo flutes, point out plants that will cure earache or delirium, gesture toward a fresh-water otter that you may miss, or point out subleties of rock or plant. They make trustworthy guides and good companions on the trail, although on a long trip one may go through three or four guides, as most know only the country within two or three days' walk of their homes.

Creel, reached by both dirt road and the Chihuahua al Pacífico Railroad, is a trading center for the Tarahumaras and a good departure point for the *barrancas*. There is also an airstrip for small planes. Twenty-seven miles northeast of Creel is Sisoguichic, a mission center in a valley which has been cultivated for three centuries. From the village, where there is a church, a boarding school and a hospital, primitive roads spoke out to small farming villages. Such tracks, although passable by pickups most of the year, turn to deep, thick gumbo after a prolonged rain or snow thaw. Perhaps twenty miles out of Sisoguichic (no maps of any credibility show the road, and when I traveled it, the odometer of the truck was broken) one will come to the Caves of Chomachi, if one has a guide who knows the right turns.

The only written material I have come across on the Caves of Cho-machi declares that they "at times reach a depth of over six miles," and were at times inhabited by Apaches. They were the hiding place, one is told, of Jesuit priests who were guided there by sympathetic Tarahumara Indians during an uprising in the seventeenth century. Sisoguichic, the most remote mission of the region, had been swept by smallpox and measles epidemics in 1693 and 1695. Indian shamans warned that the sound of church bells had provoked the plagues and that baptism spread it. There were curious occurrences the following year: an earthquake in April, the dramatic appearance of a comet in October, and finally an eclipse of the sun. Sisoguichic Mission was destroyed in 1697, although Spanish soldiers and Tarahumaras loyal to the padres recaptured the area the following year and work was started on a new mission.

The remote Caves of Chomachi lie in a beautiful canyon where steep slabs of rimrock rise from bottomlands, where oaks and juniper are scattered along a dry watercourse which has been scoured by flash floods from time to time. In September there are wildflowers—Indian paintbrush and wild species of dahlia and zinnia. What passes for a road leads to within a couple of hours hiking distance of the trackless canyon. Well provisioned, one could probably spend a lot of interesting time down there. Even the

A child of the Tarahumara Indians.

nearest Tarahumara villagers claim to know little of where the canyon comes from or goes to. Although our Mexican guide, whose Tarahumara wife had grown up in a village a few miles away, told us there were a number of caves all along the canyon, he led us to what he claimed was the largest cave.

The rock was volcanic, mostly tufa, and our hopes of probing a Mexican Mammoth Cave or a Chihuahua Carlsbad began to wane. Still, maybe there was limestone underneath. We broke out flashlights and began probing. There were several entrances. Most of them led into huge, angled cracks rather than chambers—it was rather like a movie set for *Journey to the Center of the Earth*. Once back out of the glimmer of daylight, we noted that there were interconnected levels, often honeycombed, as is the way with tufa.

"Hey!" Karl Kernberger, groping along in front of me, switched off his light momentarily. Perhaps twenty feet above us a window opened to a shaft dimly lit by outside light. He flicked his light back on. A notched log, such as were used as ladders in missions throughout northern Mexico, led from our level to the next. It was unclimbable, completely encrusted with the damp mineral deposits of decades, which caused it to gleam like a great pole of pale jade.

"The padres," commented Louis, our guide, "for years, they hid here in this darkness. They built them. Indians who were their friends brought food. After a time, they could see like bats, they say."

After exploring around, it became apparent that all the great cracks pinched out into fissures you could not pass your hand through, or joined each other even if not on the same levels. The "six-mile-deep cave" was probably once a cliff undercut over centuries into a gigantic bell-like dome which in some ancient time collapsed into a pattern of narrow, jumbled cracks, later widened by the slow seep of mineralized water.

Out in the brilliant sunlight, where bees were trafficking between autumn wildflowers, Luis told us that he thought the padres had died at that cave. "It is hard to say," he commented, "who is in which rest. The Tarahumaras in the old days placed their people here, too." He pointed out some shallow alcoves in the tufa cliff above us. "Have a look."

A couple of us scrambled up to one of the few alcoves which was accessible. Inside, obviously once neatly laid out but now only barely ordered, oddly so, were the bones of a small adult or youth.

One of the most interesting roads in all Mexico cuts south from Creel to the semiabandoned mining camp of La Bufa, deep in the Barranca Batopilas. *En route* it passes through Cuzarare, Tarahumara for "place of the eagles," where a recently restored Jesuit mission was abandoned in 1767. A couple of miles away is a waterfall of the same name that is over ninety-five feet high and eighty-five feet wide in the wet season. An attractive place to camp, but frequented, as it is only about fifteen miles from Creel over good dirt road. The next village, Basihuare, twelve miles beyond Cuzarare, is located next to a mountain whose slopes and rock pillars are banded in soft pinks and ivory. In the Tarahumara tongue *busihuare* means "sash." From both of these towns trails lead away into the outback.

Beyond Basihaure the road begins to twist its way down into the gorge of the boulder-choked Rio Urique, the river at Carmen Bridge. From Carmen Bridge one can scramble down to the river, and a brambly slide it is. Once at the river if prepared, one can head upstream or downstream; both are intriguing, both are difficult going. Few people have gone far in either direction. Downstream the river cuts its way to truly formidable depths; the deepest point of its canyon is in the vicinity of El Divisidero.

The mining road loops its way out of the upper end of the Barranca Urique and climbs onto a wooded tableland. One passes through the village of Samachique, where Tarahumaras often engage in marathon footraces in which a hand-carved globe of madrone wood is propelled by competing teams who often run day and night for forty-eight hours. Actually such races are held throughout Tarahumara country whenever the competitive *ejidos,* or regions, decide to do it. Only in Samachique, as near as I can make out, can an outsider come with a reasonable predictability as to when such an event will take place. One should write the Hotel Nuevo in Creel (Hotel Nuevo, Estación Creel, Chihuahua, Mexico) for likely dates.

Several miles of driving through more forest area brings one to Kirare, where there was, last time I was there, a man and wife from the American Bible Institute who had spent better than twenty years attempting to create a written language for the Tarahumaras, who have none, so that they might be able to read the Bible. Kirare is one of the most remote sections of Tarahumara country—many of the Indians in that region rarely have dealings with Mexicans, let alone Americans. Commonly, throughout *barranca* country, these most isolated Tarahumara people have been referred to as "gentiles." When asked about the phrase, everyone in the *barranca* outback apparently has no idea where it came from; my guess is from early Mormon miners.

Not far beyond Kirare the road begins switchbacking down into the Barranca Batopilas, which many consider the deepest of all the *barrancas*. One hairpins down better than five thousand vertical feet and in the depths of the canyon are the shards of vehicles that failed to make this tight turn or that. What remains of La Bufa clings to a slope above the south bank of the Rio Batopilas. Although most of the mines are closed and the town is largely a ghost, one can still buy a few provisions and rent mules at La Bufa. There is a fairly good trail between La Bufa and Batopilas. Even so, there are some narrow places with a lot of drop where it is prudent to lead one's mule if one is riding. The trip is a long single day's walk; a leisurely two days' saunter with ample time for exploring side canyons and taking swims in the river.

Batopilas was once a sizeable mining town, with several thousand population. Only a couple of hundred people live there now. There are magnificent old buildings scattered about, as well as abandoned stone mining structures dating from the eighteenth century. Batopilas, strung along the shallow river which has carved one of the deepest gorges in the continent, is an isolated, peaceful place. It was also one of the richest silver producers in Mexico. The La Nevada Mine produced virgin silver of such purity that it needed virtually no processing. A path of silver bars was once laid out from church to plaza so that a visiting bishop would not be forced to tread the common earth.

Batopilas is a fascinating place. From it, trails lead off into some of the most rugged and seldom-visited parts of the *barranca* country. Here again, a local guide is highly recommended as much of the region is known only to the Indians who live there.

The Barranca Urique is the most challenging of the canyons. The deepest section is often referred to as the Barranca del Cobre ("Copper Canyon"). There are few ways to get down into it, as many tributaries drop over cliffs that can only be negotiated with rock-climbing equipment. In parts of the canyon there are trails; elsewhere the bottom of this immense V-shaped chasm is a jumble of gigantic boulders. As mentioned earlier, one can get to the river by bushwhacking down from Carmen Bridge on the La Bufa road. One can also approach the river from the vicinity of Tejeban, south of Cuzarare.

Passenger trains of the Chihuahua al Pacífico pause at El Divisidero so that folks can gaze out from the rim. My favorite path descends a mile or two south of El Divisidero, where there is a superb view of the Barranca del Cobre. Donato Loya, who runs a small trading post (for Indians, not tourists) close to the trailhead, can help you find a guide and burros to carry gear down to the bottom. It is perhaps fifteen to eighteen miles from the rim to the river—a long, steep downhill if you go for it in a single day. Start early or plan to carry enough water for a dry camp midway down.

The trail drops swiftly along canyon sides that bristle with oak and underbrush. After crossing a wide meadow where there are a few Tarahumara huts, it tops a divide from which one can look down into the inner gorge. From here the vegetation rapidly becomes more subtropical and there are many species of cactus. Close to the river a steep side-path leads to a hot springs where untended orange trees, planted long ago, still thrive.

The river itself is lovely, milky turquoise in color, bunching up in long pools or squirting through rock-jams. To be on the safe side one should treat its water with halizone, I suppose, although I have always taken it as

Looking into the awesome depths of the Barranca Urique.

is without ever having any problems. Lace it with enough tequila to kill any impurities, if you're in doubt. During the wet season the river is a beautiful, thundering nightmare—impossible to run and impassable to anyone wishing to ford.

Heading upstream, one should be prepared to do a lot of bouldering and crossing and recrossing of a surprisingly strong current. A sturdy stick is useful and at times a necessity for fording. The region downriver is beautiful and wild. Only a handful of Indians live between where the trail from El Divisidero comes to the river and the isolated former mining center of Urique. I have made the trip with an inflatable kayak on the river as well as hoofing beside it. Trying it either way, plan on spending from eight to eleven days. Make sure your first-aid kit is adequate—down there you will have to be as self-reliant as if you were upon a distant planet should one of your party come down with serious illness or break a bone.

This is a varied sort of ramble. Sections, especially at first, involve bouldering along the river or following a shoreline where there may or may not be a trail. In a number of places the river plows through sheer-sided

The Chihuahua al Pacífico Railroad in the scenic mountains of the Barranca del Cobre.

gorges, and one must take to faint paths that angle up to benches hundreds of feet above the river before plunging abruptly back down to it. Most such paths seem to cover a good deal more vertical space than horizontal. It is easy to confuse such paths with goat or game trails which will, likely as not, eventually rimrock you.

As I said, it is a wild country, which is a glory in itself. There are also many exquisite things—hot springs, unexpected cold springs in cactus flats, lofty waterfalls, thickets of bamboo, towering cliffs, wild orchids, strangely decorated lizards, parrots, and one of the most rare and graceful of all predatory birds, the solitary eagle. There are remote *ranchitos* where weather-seamed Tarahumara Indians yet have the time to draw dreams in the dust.

From the village of Urique one can work back up to the railroad at San Rafael or make the strenuous trek across to Batopilas and La Bufa. The easiest way is to linger a day or two at Urique—an isolated, delightful place with cobbled streets, and catch a ride out to Chihuahua with the mail plane—not an expensive proposition. From El Divisidero one can also descend into the Rio Urique over a precipitous mule-trail leading down to the ancient San Miguel Mine. A friend of mine almost came to grief on this path when a rockslide swept across it, almost carrying him down the mountain.

The old mining center of Choix, southwest of the *barranca* country, is a good takeoff point for trips into the sierra. To reach it one drives over a thirty-eight-mile paved road which angles out of El Fuerte on the Chihua-hua al Pacífico Railroad. The former mining town of Guadalupe y Calvo, an interesting place in its own right, is at the end of a dirt road that winds for more than one hundred miles back into the mountains southwest of Hidalgo del Parral. Other excellent trailhead villages include Sinaloa de Leyva, San José de Camarones, and Revolcaderos on the Durango-Mazat-lán Highway.

Alamos, thirty-four miles west of Navajoa, is one of the most beautiful Spanish colonial cities in Mexico, as well as a gateway to the sierra. During the eighteenth century Alamos was the glittering capital of a silver empire that extended throughout the Sierra Madre. It was known for exquisite architecture, lovely women, and an elegant life-style made possible by the riches pulled from surrounding hills. Today the population of Alamos is only a fraction of the thirty thousand people who once lived there—but much of the city remains, although many buildings are either unoccupied or in ruins. It is a place where one can sometimes walk for several blocks down cobbled streets without seeing anyone, or perhaps just catching a glimpse of movement behind a curtained window.

As with all mining districts, there are curious tales. A Spanish widow, Doña Maria de Rodriguez, once worked a mine over a period of years, carefully storing the silver ingots in a protected part of her home. Finally, desiring to spend her last years in Spain, she sold her interest in the mine and packed forty mules with loads of ingots, running about two hundred pounds to the mule. Even with her small army of retainers, the trip to Mexico was a perilous undertaking. If this were a typical lost-treasure story, the pack train would have vanished somewhere in the bandit-infested mountains, but not before someone buried most of the ingots. Instead, all the silver was delivered safely to the custody of the viceroy at Mexico City, immediately after which the widow apparently vanished from the face of the earth.

Throughout the last century treasure-seekers were intrigued by a lost mine once worked in the vicinity of Arizpe. Records indicated it had been a fabulous producer before Indian attack drove away the miners. The only clue to its location was an old Jesuit map, on which it was noted that the tunnel could be seen from the door of the mission church. A number of men, figuring that the shaft had crumbled in and vegetation had masked it, sank prospect holes on hillsides within view of the church doorway. They turned up nothing of value. In 1905 a side wall of the ancient church collapsed, revealing a forgotten door that had been plastered over years ago. A prospector, using field glasses from the new vantage, soon spotted a shallow concavity which turned out to be the site of the mine. He reopened it and made a fortune.

A rough eight-mile road leads up into the foothills from Alamos to Rio Cuchujaqui, where giant sabino trees shade quiet pools of the river. At dawn and twilight a variety of birds clamor through the woods. From here, and other places east of Alamos, rough roads dwindle into trails that take one into the unique and vast wilderness that is the Sierra Madre.

Guide Notes for the SIERRA MADRE

LOCATION—Northwestern Mexico.

ACCESS—The Chihuahua al Pacífico Railroad, linking Chihuahua with Los Mochis, passes through the heart of the Sierra Madre. Only one paved road, Mexico Highway 40, crosses the range, although several secondary and primitive roads push into the mountains. There are a number of small airstrips in the Sierra Madre, and charter service can be arranged at Chihuahua, Ciudad Juarez, Hermosillo, and other urban areas of northwestern Mexico.

GETTING AROUND—There are faint paths all through the Sierra Madre: they all lead somewhere. But if one has a desire to get to a specific place in a reasonable amount of time, it is essential to hire a local person as guide. Pack and/or riding animals are usually available and inexpensive. The rainy season generally occurs in July and August.

SUPPLIES—In most mountain villages one can buy fresh vegetables, fruit, and eggs, as well as crackers, canned goods, beans, and the like. Cheese and meat may or may not be available. Mennonite cheese has been produced in commendably sanitary conditions; it is also tasty. With other local cheeses you take your chances with regard to health and flavor. It is often possible to purchase a meal or a limited amount of provisions at a *ranchito*. With the exception of dehydrated and freeze-dried trail foods, one can find just about anything in the line of food at public markets in the larger cities.

SPECIAL FEATURES—Magnificent, deeply cut canyons, vast high-country woodlands, waterfalls, and some of the more isolated Indian tribes on the continent, such as the Tarahumara.

SOURCES OF INFORMATION—Not a great deal has been written about this region. The best way to find out about it is to go there and ask questions. The map sources listed for "Rim of the Sea of Cortéz" apply to this chapter also.

NINE

Rim of the Sea of Cortéz
(Mexico)

The Sea of Cortéz, otherwise known as the Gulf of California, pokes a long, gnarled finger into the northwestern corner of Mexico. Anglers have long praised the multitude, size, and variety of fish that live and can be caught in it. Botanists marvel at the many unique and interesting plants that can be found on the rim of the Sea of Cortéz and upon islands that appear completely barren from the air. It is a region of strong earth forces—sudden storms, like the dreaded *chabusco,* that rip the surface of the water into massive, heaving, white-combed waves; the infinitely slow movement of land across sea floor that geologists feel pulled open what once was merely a large bay between Cabo San Lucas on what is now the tip of Baja California and Cabo Corrientes on the mainland. In the space of a hundred million years the gap widened, islands broke away from the mainland, and the breach deepened, until today there are places in the Sea of Cortéz where a piece of iron would sink over 10,500 feet before touching bottom. The journey of a hundred million years has taken Cabo San Lucas three hundred miles away from Cabo Corrientes, which it once almost adjoined.

The animal life of the Sea of Cortéz is prodigious: teaming sea lion rookeries, flocks of brown pelicans that flap languidly in squadron until they peel off like dive bombers to crash into the shallows after fish. On Isla Raza there are thousands of aristocratic terns crowded into an area of less than half a square mile. Tide pools are filled with an infinite variety of life—starfish, sea urchins, rock oysters, sea snails, anemones, peanut worms, sea cucumbers, and crabs of all sizes and characteristics, including the Sally Lightfoot—a small, beautiful red, blue, and soft brown creature that moves in any direction as fast as thought and is as hard to catch as a dust mote.

For many years sailors in the Sea of Cortéz did not land on Isla Tiburón ("Shark Island"), home of the Seri Indians. Although early-day mariners probably exaggerated their propensities for cannibalism, the Seris did not welcome strangers. More than one Spanish explorer, pirate, or a combination of both apparently came to fatal grief there. And back behind the sand beaches, on the Baja California side where the Sierra Juarez, Sierra de San Pedro Mártir, and the Sierra Giganta push rocky spines skyward, there are gaunt canyons with surprising palm-tree oases where ancient Spanish missions crumble under a persistent sun, and powerful rock art of a vanished people festoons the walls of shallow caves.

Perhaps the grandest way to visit the Sea of Cortéz and its long, remote beaches is by boat. Several fine books have been written from this vantage and two of the best, in my opinion, are listed in the Bibliography. Yet as this book concerns itself principally with places one can get to in a rugged vehicle, on horseback, or afoot, I shall let the fine nautical possibilities of the Sea of Cortéz remain in other, highly capable hands.

Joseph Wood Krutch once wrote: "Baja is a splendid example of what bad roads can do for a country. It must be almost as beautiful as it was when the first white man saw it in 1533." Until recently the eight-

The mountain spine of Baja California rises precipitously from the sea.

hundred-mile-long peninsula was linked to the rest of the world by a corrugated, sandy, rocky track that was one of the great driving adventures upon the continent, much as the Alaska Highway once was. Today this road, which squirms across volcanic passes and through miles of cactus and scrub country, has been paved. Predictably, most of the places along the highway are beginning to be infected with heavy tourism—camper trucks and house trailers sit cheek by jowl upon certain favored beaches.

Nevertheless, much of Baja is still accessible only by four-wheel-drive vehicles, on horseback, or afoot. The mountain spine of Baja rises precipitously from the Sea of Cortéz, sloping off gradually to the Pacific coast. A good place to start looking at some of the unspoiled outback of Baja is by heading into the palm canyons of the Sierra Juarez. A few miles west of Mexicali the road to Tijuana (Highway 2) crosses the upper end of the Laguna Salada, a dry lake that extends some thirty-five miles to the south. It is perhaps ten to twelve miles wide, crisscrossed with tracks, as the surface is firm enough to provide a good road for vehicles when dry. Like California's Salton Sea, the area was once an arm of the Sea of Cortéz. It is below sea level, blisteringly hot in the summer. The lake bed is rimmed with sandy hummocks, and most of the palm canyons, which open out of the steep, rocky slopes to the west, can only be reached by four-wheel-drive vehicles or on foot.

The two most accessible canyons are Cantu Palms and Guadalupe. Guadalupe, in fact, is so readily reached that the bottom end of it has been commercially developed in a modest way. One pays a fee to camp near the hot springs whose mineral water tumbles down cliff faces. One can soak in small pools shaded by thatched cabanas or swim in a large pool created by the damming of a spring's runoff. Up from the hot springs the canyon becomes steep, rugged, and wild. A stream of sweet water flows between rocky clefts and stands of palm. As the granite walls lift higher on either side, there are waterfalls—short musical drops at first, and later, where the canyon closes into a series of boxes, the plunges are in places so high that the wind swings upon their slender fall as a child upon a rope. One can backtrack a bit from each of these lovely cul-de-sacs and attain ledges leading to the next level.

Eventually one will come to the crest of the Sierra Juarez. Westward the view is over timbered ridges that successively lower as they approach the Pacific Ocean, just as the swells of the ocean generally lower as they approach the land. On a good day the deep blue of the Pacific will be wrapping its arms around headlands, sneaking into coves. On a bad one the air pollution from southern California industry and the exhausts of its hyperactive motorists cover the land like a layer of bacon grease that has been fried far too long. Off to the east, over the sun-sucked back of the Cocopah Mountains, the rich brown of the Colorado River delta fans its muddy channels into the turquoise of the Sea of Cortéz.

I remember as a child throwing out doughballs for catfish into one of the irrigation mains of southern California's Imperial Valley. The catfish usually hit just as the sky was going from a dull gunmetal to a luminous blue. The bluegill liked to breakfast just as the rising sun colored knobby peaks directly west beyond Coyote Wells, as it did summits to the south, over the border—the Cocopahs and the Sierra Juarez. The white-haired, single-jackass prospector who had shown me the best holes in the canal was a former Mount Holyoke College literature professor locally known as Sandhill Sadie. Sometimes, fishing with me in the dawn, she would talk of prowling canyons down to the south, where there were washes full of placer gold, petroglyphs, Indian ruins, and treasure.

There are several palm canyons that open into the Laguna Salada—La Mora, Santa Isabel, Tajo, and Palomar—that are difficult to find, rewarding to hike. Carry lots of water, gasoline, and food into this country. When you have come back out of the sierra, returned from the heights to the mouth of a canyon and your jeep, it may be that sudden rains have made the *laguna* surface impassable. Even in winter, mirages may lead you upon a devil's dance.

Up these twisting gorges there are palm trees, palos verdes, tamarisks, and elephant trees, whose contorted, silvery limbs seem to have been inflated like a complicated child's balloon. Green twigs splay out from the stumpish ends of the limbs: after the rare rains which come here, tightly clenched leaves unfold and blossom in a riot of pink fruition. Cocopah Indians lived in these canyons for better than a decade after the turn of the century. For all practical purposes the proud and desert-wise Cocopahs are extinct today. Yet in isolated bends of the palm canyons, their rock shelters, *metates* for grinding mesquite beans, and other artifacts remain. Most of the canyons contain petroglyphs and pictographs, scatters of pottery shards. . . .

When the Spaniards came to Baja California in the sixteenth century there were thousands of Indians there. Projecting that people living in such a harsh land would be receptive to conversions that would lead them to a perpetually watered and green Eden in the afterlife, missionaries toiled hard for their immortal souls. The friars, often men of great courage and determination, labored alongside the Indians to build adobe churches. But as with tribes to the north in California, such as the Chumash, dependency upon mission handouts dulled the Baja peoples' ability to deal with an environment both physically and emotionally demanding. When the songs or paintings necessary to placate the spirit of the deer before they hunted it were imperfectly remembered, they could rarely kill a deer, even though some of them now had rifles.

Diseases for which they had no antibodies swept across entire villages and tribes like a scythe. Today there are perhaps five hundred native Baja Californians. Most that remain are of the Paipais, Tipais, and Kiliwas tribes, who live in the highlands of the Sierra Juarez.

The village of Santa Catarina, on the western flank of the Sierra Juarez, is where the Dominicans built their last mission in 1797. The Paipais, who then numbered about 1500 tribal members, began a series of rebellions that eventually drove the last Spaniards out of the region. Today the mission is merely an outline of brown walls. A maze of trails leads from Santa Catarina to outlying *ranchitos* of all three remaining Baja tribes. One can also come into that country through the sky-kicked canyons out of the east, walking up over the spine through Constitución National Park, which lies some twenty-five miles south of Laguna Salada.

Not far south of Valle Trinidad the Sierra Juarez officially becomes the Sierra San Pedro Mártir, even though there is no real break in the cordillera; the same humped volcanic rocks continue all the way to Cabo San Lucas. Part of the Sierra San Pedro Mártir has been set aside as a wilderness area. Access from the east is from the dirt roads that connect Valle Trinidad and the fishing village of San Felipe. Here the mountains rear up from the sea plain like a gigantic wall furrowed with precipitous canyons. El Picacho del Diablo looms 10,156 feet above the Sea of Cortéz. It is the loftiest summit upon the peninsula. The eastern flank of the mountains is rarely traveled, poorly mapped, and thoroughly delightful.

An easier way to get into this range is to drive south from Valle Trinidad for some fifty miles to the Meling Ranch, a cattle spread high on the wooded western slope. From this guest ranch one can trek into the mountains or arrange for a pack trip to the ruined mission of San Pedro Mártir, to spring-fed trout streams, or wherever your fancy directs. Mike's Sky Rancho, a few miles northeast of Meling Ranch, offers similar accommodations and services. Gemstones are scattered throughout the nearby hills—fine opals, garnets, and topazes.

Some of the most beautiful beaches in Baja are reached by very poor roads or no roads at all. The 127-mile stretch of highway from Mexicali to San Felipe is paved; the fifty-two-mile continuation on to Puertocitos is unpaved but easy on the shock absorbers. This is the end of the line for passenger cars, house trailers, and boat trailers. Quite a few house trailers are usually nestled in right there, their owners renting lots by the month. Beyond town, the road snakes its way over low coastal hills for some ten miles and then climbs over steep volcanic ridges. The entire stretch of twenty miles has been described as the "worst major road in Baja." If you like a little solitude when beach-camping, you will look upon the first portion with fondness. There are a number of lovely beaches there—white sand crescents that dip into turquoise water which shades into a deep blue with depth.

Provisioning for a beach camp in Baja, or on the coastal mainland, is a tasty and inexpensive proposition if you enjoy seafood. At the nearest village one can stock up on water, beer, or soft drinks, fruit juice, eggs, beans, tortillas, fresh fruit (including plenty of limes), a little cooking oil, tomatoes, potatoes, and a few canned goods for variety or emergencies. In many areas, such as the headlands below Puertocito, rock oysters can be gathered when the tide is out. These fist-sized delicacies can be knocked loose from the rocks with a hammer and chisel. One can eat them on the spot with lime juice for seasoning, or marinate them for an hour or two in lime juice, onions, and chili for a zesty *seviche*. Pen shells, which average about a foot in length and five inches wide, are also great *seviche*-makings. They are usually obtained by diving. A number of beaches beside the Sea of Cortéz have butter clams that are mighty fine when steamed. The culinary joys of lobster, which can be dived for in most areas, need not be elaborated on.

"Baja is a splendid example of what bad roads can do for a country," wrote Joseph Wood Krutch.

There are more than 650 species of fish in the Sea of Cortéz, most of which are edible. A few are downright poisonous. Ask local fishermen. The beach-camper can obtain a tasty meal by shore casting, spearfishing, or even by hand when the grunion are spawning. On beaches in the northern area of the Sea of Cortéz the grunion make spawning runs from February through May. Vast numbers of the blue-green luminous fish hover close to a sandy beach. At the precise crest of extreme lunar high tide, the fish flop ashore. The female quickly burrows her five- to eight-inch body into the sand, depositing eggs upon which a male, curled around her head, discharges milt to fertilize them. The grunion then flip back to catch the next, and shorter, wave upon its retreat. In two weeks, when the next lunar high tide sends a wave over them, the eggs hatch and the larvae are swept back to sea, where they soon grow into fish.

The undersea world along the rim of the Sea of Cortéz is magical. Fish of every imaginable hue and shape glide past coral formations, in and out of sea caves, and over beds of rippled sand. The trigger fish has strong buck teeth set in a ridiculously small mouth. Schools of drab leopard groupers are always led by a fish whose body is a shimmer of soft gold. Seri Indians call them the "goddesses of all the fishes." Until they are about ten inches long these strange fish are the same greenish brown color as the rest of the leopard groupers. Quite suddenly, by a genetic process not yet fully understood by scientists, three or four out of a spawn of several hundred will undergo the color change so sought by medieval alchemists. The Southern jewfish, a cousin of the leopard grouper, lurks in the rocky deeps and may weigh up to one thousand pounds. The goatfish is a vivid yellow when alive but turns bright red in death. One of the most decorative fishes in the Sea of Cortéz is called *chino mero* by the Mexicans, who liken its masklike face design to that of a Chinese actor. Designs upon the body of the fish resemble calligraphy. An American fisherman copied the odd designs and later showed them to a friend who was a Chinese scholar. The scholar pronounced them to be in the early Ming style of writing, which translated into an old classic proverb: "Two farmers, one wife, no peace."

If you bring nothing else, at least bring a facemask, snorkel, and fins to the Sea of Cortéz. They will open the door to magic and beauty.

A small rubber raft is another great item to bring to Baja. From it one can dive, fish, and explore the shoreline and nearby islands. You will probably not make many raft excursions before the playful bottlenose dolphins will besport themselves around your craft. Dolphins, when feeling especially splendid, have been known to leap right over small craft. Giant manta rays sometimes burst through the water to soar, wings flapping, several feet above the sea, before falling back again with tremendous splashes. Scientists theorize that the spectacular acrobatics may be efforts to dislodge parasites.

One should have some sort of large ground tarp, preferably light and compact, such as ripstop nylon, which will keep the sand out of your bed by night and can be hoisted upon poles to form a square of shade by day. If you possess a small fish smoker, or can buy or read up on how to construct one, by all means have it at a Baja beach camp. As well as adding variety to your own table, the smoked fish can be traded to occasional passersby for all manner of useful things, like water and other supplies.

There are other good beach campsites in the vicinity of Bahía San Luis Gonzaga, before the road swings inland to cross sandy flats which, in February and early March, are often a dazzle of color—blooming purple sand verbena, yellow poppies, and blue lupine. The long, prickly tentacles of ocotillo are tipped with red flowers in mid-spring. Look for the adobe house which is Las Arrastras, sixteen miles from Bahía San Luis Gonzaga.

Heading toward the mountain wilderness of central Baja California.

The well in the arroyo provides the first good water supply after Puertocitos. The road moves up the broad valley before descending into the
deeply slashed, multicolored gorge of Calamajue. Of Mission Calamajue,
founded by Jesuits in 1766, there are only ragged foundation walls left. At
the head of this slab-sided canyon, one emerges into a vast, spiny forest.
There are massive cardons, world's largest cactus, which may tower up to
sixty feet in the air and weigh tons. Here one finds the upswept, slender
tentacles of the ocotillo, as well as the sprawling, thicker arms of the sour
pitahaya. The sour pitahaya has a white and yellow flower and bright red
fruit with a citruslike flavor. The *cirio* (Spanish for "wax candle") is
abundant along this stretch. Botanist Godfrey Sykes nicknamed this curious
plant the Boojum, after the imaginary creature dreamed up by Lewis
Carroll in *The Hunting of the Snark*. Some of the plants poke slender,
graceful fingers sixty feet straight up from the ground. Others rise for a
certain distance and then send out branches that arc and curl off in all
directions. The branches may droop back to the ground and take root—
good plants to drape the limp watches of Salvador Dali from.

Thirty-one miles from Las Arrastras the Gulf route joins Highway 1,
the Baja Highway, at El Crucero, important upon maps because gasoline
can be purchased from drums stored in the single adobe that is the town.

Six miles below El Crucero a forty-six-mile road winds off to Bahía de
los Ángeles. Flanked by a sweep of white beaches, the village for many
years was principally a turtle-fishing center. The green sea turtle, which will
go to two hundred pounds, has long been hunted for its meat. In recent
years the catch has dwindled, and the Mexican government prohibits
fishing for them from May through September when they are closer to
shore and thus easier to catch. In season, 150 to 200 turtles a month are
still brought into Bahía de los Ángeles, where they wait in shaded watery
pens for shipment out by truck. The income of the three hundred villagers
is augmented these days by the tourists and fishermen who stop there,
coming principally by boat or small plane. Few of them roam far from the
village, however, preferring the comforts of the Casa Diez, a hotel, to
beach camping. That leaves a lot of beautiful shore country for those who
like to rough it with some privacy. One looks across the Canal de las
Ballenas ("whale passage") to Isla Angel de la Guarda—the archetypical
desert island.

In Canal de las Ballenas, as elsewhere in the Sea of Cortéz, one often
can see pods of whales finning and occasionally blowing as they cruise.
One may see twenty-foot pilot whales, the black and white killer whales
that are the terror of other sea mammals yet have rarely, if ever, attacked
man; the massive sperm whales, once hunted for ambergris, an ingredient
of perfume whose value, fortunately for the species in these waters, has
dropped from forty dollars an ounce to about a dollar; and finback whales,

the second largest animal on earth. Only the gray whale is larger. A pod of about 150 finbacks apparently regard the narrow (eight to ten miles wide) Canal de las Ballenas and the Canal Sal Si Puedes to the south as home territory. When walking these shores a pair of binoculars is a fine thing to have.

Forty-five miles south from El Crucero, at Rosarito on the trunk highway, a twenty-two-mile dead-end road forks off to San Borja. The magnificent stone block mission, finished by the Jesuits in 1801, dominates a small village where a handful of families grows dates, olives, and pomegranates. There is no longer a priest at the mission, nor pews, yet one finds flowers upon the altar and vivid children's drawings. One would be hard-pressed to find a more lovely place to worship.

San Borja was founded by Jesuits in 1759. Their crypts, long since looted by treasure-seekers, lie beside the mission. This mission, like others to the north and south of it such as Calamajue, Santa Gertrudis, and San Ignacio, are all close to the wild country of the central Baja crest—a wild and little-known region of mesas, abrupt desert mountains, and deeply slashed, almost inaccessible canyons. The missions were started at oases deep in these canyons. It was demanding, lonely country. Calmajue was abandoned only months after its completion; missions San Borja and Santa Gertrudis dominate lonely villages that are all but deserted. Only San Ignacio flourishes. Springs welling out of lava rock have been channeled to water some eighty thousand date palms and two thousand orange trees in the area. Yards are verdant with banana, papaya, fig trees, grape vines, bougainvillea, hibiscus, and blackberry vines.

The Jesuits and the Dominicans who followed them heard of other oases deep in the crosshatching of canyons—places of natural palm trees, life-giving springs, and shallow caves where a race of giants had painted scale likenesses of themselves. Although the Indians knew of these places and lived at them from time to time, they attributed the paintings to an ancient people who were strong and steeped in magic—a people who had gone to another mysterious place. The myth of a race of giants lost little in the telling from the fact that today many of the missions where friars listened to the stories of the painted caves are in ruins, and the path used to connect the missions, the "Lost Jesuit Trail," has yet to be completely retraced.

Remarkable cave paintings have been discovered in deep, almost inaccessible canyons of the Sierra San Francisco, immediately north of the village of San Ignacio. Animal and human figures, rendered in white, black, red, purple, and yellow, decorate the walls of shallow caves. Most are life-sized or larger, and some have arrows painted across or imbedded in them. Deer, rabbits, and mountain sheep are usually portrayed in two areas of color, with black or red covering the top portion. Mountain sheep might have one horn of black and the other of red. The figures may well have been associated with hunting-magic, especially those with arrows across them. Curiously, the arrows shown in human figures were apparently painted at a later time. Sorcery would thus seem a more likely motive for the arrows than warfare.

From the fact that a number of paintings are superimposed upon others while there is blank wall space nearby, anthropologists surmise that the act of creation was more important to the vanished artists than the finished product. They were done, it is estimated, during the late fourteenth and fifteenth centuries. Some paintings are thirty feet above the shelter floors; others are upon projecting lips that overhang sheer drops of several hundred feet. The value of such paintings, apparently, was enhanced by the act of creating them in difficult and dangerous places.

Mystery writer Erle Stanley Gardner, whose interest in real-life puzzles has often drawn him into the rugged Baja outback, discovered some of the most dramatic panels of the Sierra San Francisco only a couple of decades ago. One of the largest of the decorated caves now bears his name. On his first expedition to the region, he passed through a remote village where an old man told him: "I have lived here all of my life. Your party is the first. No one has ever come into this country." Few have since, as getting into this roadless and wild outback is still as challenging as when the discovery of the caves was first made.

The region of Punta San Francisquito, fifty-two miles northeast of El Arco, offers numerous fine, unspoiled beaches. For much of the distance the dirt road is gentle upon the tire treads and oil pan of your vehicle. Forests of cardon, the gigantic saguarolike cactus, line the road. Beautiful country to walk in. Thirty-one miles out of El Arco one comes to an unlocked gate: beyond, the smooth dirt track becomes a jeep-trail that plunges headlong toward the sea: tough, tight turns upon granite make it four-wheel-drive country.

Water can be obtained at the El Barril Ranch, as well as fish, turtle meat, and vegetables, if they are in season. El Barril is known for smuggling and sharks. Four hundred and twenty-five sharks were caught close to El Barril during a twenty-seven-hour period in 1970. A couple of decades earlier Mexican fishermen went after sharks mainly because the American health market depended heavily upon shark liver as a vitamin source. Never a people to let things go to waste, the fishermen began drying shark meat and selling it as a food. There is at least one Chinese merchant in any Mexican village of any size, and their culture has prized dried shark for centuries. On our side of the border synthetic vitamins have largely killed the market for such exotics as shark livers, yet dried shark meat (*muchaca*) has become an ingredient in many Mexican dishes. Upon several occasions it has been my pleasure to have had some dried, salted

Boojum trees are among the most bizarre plant life of Baja California.

shark cooked up in a chili sauce, generally served with rich, muddy coffee and endless corn tortillas, inside some wind-battered thatch hut upon the rim of the Sea of Cortéz.

There is an old, abandoned three-story house on a beach near El Barril that was once used by smugglers and is now said to be haunted. Until disease destroyed the oyster beds around 1919, the remote region of San Francisquito Bay was a center for pearl smuggling. Later, when the Mexican government prohibited the export of lobsters, small planes made runs between the United States and various remote coves along the Sea of Cortéz to pick up cargoes of the illicit delicacy. One such pilot, it is reported, camped by the old house when a lobster shipment did not arrive as scheduled. It began to drizzle, and so he carried his sleeping bag into the stone structure and laid it upon a dilapidated pool table. He closed the door and dozed off. He was awakened by the barking of a dog. The door was now wide open. A man and a small dog were clearly illuminated by a full moon that had risen. The stranger lifted his arm as if pointing a gun, and the flier, ever on the alert for *bandidos* and *federales* alike, drew his own gun and fired point-blank.

It was suddenly coal-black. The pilot, fearing that a misfire had blinded him, groped for his flashlight and pointed the beam at the door, which was now firmly shut. His bullet had pierced it. Outside, the full moon shone upon the bay and the crude landing strip.

The lobster smuggler, concluding he fired while emerging from a nightmare, resumed his slumber down on the beach. Next morning the fishermen arrived, and as they loaded the lobsters into his plane the flier remarked upon his strange dream. It had been been no dream, they told him. He had simply seen the ghost of Señor Viernes, who, with his dog, often hung around his former house on nights of full moon.

Viernes and his two grown sons had squatted at the stone house after the pearl smugglers left for good. Viernes raised goats and produced goat cheese, which his sons sold in El Arco. The younger son, Manuelito, returned from El Arco one day with a young bride. This ambitious woman soon observed that the Viernes clan seemed to live far better than might be expected of a humble family of goatherds. Her husband was unable to explain it, but did comment that his father would periodically head up into the mountains, and, upon returning, would go to El Arco or even the border towns, on a buying spree. She convinced her husband that his father had a stash of treasure hidden—gold, or pearls, perhaps—and that he should demand a share of it. Manuelito confronted his father. They argued. The son lashed out at his father with a bung hammer, crushing his skull. The woman and both sons fled, never to return.

Only Señor Viernes, say the fishermen, still remains—a ghost who is always seen raising his arm as if to ward off the blow of the hammer, or

The Sea of Cortéz south of Santa Rosalía.

perhaps to point in the direction of the treasure.

If you camp north of Punta San Francisquito you will be upon a cove facing the Canal Sal Si Puedes ("Get Out if You Can"). When the lunar tides are high, water rushes through this narrow, deep trough. Upwellings may push an area of sea, half a mile wide, ten feet above the surrounding water. Huge whirlpools form. Early-day navigators spoke of sailing craft being "gulped down into great and fearful maws." There is little substantial evidence of any vessel being thus swallowed, yet such a rage of sea is exciting to watch, and its effect upon sea-life—fish, mammals, birds—is always unpredictable, always interesting.

Beyond San Ignacio the Baja Highway crosses the mountains and drops to the Sea of Cortéz at the copper mining and smelting town of Santa Rosalía. If you wander around after a couple of tequilas, the place has a surreal quality. The old frame buildings and houses, with their screened verandas, seem to have been dropped there from another time and place. The fact that Mexicans are doing Mexican kinds of things in and around these thoroughly un-Mexican buildings only makes the set-up seem more unreal. Like most communities south of the border, the Santa Rosalía skyline is topped by a church. But this one is made of prefabricated iron and was built by Alexandre Gustave Eiffel, who is better known for an iron tower he constructed to top the Paris skyline. Santa Rosalía was, in fact, built by a French mining company around the turn of the century. Although most of the Frenchmen who once staffed the mines (which are now operated by Mexicans) have left, ghosts of a vanished era linger.

Forty-two miles south of Santa Rosalía the town of Mulegé strings along the banks of the Rio Santa Rosalía, the only watercourse in Baja that really looks like a proper river, even though it is scarcely two miles long.

The palm jungle that lines the river is astonishingly lush in contrast to the arid country through which it winds. A walk up one of the burro trails that follows the river is a pleasant experience—one passes thatched huts nestled in thick, flowering vegetation, and the narrow river and bank strip are clamorous with birds. Green heron fish the shallows, large flocks of ducks ride the calm water or beat up into flight if too closely approached, and orioles dart among the trees. In the dry, rugged country to the west of the river's source there are cave paintings and spectacular overlooks of the Sea of Cortéz.

At twilight the pulse of life along the short river quickens—birds become strident, the placid surface of the river is repeatedly broken by feeding fish such as the giant black snook, and one may even hear the mournful call of a conch shell trumpet, summoning inmates back to the territorial prison that perches upon a hill above Mulegé. During the day prisoners are allowed to leave the jail for jobs in town or the fields. Many of their families live in Mulegé. At night they return to the lock-up.

Below Mulegé the Baja Highway follows the western shores of beautiful Bahía Concepción. The twenty-five-mile long bay has a number of sheltered crescent beaches that are excellent campsites. Snorkeling and diving are superb in the warm, clear water, where multicolored fish glide as if in a huge natural aquarium. Predictably, the beaches with easy access from the highway are beginning to feel the press of visitors. Last year I stayed at one beach where the government has constructed thatch cabanas for the convenience of campers and set out trash barrels. When workers came for the trash barrels, they simply carried them twenty or thirty yards back into the sand and brush behind the beach and up-ended them. No matter where you camp in Mexico, be prepared to dispose of your own trash. Scatter organic material well away from camp—birds, small animals, and insects will make short work of it—and burn and bury cans. As elsewhere in Baja, the seldom-visited beaches are well off the main highway on rough dirt roads. The mountainous peninsula that separates the bay from the gulf is wild and unoccupied except for a couple of fishing camps. A rough dirt track follows the bay side all the way to the tip at Punta Concepción. Excellent, remote campsites. Bring plenty of water. Sundown at Bahía Concepción always weaves a magnificent set of colors, tinting octaves of blue in the bay, casting long shadows from cactus and desert trees, glowing finally behind the Sierra Giganta to the west.

For more than two hundred miles the rugged crest of the Sierra Giganta parallels the Sea of Cortéz. Most of the range is accessible only by mule-trail or footpath. Back in the granite folds of this exquisite range there are deeply carved canyons, small springs and palm oases, remote *ranchitos,* and a variety of plant life. Deer browse the slopes of the sierra and in remote canyons one occasionally hears the scream of a mountain lion. Bighorn sheep are found on high, rocky crags, some of which have never been climbed by man.

Loreto, a tranquil thatch and adobe village that was Baja's first permanent settlement, is a good place to ask about routes into the Sierra Giganta. As in most of Mexico, inquiries will probably lead to someone who will serve as a guide for a reasonable rate as well as rent mules or burros. West of Loreto a twenty-six-mile dirt road winds up the Arroyo de las Parras to the village of San Javier, crossing and recrossing a stream. Beside the stream, which occasionally drops over ledges as waterfalls, native fan palms grow as well as huge *zalates,* wild fig trees. Ranches in the steep-sided canyon grow figs, sweet lemons, sour oranges, dates, and mangoes. At the Rancho de las Parras olives are cured in cowhide vats. The mission of San Francisco Javier de Vigge is the best preserved of all the Baja missions. A monumental building constructed of lava blocks, it dominates a quiet village hemmed by black lava cliffs. It was completed in 1758, six years after the mission of Loreto. Fortunately it has escaped the looting that has victimized so many Baja missions—even the gold-plated altar is intact.

The shoreline south of Loreto, an almost uninhabited region of white sand beaches, plunging headlands, and tranquil bays, is one of the most beautiful in all of Baja. The Sierra Giganta looms above a narrow coastal shelf where vegetation seems greener and thicker than is common along most of the Sea of Cortéz. Although there is no running surface water on the coast except during storms, underground seepage from mountain springs provides some moisture to the area.

When Spanish *conquistadores* contacted Indians in what is now the vicinity of La Paz, they were told that a tribe of tall, lovely women lived in an idyllic setting to the north, where impenetrable mountain cliffs sealed off the approach of potential enemies by land. The Amazons, who wore only aprons of black pearls, sailed a gentle, fish-filled sea between islets where precious stones lay about like pebbles. Ashore, trees drooped with the weight of succulent tropical fruit, and there was an abundance of wild honey and game. The only men with this tribe were occasional captives used for breeding purposes.

In 1633 Francisco de Ortega ventured into the region, seeking pearls and treasure. He reported finding a tribe of giant Indians at Bahía Escondida, whose dancing and flute music impressed him. But the women were not wearing black pearls anywhere, and there were many large men. The expedition left, Ortega disappointed in the lack of pearls, while his men, who would have shared little in the rewards of the pearls anyway, were, perhaps, disappointed that they had not temporarily been made captive for breeding purposes.

The wild coast south of Loreto is no longer occupied by Indians, of huge stature or otherwise. Tales of treasure persist. Some years back Ray Cannon, who retired from the movie industry to prowl the Sea of Cortéz, listened to an old fisherman who spoke of a hot spring in the vicinity of Punta San Telmo that gushed forth with so much gold in solution that it plated downstream boulders. This was the major source of the gold which was brought to the mission at Loreto, he claimed. When Spaniards followed the Indians to discover the location of the spring, the Indians were aware of them and buried the spring and stream-bed with rocks and earthen fill. All of this tribe died out without revealing the location.

Just before the fisherman shoved his dugout into the water, he pulled from his pocket an oblong pebble that was coated with what appeared to be gold.

"Vaya con Dios—acaso" ("Go with God—maybe"), he said, and paddled off into the Sea of Cortéz.

For some twenty miles south of Loreto the highway to La Paz follows the shore before swinging inland, close to Puerto Escondido. *En route* one passes a mangrove lagoon at Nopolo, where herons and egrets wade in the shallows, and Rancho Juncalito, with its salted sharks hanging upon lines to dry. Once the main highway begins to climb into the Sierra Giganta, one can continue for a short distance down the beaches of Bahía Escondida by vehicle. The coast is a wild sweep of craggy headlands and lonely beaches.

A segment of the trail which once connected a chain of missions from Loreto to La Paz winds into this wild country from the vicinity of the ruined Ligui Mission on Bahía Escondida. The path, although rarely used today, is passable at least as far as Bahía Agua Verde, where there is a small village in a cluster of palms. It is perhaps twenty-five miles by trail from Bahía Escondida to Bahía Agua Verde. The path crosses two mountain spurs where cliffs lean against the sky and hawks soar. It dips in and out of countless sandy coves. On such a trail it is good to have coffee and a light breakfast in the dawn, snack upon biscuits, cheese, jerky, and the like at midday, and make camp in the early afternoon when the heat is strongest: time to throw off the packs and plunge into the balmy sea. The beaches are strewn with all manner of seashells. Sometimes there are dry, spiny pufferfish lying on the sand, and old turtle shells. From certain shelves of rock one can gaze fifteen or twenty feet down into clear water, where colorful fish swim by in an endless, exotic parade.

Drinking-water is a problem. There is an old Indian well at one place along the trail. Pottery shards and *metates* are scattered about the vicinity. The stagnant water, skimmed with algae, should be treated with halazone. Elsewhere, there is no fresh water. A good way to make this trip is to hire a fisherman at Puerto Escondido to carry you to Bahía Agua Verde by boat, caching water at selected camping places along the way. One can then hike back from Bahía Agua Verde without hauling a lot of liquids upon one's back. Another sensible solution is to rent a burro which can carry water enough for the round trip.

This fine backpacking jaunt is but a sample of the hundreds that are possible in the gaunt, beautiful Baja peninsula, once you trek away from the main highway.

At the extreme northern end of the Sea of Cortéz is a no-man's-land that is ruled and shaped by constant floods of water: the Colorado River Delta. Ebb tides roll back off of brushy hummocks, marshlands and mudflats with great, sucking currents. But before the land can dry, and plant and animal life can adjust to it, a new surge of water sweeps in from the sea. West of the mouth of the Colorado is one of the most scorched, desolate and arid regions in the world. The Gran Desierto, an artfully rumpled sea of sand dunes, stretches back from the coast toward the crumbled lava that surrounds 3957 Pinacate Peak, dead embers of an ancient forge. There are bands of dunes forty miles wide in the Gran Desierto; a temperature of 134 degrees has been recorded in a barren rift of the Pinacates. Only a temperature of 136 degrees, logged at a desert weather station in Libya, has been higher.

Mexico Highway 2, which passes immediately to the north of the Pinacates and the Gran Desierto, is known as the *Camino del Diablo* (Devil's Highway). In the last century, it was a trail used by California gold stampeders as well as Mexican traders. Many an argonaut or merchant died on that stretch—wandering lost in corridors of lava as their tongues thickened from thirst and their stock was picked off by Indians related to the Papago tribe. Other tribes considered the Indians of the Pinacate to be sorcerers. Perhaps they were. The next-to-last member of the band died of yellow fever in 1851—the last one simply disappeared many years later.

Of the region, explorer William Hornaday said: "There were hills and valleys a-many, of piled-up hell-fire suddenly gone cold; the lava glowered and scowled at the heavens and dared us to come on."

In probing his own fascination with the Pinacates, Edward Abbey (in *Cactus Country*) comments that perhaps the appeal of this region "lies in its total lack of any obvious appeal. In its emptiness, in its vast, desolate nothingness." Such places have drawn men since someone first realized that God, if there be such, would not approach them in an easy dream, and that heaven, if there be such, might be the green strength of a single plant in a seared seam of rock.

The road to El Desemboque leaves Mexico Highway 2 at Caborca. You should fill your gas tank here and buy provisions, as little can be purchased at El Desemboque. The fifty-five-mile road to the coast seems longer, as it is laid across a vast plain, some of it cultivated, much of it a thorny scrub where lean cattle browse. After crossing a low, sandy ridge, quite suddenly the sea and the village lie before you. The single dirt street is lined with shanties that have been thrown together out of scrap lumber, driftwood, palm fronds, sheets of tin, and whatever else was at hand. Wide, white beaches sweep off to the north and the south. There are good sheltered campsites in either direction if one trails out across the dunes for a half-mile or so.

On a visit to El Desemboque last winter we paused at one of the two shanties that serve food. The unwritten menu consisted of beer, coffee, soft drinks, eggs, beans, and tortillas. If you bring in seafood, they will cook it for you. In small villages such as this I have found it is usually best to stick to the first café you go to—if you try the other one, it will probably be inferred that you found the food or the proprietors unpleasant at your first stop. As we had cold beer and bean *burritos,* we watched, along with several other kibitzers, a marble game in which children were intently competing upon the dirt floor. The game, we were to learn, apparently goes from daybreak to sundown in that café, with rotating participants. Occasionally the marble arrangement of the moment would be destroyed by a scratching chicken, and the bird would be chased away with mock indignation. We watched a jeep drag a skiff some fifty yards across the damp tideflat to the water line, where a fisherman and some companions unhooked it and pushed it into deeper water. In this upper end of the gulf tides have a rise and fall of over fifteen feet. If there is only one jeep in a fishing village, as in El Desemboque, the owner is a person of considerable stature in the community.

Down the street from the café was the home of Ramón Mexia. His shanty was grandly surmounted by a large shark's fin mounted upon a board. The following morning we helped Ramón push his long, narrow skiff into the water after unhooking from the jeep tow. We headed south over a smooth turquoise sea. I was at the control handle of the outboard. Karl Kernberger and my son, Sean, sat on the middle seat, while Ramón balanced on the bow. After some casts with a hand-net that produced meager results, he indicated he would like me to steer the boat as close to the sandy shore as I could. Ramón now had his harpoon in hand—a homemade unit made from a round iron construction bar welded to a trident spearhead.

"Que busca? ('What are you looking for?')" I yelled over the growl of the motor. *"Mantas,"* he replied, eyes intent upon the glassy water to each side of the prow's clean slice. Suddenly he hurled the harpoon with his right arm and dropped his left hand, the signal for me to kill the engine. He hauled at the jerking rope attached to the harpoon and soon landed a fair-sized manta ray.

"Buena comida ('a good meal')," Ramón grinned, balancing upon the nose of the skiff with the supple legs of a circus performer who rides two horses while standing upright. The manta ray was dropped onto the floor of

the boat, where it periodically thrashed its wings. Its wingspan was about three feet across; it rather resembled a huge, fleshy bat.

After there were four mantas in the boat, Ramón motioned that we should head out to sea. A couple of miles offshore we cut the engine and the skiff rocked gently in long, easy swells. Nearby, some seals frolicked, bunching in clusters and then plunging away, chasing each other as if playing tag. A pair of gulls hovered in the sea breeze, patiently waiting for whatever we might throw overboard. Ramón cut off a slab of manta, baiting a hook one might expect to find in a butcher shop, and dropped it overboard.

"Tiburones ('sharks')," he explained. *"Muy grandes aquí."*

Since we were already having a tough time keeping our feet off the spines of the still lively mantas, we wondered upon whose lap we should

After crossing a low, sandy ridge, suddenly the sea and the village of El Desemboque, in Mexico's state of Sonora, lie before you.

stow the shark, or sharks, should they be hauled in from the deeps. The sharks, as it turned out, were not snapping at manta that day, and so, after a bit, when the smooth sea feathered into choppy waves, we headed in. The manta wings, fried and served with flour tortillas, lettuce, and tomatoes, were good; they tasted like mildly fishy pork chops.

Pitiquito, six miles southeast of Caborca on Highway 2, is where a seventy-three-mile improved road spikes off toward the fishing village of Puerto Libertad. This is lonely country with scattered ranches in thornbush hills and occasional forests of tall cactus—ocotillo, agave, yucca, slender saguaros, and the taller, more massive cardon.

Most of the Puerto Libertad fishermen are Seri Indians, those fierce people who formerly lived on the gaunt, mountainous island of Tiburón to the south. For many years, as already mentioned, Tiburón had an evil reputation among seafaring folk. The Seris, it was known, had killed people attempting to land there or having the misfortune to be shipwrecked. The victims, it is rumored, were cannibalized. Until a couple of decades ago, Mexicans and American sport fishermen occasionally reported being persuaded not to beach on the island by Seris brandishing shark spears. Thoroughly contented in their harsh environment, they simply wanted to be left alone. In 1956, however, two Mexican fishermen disappeared in the vicinity of Tiburón. The Seris were suspected of killing them, and the ancient fears of cannibalism were revived. Mexican troops landed in force and rounded up the remaining Seris, who then numbered about 250, and deported them to the mainland. They now mostly live in Puerto Libertad (an ironic name for an exiled people) as well as in Desemboque and Bahía Kino to the south. Desemboque of the Seris is not to be confused with the El Desemboque that is southwest of Caborca.

In these villages the Seris live in primitive shelters next to the beach. The men have high, dark cheekbones, watchful eyes, and wild, long hair. They hunt shark and green sea turtles with harpoons. Older girls and unattached women ceremonially paint the portion of their faces below the eyes in delicate designs with bright colors and white spots that seem like beadwork.

Remote villages on the Sea of Cortéz, like Puerto Libertad, are sometimes visited by men in dugout canoes equipped with triangular sails. These are bearded, rugged men whose faces are seamed from the glare of sun upon sea. Their eyes have a dreaming quality, as if seeing some distant, half-forgotten thing. Quietly they trade turtles and dried shark meat, sometimes small pearls, for the few things they do not obtain from the sea and the shoreline—beans, *maíz* for tortillas, dried chili peppers, salt, matches. After filling wine bottles with water, perhaps squatting in the shade of a wall or tree to smoke and watch the villagers, they paddle away in their dugouts and are soon lost in the blue and white immensities of sky, sea,

Ramón Mexía, fisherman of El Desemboque, casts his handnet into the Sea of Cortéz.

and shore. *Vagabundos del mar,* "sea gypsies," they are called. Their homes are where the winds and their whim take them. Their possessions are stripped to bare necessities: rope, hooks and handlines, harpoons, a couple of cooking utensils, blanket, and machete. Some may even have a book or two, for some *vagabundos* have come to the wild freedom of the sea from a very different sort of life.

A sandy track leads south through wild desert country to the village of Desemboque on the Rio San Ignacio, which is usually dry. Although not shown on most maps, the jeep-trail continues to the south, sometimes swinging inland, at other times skirting beaches whose dunes have rarely, if ever, been tracked by man. In lonely coves predator fish sometimes drive schools of small fish close to the surface, and then dozens of pelicans dive down to gorge themselves. Fish are often stolen from the pelicans' pouches by fierce-looking frigate birds. The male frigate, with its black body, red throat-pouch, large hooked beak, and angular wings that may have a span of eight feet, is one of the most beautiful of all the sea birds.

The rough track continues down the coast, around points, across dry lakes, and beside the mountainous hulk of Isla Tiburón, split from the shore by the narrow Canal el Infiernillo—mile after mile of beauty and solitude. Gaunt ranges loom up from a dramatic shoreline: in places, cliffs plunge forty fathoms beneath the surface of the sea. The road, such as it is, finally emerges at New Kino, a mushrooming resort. Puerto Kino, a decrepit fishing village three miles to the south, is more my sort of place: good beaches, excellent fishing and crabbing. A sixty-nine-mile paved road takes one back to the drab and modern city of Hermosillo. The Puerto Libertad–to–New Kino route should only be attempted if one has four-wheel drive, lots of water and supplies and preferably someone along who knows the region. To become lost or have a breakdown would mean a long hike to the nearest village.

Although in places the beaches of the Sea of Cortéz are lined with hotels, house trailers, condominiums, and gregarious campers with motorcycles, dune buggies, folding chairs and card tables, much of the region is as wild as when Spanish explorers first came there: a parched and rugged area where there are more mountain lions than resorts, coyotes than people, and the solitude of sky, sea, and land is as great as that of the imaginations of men and women who would go there to dream.

Guide Notes for the RIM OF THE SEA OF CORTÉZ

LOCATION—Northwestern Mexico. The chapter addresses itself to those Mexican states which front the Sea of Cortéz, or Gulf of California: Sinaloa, Sonora, Baja California Norte, and the Territory of Baja California Sur.

ACCESS—Principal access upon the Baja Peninsula is Mexico Highway 1, which runs from Tijuana to Cabo San Lucas. Once one of the great motoring adventures upon the continent, all of it has now been tamed by blacktop. Nevertheless, throughout most stretches there is little or no shoulder, livestock wanders freely, and Mexican truck drivers jockey their rigs like moonshine runners. Here, as upon the mainland of Mexico, one is advised to drive by day: more enjoyable—and much safer. One should bear in mind that hitting another car, animal, or (God forbid) a person in Mexico is not merely a civil offense, but a criminal offense. The latter, as a friend of mine once discovered, can all but get you lynched if the person you bump, no matter how blamelessly, is a resident of a small town. The purchase of Mexican insurance upon your vehicle is a must before you cross the border. Passport or birth certificate is also necessary, as well as vehicle title documents.

Virtually every spur blacktop or wagon-track in Baja twigs off Highway 1, or at least is a connecting loop. On the mainland the same is true of Highway 2, running between Tijuana and Santa Ana, or Highway 15, the west coast route of Mexico.

GETTING AROUND—Away from the trunk routes given above, most road maps are not entirely accurate; some of them lean toward the mythological in outback regions. Roads are shown that do not exist, or are mule trails: perfectly good dirt roads or jeep-trails are not indicated at all. Baja has been reasonably charted by certain guidebooks (see Bibliography). The mainland west coast of Mexico is another matter. The American Automobile Association map of Mexico is generally the most accurate road map available, but even it leaves much to be desired. The new AAA road map of Baja California, however, is excellent. Best always to inquire locally.

Four-wheel-drive vehicles are required to get to many of the places described in the text. If you are hiking along the shore for any distance, or back into the mountains like the Sierra Giganta, the rental of a burro or mule to carry water and supplies is an inexpensive proposition. Often a guide, usually a small boy or youth, will be included in the deal. A small rubber raft is a handy item for diving and short trips. In most villages fishermen can be found who will take one on longer jaunts for a reasonable rate. Most villages on the Sea of Cortéz are served by buses. Ferries connect Guaymas and Santa Rosalía; Guaymas and La Paz; Topolobampo and Loreto; Topolobampo and La Paz.

CAMPING—The summer months, although the best time for fish-watching or catching, are very hot upon the Sea of Cortéz and its rim. The remaining three seasons are delightful. The waters of the upper Gulf, however, are somewhat nippy from mid-December through the end of January. There are countless good camping spots upon the beaches and in the mountains of Baja. Tents, as in most of the Land of Clear Light, are superfluous, although light ponchos are always useful—for ground tarps, shade, and the infrequent rainstorm.

SUPPLIES—The Sea of Cortéz itself is an endless source of food if one brings fishing gear of some kind, a shovel for getting clams, and a hammer for knocking loose rock oysters. If you enjoy seafood but do not want to fish, watch for where and when fishing boats return to the village; fish and sometimes turtle meat can be purchased very reasonably from them. Most of the larger villages discussed in the text have outdoor markets as well as *tiendas* specializing in meat, vegetables, and the like. You will not find any dehydrated or freeze-dried foods, nor, in most places, will you miss them. Since the rim of the Sea of Cortéz has little drinking water, you would have to pack the water necessary to reconstitute backpacking chow, and so you might as well carry real food.

SPECIAL FEATURES—A magnificent coastline with numerous fine, seldom-visited beaches. The water is warm and relatively calm, filled with an abundance of interesting sealife. Excellent tidepool areas. Three high and unspoiled mountain ranges (Sierras San Pedro Mártir, Juarez, and Giganta).

SOURCES OF INFORMATION—There are a number of books on Baja, a few about the mainland shores (see Bibliography). Contour maps can be ordered which have contours at two-hundred-foot intervals. Information and the maps themselves can be obtained by writing to Dirección de Geographía y Meteorología, Avenida Observatorio No. 192, Tacubaya 18, Mexico, D.F. Information and road maps can be obtained by writing Librería Patria, S. A., Avendia 5 de Mayo 43, Apartado 2055, Mexico, D.F.

Epilogue

It is not without irony that during the period I was writing *Land of Clear Light* a large portion of the region, Utah's Canyonlands, was threatened with widespread air pollution. Not mere haze, but an eye-stinging mirk that would have cut visibility to as little as fifteen miles on occasion, the soiled atmosphere one associates with industrial cities. Electric companies in Southern California and Arizona had proposed to build the largest coal-fired power plant in the United States—a three-and-one-half-billion-dollar project to be situated on the Kaiparowits Plateau. Within a 250 mile radius of the power plant site are 8 National Parks, 3 National Recreation Areas, 26 National Monuments, and several Indian Reservations.

In 1973, then Secretary of the Interior Rogers Morton had turned down the Kaiparowits proposal on the grounds that environmental problems "cannot be overcome."

Well-financed power plant developers and most Utah politicians saw this merely as a temporary stumbling block and continued to press their proposal. The Sierra Club and a host of other environmental groups vigorously opposed the project, pointing out its destructive potential to one of the most magnificent wilderness areas in America. They questioned the economics. Studies indicated that not only had specific power needs been over-estimated, but that the same amount of money invested in energy conservation (more efficient industrial power usage, improved air conditioners, and the like) would result in three times as much power in the long run. Stalled repeatedly by litigation, the electric companies withdrew their proposal in the spring of 1976. The project collapsed of its own economic weight.

Undoubtedly, there will be other proposals for Canyonlands power development in the future. This scenic domain is secure only as long as there are people who value wild country enough to successfully protest encroachment.

This is true for all of the Land of Clear Light.

Under the banner of "Progress and Prosperity," America has brutalized its landscape—slashing down entire forests, strip-mining graceful, wooded hills into rubbles of sterile rock, turning rivers into open sewers, and overplanting the soil until much of it has blown away in clouds blotting out the sun.

Until recent years most of the Land of Clear Light was deemed to have little value, except beauty, and the captains of commerce turned their attention elsewhere. National Parks, Monuments, and Recreation Areas were established with minimum fuss. Over the past couple of decades, however, business interests are beginning to gaze at the commercial possibilities of the region as if it were a ruby plucked from a mound of gravel. All that coal under the desert, timber in the mountains, waterless sage and saguaro flats that can be peddled in lots to retired Easterners, chilled to the marrow from lifetimes of frigid winters. Money men circle Southwestern wilderness areas like sharks.

Those who love the wilderness have drawn a dusty line around the Land of Clear Light. They will fight to preserve the land that has been given to all Americans—the few remaining places where one may go for solitude. They patiently file legal briefs and try to explain to local people, who are excited by the possibility of jobs and an expanded tax base for schools and hospitals, that the real money, now as in the past, will go to the captains of commerce who will move on when the land has been looted, leaving them jobless in a land scarred for decades.

How does one preserve something as unique, strong, and yet fragile, as the Land of Clear Light? The debate is at least a book in itself. Yet a few things are clear. In terms of human needs, the scarcity of wilderness is making it one of the most valuable commodities around. *The New Yorker* ran a cartoon a while back in which innumerable people, stretching off to the horizons, were standing in tiny squares, staring blankly. One gentleman was leaning toward someone on a neighboring square: "I am prepared to make you an attractive offer for a portion of your square." In an age where one must reserve camping space at the more popular National Parks a good deal in advance, as with hotels, the jest is a bit too real for a belly laugh. The need to set aside more public wilderness is imperative.

Over the last three or four years the companies most eager to tear out profitable hunks of the Land of Clear Light at minimal corporate expense have barraged the public with television and magazine ads, which express their image as that of Thoreau mouthed by a Marlboro cowboy. Be not deceived. Large corporations, public relation gambits aside, are in business to make profits. Period.

Finally, then, one comes to the psychology of roads. Anyone who has spent some time in backcountry knows that where the paved road ends and the jeep or foot-trail starts, you will find piles of discarded cans. One can only conclude, since the litterers could easily have carried the cans out, that they are left there as a sort of monument to the joint effort of man and machine. *We have conquered this landscape.* Back on the trails one rarely finds trash, even though the packaged goods that are taken there require more effort to bring out. The old axiom, "If it is too easy you will not respect it," has absolute validity in the backcountry.

The Land of Clear Light is a magic region. But magic, like everything else worthwhile, must be special, worked at in some dancing dream. To be able to walk, listen, smell, and simply be in such a place is only as important as how you come to it. At some point you must leave your car and walk.

Earlier this year, kneeling beside the Sea of Cortéz, I picked up an old bottle in which was a message written on a page torn from a schoolchild's notebook: "I think I have perfected a species of asphalt-eating-ant. . . ."

In my garden in Santa Fe tonight, where the light is yet clear, I toast the possibility.

Selected Bibliography

BOOKS

Abbey, Edward. *Cactus Country*. New York: Time-Life Books, 1973.
————. *Slickrock*. San Francisco: Sierra Club, 1971.
Austin, Mary. *Land of Little Rain*. Boston: Houghton, 1903.
Baker, Pearl. *The Wild Bunch at Robbers Roost*. New York: Abelard-Schuman, 1965.
Bandalier, Adolph. *Delight Makers*. New York: Dodd, Mead, 1918.
Barker, Eliot S. *Beatty's Cabin*. Albuquerque: University of New Mexico Press, 1953.
Bates, Ken and Caroline. *Sunset Travel Guide to Baja California*. Menlo Park, Calif.: Lane Brooks, 1971.
Bates, Margaret. *A Quick History of Lake City, Colorado*. Colorado Springs: Little London Press, 1973.
Bernheimer, Charles. *Rainbow Bridge*. New York: Doubleday, Doran and Co., Inc., 1929.
Bolton, Herbert E. *Pageant in the Wilderness: The Story of the Escalante Expedition*. Salt Lake City: Utah State Historical Society, 1950.
Boudreau, Eugene. *Trails of the Sierra Madre*. Santa Barbara: Capra/Scrimshaw, 1973.
Bradley, Zorra A. *Canyon de Chelly*. Washington, D.C.: Office of Publications, National Park Service, 1973.
Bullock, Alice. *Living Legends of the Santa Fe Country*. Santa Fe: Sunstone Press, 1972.
Cannon, Ray. *The Sea of Cortez*. Menlo Park, Calif.: Lane Publishing Co., 1966.

Corle, Edwin. *The Gila River of the Southwest*. New York: Rinehart and Co., 1951.

Crampton, C. Gregory. *Standing up Country*. New York: Alfred A. Knopf, 1964.

Crum, Josie Moore. *Rio Grande Southern Railroad*. Durango, Colo.: Hamilton Press, 1961.

Eberhart, Perry and Schmuck, Philip. *The Fourteeners: Colorado's Great Mountains*. Chicago: Swallow Press, 1970.

Federal Writer's Project. *Arizona, A Guide to the State*. New York: Hastings House, 1941.

————. *Utah, A Guide to the State*. New York: Hastings House, 1941.

Franz, Carl. *The People's Guide to Mexico*. Santa Fe: John Muir Publications, 1972.

Freitz, Leland. *A Quick History of Creede*. Colorado Springs: Little London Press, 1969.

French, William. *Some Recollections of a Western Ranchman (1893–99)*. New York: Argosy-Antiquarian, 1965.

Gilmer, Francis and Wetherill, Louisa Wade. *Traders to the Navajos*. Albuquerque: University of New Mexico Press, 1963.

Hornaday, William T. *Camp-fires on Desert and Lava*. New York: Charles Scribner's and Sons, 1925.

Kelly, Don Greame. *Edge of a Continent*. Palo Alto: American West Publishing Co., 1972.

Krutch, Joseph Wood. *The Forgotten Peninsula*. New York: W. Sloane and Associates, 1961.

MaComb, J. N. *Report of the exploring expedition from Santa Fe, New Mexico, to the junction of the Grand and Green Rivers of the Great Colorado of the West (1876)*. Washington, D.C.: U.S. Government Printing Office.

McFarland, Elizabeth. *Wilderness of the Gila*. Albuquerque: Publication Office, University of New Mexico, 1974.

McKenna, James A. *Black Range Tales*. Chicago: Wilson-Erickson, Inc., 1936.

Montgomery, Arthur and Sutherland, Patrick K. *Trail Guide to the Upper Pecos*. Socorro, N.M.: New Mexico Institute of Mining and Technology, 1967.

Porter, Eliot. *The Place No One Knew: Glen Canyon of the Colorado*. San Francisco: Sierra Club, 1963.

Powell, J. W. *The Explorations of the Colorado River and its Canyons*. New York: Dover Publications, 1961.

Steinbeck, John. *The Log from the Sea of Cortez*. New York: Viking Press, 1962.

Underhill, Ruth M. *The Navajo*. Norman, Okla.: University of Oklahoma Press, 1956.

Wampler, Joseph. *New Rails to Old Towns*. Berkeley, Calif.: private printing, 1969.

Waters, Frank. *The Colorado*. New York: Rinehart, 1946.

Watkins, T. H. et al. *The Grand Colorado*. Palo Alto: American West Publishing Co., 1969.

Wolle, Murial S. *The Bonanza Trail.* Bloomington: Indiana University Press, 1958.

————. *Stampede to Timberline.* Denver: private printing, 1949.

PERIODICAL LITERATURE

Bailey, Alfred M. "Desert River through Navajo Land." *National Geographic,* August 1947.

Barnes, F. A. "Dinosaur Hunting." *Desert,* June 1974.

Barney, James A. "Steamboat on the River." *Arizona Highways,* February 1952.

Breed, Jack. "First Motor Sortie into Escalante Land." *National Geographic,* September 1949.

————. "Utah's Arches of Stone." *National Geographic,* August 1947.

Coughlan, Robert. "Vernon Pick's $10 Million Ordeal." *Life,* November 1, 1954.

Goodman, Jack. "Uranium Millionaire." *The New York Times Magazine,* October 17, 1954.

Hoffman, Velma Rudd. "Lt. Beale and the Camel Caravans through Arizona." *Arizona Highways,* October 1957.

Ingalls, Huntley. "We Climbed Utah's Skyscraper Rock." *National Geographic,* November 1962.

Jenkinson, Michael. "The Glory of the Long-Distance Runner." *Natural History,* January 1972.

Judd, Neill M. "Return to Rainbow Bridge." *Arizona Highways,* August 1967.

Litton, Martin. "Lost Garden of the Kofas." *Arizona Highways,* February 1948.

Lyon, Fern. "The Gila High Country." *New Mexico,* Holiday Issue 1971.

Mays, Buddy. "Backpacking in the Arches." *Desert,* June 1974.

Moore, Robert. "Cities of Stone in Utah's Canyonland." *National Geographic,* May 1962.

————. "Escalante: Utah's River of Arches." *National Geographic,* September 1955.

Off Belay Editorial Staff. "Colorado's Lizard Head." *Off Belay,* October 1972.

Pepper, Jack. "Organ Pipe." *Desert,* October 1973.

Pope, Elizabeth. "The Richest Town in the U.S.A." *McCall's,* December 1956.

Reinhart, David. "Desert Trekking." *Hiking,* Spring 1974.

Schneeberger, Jon. "Escalante Canyon—Wilderness at the Crossroads." *National Geographic,* August 1972.

Townley, John. "Boats that Sailed the Colorado in the Early Days." *Nevada,* Summer 1970.

Weiss, David. "The War Waged to Make a Movie." *Coronet,* February 1952.

NEWSPAPERS

Albuquerque Journal, Creede Candle, Denver Post, Denver Republican, Mining Register (Lake City), *Ouray Times, Santa Fe New Mexican, Silver City Enterprise.*

Index

Page numbers in **boldface** type refer to photographs.

M

N

U

V

W

Y

Z

About the Author

Michael Jenkinson is well qualified to write about the Land of Clear Light, for he has lived there most of his life and has personally explored all of the wild regions discussed in this book. Though born in England, he was brought to America as a small child and has resided in the West ever since. A graduate of the University of New Mexico, where he majored in anthropology, he now serves the state of New Mexico as Projects Coordinator of its Arts Commission. Besides *Land of Clear Light,* Michael Jenkinson has written three other books on wild regions of North America, and their history and traditions: *Wild Rivers of North America, Ghost Towns of New Mexico* (with Karl Kernberger), and *Tijerina: Land Grant Conflict in New Mexico.* He has also authored many articles on exploring wilderness regions and river running, besides contributing poetry to numerous publications. In the past he has worked as a teacher, book salesman, ranch-hand, ghost writer, camping equipment manufacturing executive, professional actor, and game warden. Married and the father of three children, his home is in Santa Fe.